WINDJAMMERS
of the Pacific Rim

SCHOONER INCA

WINDJAMMERS

of the Pacific Rim

(The coastal commercial sailing vessels of the yesteryears)

By Jim Gibbs

West Chester, PA 19380

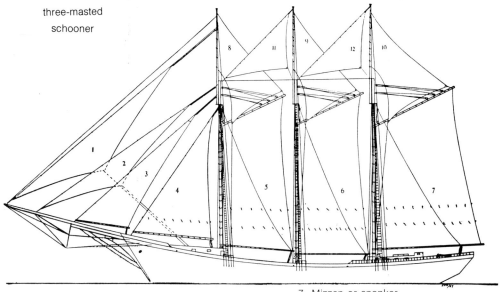

three-masted
schooner

1. Flying jib.
2. Outer jib.
3. Inner jib.
4. Fore staysail (jumbo).
5. Foresail.
6. Mainsail.

7. Mizzen or spanker.
8. Fore gaff topsail.
9. Main gaff topsail.
10. Mizzen gaff topsail.
11. Main masthead staysail.
12. Mizzen masthead staysail.

The sails of a commercial three-masted schooner.

Copyright ©1987 by Jim Gibbs.
Library of Congress Catalog Number: 86-63762.

Printed in the United States of America.
ISBN: 0-88740-086-8
Published by Schiffer Publishing Ltd.
1469 Morstein Road, West Chester, Pennsylvania 19380

Ship

The designation "ship" is properly restricted to the full-rigged vessel — large, square-rigged, with three masts each carrying a full complement of square sails. Each mast is composed of three separate spars — a lower mast, a top-mast, and a topgallant mast. In addition to the square sails on the mizzenmast (closest to the stern), this example also carries a schooner-type gaff-sail called the spanker.

Bark (Barque)

A bark is traditionally a three-masted vessel having her foremast (closest to the bow) and mainmast (in the middle) square-rigged — that is, with rectangular sails hung from yards. The mizzenmast (third from the bow, the last one in this example) is rigged with fore-and-aft sails. In recent times, huge four-and five-masted iron barks were built.

Barkentine (Barquentine)

The barkentine is a three-masted vessel having only the foremast square-rigged and the main and mizzenmasts carrying fore-and-aft mainsails and gaff topsails — rigged and designed to be handled by a small crew. Sometimes one or two additional schooner-rigged masts were added to make a four- or five-masted barkentine.

Brigantine

As a class of brig, the brigantine has two masts. The foremast, made of three separate spars, is square-rigged. The mainmast, however, is made up in two spars and carries a fore-and-aft mainsail, over which are two or three yards from which are rigged a square main-topsail and (when there are three yards) a topgallant-sail. No sail is carried on the lower, or main yard.

Hermaphrodite Brig

This type vessel has the foremast of a brig and the mainmast of a schooner. The mainmast is made up of two spars and carries no yards or square sails (as does the foremast). It has a fore-and-aft mainsail and a gaff topsail. With the complicated squaresail rig only on the foremast, this rig offered the advantage of a small crew.

Schooner

The schooner has two or more masts, all of which are fore-and-aft rigged. The sails can be either full triangle or gaff-rigged (as above). Schooners were popular in coastal trade work and as off-shore fishing boats — widely used off North America. Most popular of the rigs were the three-masted schooners (above) which could be handled by a captain, mate, cook, and four crewmen. Many four-, five-, and six-masted schooners were built. One seven-masted schooner was constructed.

SAILING VESSEL RIGS

Brig

The brig is a graceful craft having two masts, both of which carry square sails. On the mainmast there is a small, schooner-type gaff-rigged sail. There are three types of brigs — the full-rigged brig (above), the brigantine, and the hermaphrodite brig (both pictured elsewhere). In all three types, the foremast is made of three separate spars and rigged with square sails, but the main (or after) mast has a different sail rig in each case.

Topsail Schooner

The topsail schooner is a schooner with a little of the squaresail on the foremast. The foremast and its sail plan are nearly identical to the mainmast of the brigantine: a square fore-topsail and fore-topgallant sail over a fore-and-aft foresail. Both masts are composed of two spars, but the lower foremast is a little shorter than the corresponding spar of the mainmast.

Silhouettes drawn by Charles G. Davis. Courtesy of Peabody Museum, Salem, Massachusetts.

Introduction

The breath of heaven must swell the sail
Or all the toil is lost.

----Wm. Cowper

It was another era, another season in the passing parade of time.

Ubiquitous, was the West Coast commercial sailing schooner of yesteryear. Even as the so-labeled canvas covered "prairie schooner" drawn by horse or ox team made its way across the vast interior of the United States so was the sailing schooner pioneering Pacific coastal waters carrying supplies for new settlements and hauling back urgently needed lumber for the growing established centers. The turbulent seas between destinations often tested ships and seafarers to the utmost.

"See how she scoons!" excitedly exclaimed a bystander as a Gloucester sailing vessel slid into the bay in 1713. "A schooner let her be," retorted Captain Andrew Robinson, and so it was. That standing yarn whether it be true or false was not however, the birth of the schooner, nor was it a Yankee invention.

According to the eminent Captain Alan Villiers, fore and afters plied the North Sea in the 1600's, "skimming over shoals with leeboards raised." Yankee knowhow is nevertheless credited with several innovations perfecting such vessels for the coastal trades. Sails abaft the masts allowed the schooner to lie close on to the wind and tack with relative ease in narrow waters. Some had centerboards allowing them to sail up rivers and into shallow portals.

The initial schooner built on the West Coast of North America was the little 40 ton *Northwest America*. Under the direction of Captain John Meares, the vessel was constructed of native woods at Nootka Sound on Vancouver Island, some of the laborers being Chinese. Completed in the early fall of 1788, the vessel was later seized by the Spaniards and renamed *Gertrudis*. Following a treaty between Great Britain and Spain, the vessel along with others was returned to the British.

The first Yankee schooner built on the Pacific Coast was the effort of several pioneer Oregon farmers. She was the 53 ton *Star of Oregon*, built on the Willamette River in 1841.

The winged clipper ship, native to the east coast, brought throngs of prospectors to the Pacific slopes to search for gold in the wake of the big strike in 1848 near Sutter's sawmill in California. Few treasure seekers found mineral fortunes but many settled in the area, homesteading farms and getting the wheels rolling on new industry, all of which was solely dependent on supply by water transport.

A distinctive type of sailing schooner was developed, mostly by skilled artisans whose roots were on the New England coast, men who learned great wooden shipbuilding skills from crafty forebears and added their own knowhow to create a schooner with a West Coast hallmark, one that would become the lifeline for coastal pioneers. Not only was it a distinctive vessel but one that demanded rugged, fearless hands before the mast and a steady hand at the helm. A glorious yet tragic record was accomplished, one ideally suited to the trade and geographic requirements of the western coastal waters.

Numerous sailing vessels were constructed on the Pacific Coast after the 1840's, mostly to bring lumber to San Francisco from the Mendocino and Sonoma regions of northern California and from the forested hills of the Pacific Northwest. Others brought coal from

7

A sight for sore eyes. A bark, a three-masted schooner and a
two-masted schooner are pictured on sun drenched Pacific
waters as seagulls soar gracefully above.

ports in British Columbia and Puget Sound. Northbound, the coasters carried general
cargo and supplies of all descriptions to new logging camps and settlements. Offshore
voyages turned the compass westward to the Sandwich (Hawaiian) isles for sugar,
northward to Alaska for pelts and fish or on long hauls to timber-starved Australia.

Lumbermen using beasts of burden hauled their products to the shoreside utilizing the
most direct route that was feasible. Logs either came over land or were floated down
water-filled chutes for several miles. High wharves on trestles were built out across craggy
promentories and rocky outcrops. From the bitter end of the wharves inclined wooden
chutes were slung, down which a torrent of lumber cascaded to the decks of the schooners
moored precariously with large anchors forward and aft and sometimes to port and
starboard, open as they were to the full fury of the seas.

By the 1870's high strength wire cable became available which permitted more flexible
and innovative loading, giving rise to the oft repeated phrase, "coming in under the wire."
This often dangerous method frequently left defenseless vessels at the mercy of coastal
obstructions when iracible seas rose with sudden momentum whipped by squalls or gales,
sometimes scattering helpless seamen and their ships upon hostile tentacles.

When more conventional modes of stevedoring were developed and harbor facilities
were erected at the mouths of rivers or inside safe portals, lumber schooners were often

moored, stern first, into piers and loaded from lengthy ramps over the poop or through special loading ports located near the transom.

Prevailing westerly winds blowing directly onshore demanded a capability of the windjammer to beat to windward, and the requirements of specific trades resulted in features foreign to the east coast sailers. There were few with centerboards, most being keel vessels, yet it was remarkable where the keel vessels were able to go, such as the schooners that hauled tanbark, slithering into places like Frankport on the southern Oregon coast, north of Gold Beach, anchoring among tall ominous seastacks.

Though the versatility of the schooner received wide recognition in nautical circles they also had their setbacks, for no matter how ingenious the rig, every vessel of sail was entirely dependent on wind. When becalmed or clawing up the coast against adverse winds and contrary seas it was difficult with a capital D. All good things must come to an end, the basic stumbling block being the birth of the steam schooner which would eventually push the traditional sailing schooner into near oblivion on the coastal routes. The economic factors of sail versus steam allowed them to hang on tenaciously for a few more decades, most going into various alternate trades. They became South Seas Island traders, sealers, codfishers, etc., all of which brought about new combinations of sail best suited to the individual trades. For instance, the Alaska schooners were among the first to adopt the Pacific Coast leg-of-mutton rig featuring, "a triangle sail set on the topmast and sheeted to the boom end—a combination of topsail and ringsail, "according to Howard Chappelle in his *History of American Sailing Ships.* Similar to Essex, Massachusetts-built fishing schooners of the 1870's, though fuller ended, the Pacific fishing schooners were somewhat unique as were the South Pacific trading schooners which bore some of the features of the Grand Banks Gloucester codfish schooners, plus some of the swiftness of the Baltimore clippers, though marked by high quarter decks or large houses aft. The sugar packets, probably the fastest commercial sailing vessels in the Pacific in the bygones, featured all the best sailing qualities of the above mentioned vessels, setting highly enviable records between the West Coast and the Hawaiian Islands.

Then there was the San Francisco Bay exclusive—the clumsy yet economical scow schooner, flat-bottomed and square-ended, fitted with two fore and aft rigged masts. Mostly they worked the waters of the bay area and environs, but some inadvisedly served as coasters. They were by no means an open sea craft but were very handy at carrying a wide variety of cargo on the bay.

According to Chapelle, "the rig of many Pacific Coast constructed schooners featured many details not seen elsewhere. The square course when not set on schooners was furled up and down the mast rather than on the yard, the sails being on rings. When sail was to be set it was hauled out along the yards by out-hauls to the yard-arms. There were many variations of this rig, but all on the same principle. Though this method of setting a square sail was used abroad, it was not seen in the United States except on the Pacific Coast."

Schooner skippers took great pride in their commands and enjoyed fast passages, boasting loudly of record voyages, and certainly some remarkable voyages were recorded. For instance, the schooner *Sadie*, around the turn of the century, sailed 940 miles from San Pedro, California to Oregon's Umpqua River port of Gardiner, took on a full load of lumber and returned to San Pedro in just under 17 days.

Not totally content to rest on those laurels, the skipper took his 311 ton three-masted *Sadie* on a voyage laden with 400,000 board feet of lumber, Umpqua River to San Pedro, in just three days, 14 hours. Such passages coastwise were the exception however, for often contrary winds and cantankerous seas caused serious delays such as the shorter distance route of the schooner *Wing and Wing*, which in 1883 required 40 days to sail from Santa Cruz, California to Coos Bay, Oregon.

Expert seamanship was required to take schooners across a bar entrance for swells, currents and wind all had to be carefully calculated. Though tugs were of great assistance, many tough shipmasters made hundreds of crossings completely on their own. Wrecks and strandings were numerous. Wind is a fickle commodity.

Captain Oliver Peterson, master of the *Lucy*, a seasoned salt, tried for four weeks in 1907 to get across the Umpqua bar. Time after time he had to come about when adverse weather, high seas and contrary currents and bar swells prevented transit over the bar. Finally, in desperation, with a crew facing near starvation, Captain Peterson took his vessel up the coast, entered the Strait of Juan de Fuca and the protection of Puget Sound.

Artist's rendering of the two-masted sailing **SCHOONER SAN BUENAVENTURA,** 180 tons, built by Hans Bendixsen at Fairhaven, California in 1876. For several years she was operated by Daly & Rodgers and was considered a swift sailing vessel her skippers always carrying the maximum of sail. Under the ownership of C.P. Overton and commanded by Captain John Madison she was totally wrecked at the entrance to the Rogue River, near Gold Beach, Oregon January 14, 1910.

A considerable evolution in sailing vessels took place in America through the age of sail. Though several full-rigged ships, barks, barkentines, brigs and brigantines were turned out on the coasts of America, the schooner, due to its more simple rig, economic factors and smaller crews made it the sweetheart of the domestic trades and to some extent in offshore routes as well. Though most of the early schooners on the west coast were two-masters, evolution moved swiftly to three, four and five-masters. Then came the ultimate during the World War I period when the Kruse & Banks Shipbuilding Company in North Bend, Oregon turned out the six-masted schooner *Fort Laramie,* 2,240 tons, the first of three six-masters built on the Pacific Coast. She was one step up from the many five-masted schooners and barkentines turned out in the same time frame. The massive wooden vessel found only limited usage following the war and was finally burned for scrap on Puget Sound in 1935.

The other two six-masters built were the sisterships, *Oregon Pine* and *Oregon Fir* by the Peninsula Shipbuilding Company in Portland. They went down the ways in 1920 and were slightly greater in tonnage than the *Fort Laramie.* Later renamed *Dorothy H. Sterling* and *Helen B. Sterling* respectively, both ended their days under the breaker's hammer in Australia in the early 1930's.

It was basically the end of an era. The past is often pictured through a romantic haze compounded of selective contemporary discontent and forgetfulness. Gazing at a cloud of canvas gliding gracefully along the horizon brings longings for days that will never again return. There comes a yearning for the days of wooden ships and iron men and of gnarled old salts telling their yarns and adventures along a rugged and demanding coastline and in offshore ports of intrigue. Actually, economic realities were the same then as they are today, and a ship was a means for satisfying commercial desires. Its form and composition changed in conformity with those desires and with advances in technology.

In all of America, there were only ten six-masted sailing vessels constructed, three of which were on the west coast. A few others were converted from five-masters. The first six-master was the *George W. Wells* built at Camden, Maine at the turn of the century, of nearly 3,000 tons, with a length of 342 feet. The greatest schooner ever built in America, or for that matter in the world, was the only seven-masted vessel of that rig, the *Thomas W. Lawson.* She however, had a steel hull. Built in 1902, at Quincy, Massachusetts she carried a 16 man crew, aided by steam machinery to handle the sails. She capsized in an Atlantic gale in 1907, carrying all but two of her crew to a watery grave. The mammoth fore-and-after measured more than 375 feet between perpendiculars and had a tonnage exceeding 5,000.

In our present day maritime world of super ships one can hardly realize that for nearly seven decades the basic commerce on the West Coast was carried on to a great degree by sailing vessels. Most were created by master craftsmen without the aid of blueprint or power tools; manned by daring and rugged men of the sea and owned by empire builders great and small. Upon such ships of sail was the West Coast of the United States largely developed. In their time some sixty percent of the coastal schooners stranded, were in collision, foundered or burned, and many lives were lost.

Shipyards from northern California to British Columbia fashioned the ultimate in windjammers to carry on the trade of the Pacific—and a golden era it was. Today only reflections and memory remain and indeed these are perishable and intangible items.

As a youth the writer spent much of his time exploring the rows of idle sailing vessels moored in Seattle's Lake Union. It was great adventure to roam the deserted decks of the tall square-riggers riding at anchor at historic Eagle Harbor on Bainbridge Island, to size up the windjammers crowded into Astoria's Youngs Bay and to vagabond among the derelicts in rotton row on San Francisco Bay. The writer was present as they touched the torch to numerous old sailing vessels on the shores of Puget Sound—at Richmond Beach and Picnic Point. It was indeed a fascinating segment of one's life to be a witness to the last chapter of the windjammer—the closing of a glorious era which children of the space age will never be privileged to enjoy. From early Bible times sail had reigned until the twentieth century.

As one watched the great pillars of orange flame and curling smoke spiraling skyward from oil-soaked sailing ship hulls in the 1930's it was like watching thousands of years of history brought to a sudden, jarring halt. The sweat and toil that had gone into such wooden sailing craft was snuffed out in minutes as massive infernos left beaches littered with twisted bits of metal fittings. Sometimes through the flames one could imagine the glorious years when the sailing ships reigned supreme in the world of marine transportation: the rough, tough men who sailed before the mast; the strident commands of skipper and bucko mate; the yarns spun in the damp musty fo'c's'les; the creaking and groaning of block and tackle; the overpowering sou'westers and the bitter nor'easters; the pulsating gray seas; the chantey sung around the capstan; the romance of foreign ports with exotic sights; of palm-fringed South Sea Islands with their chocolate colored maidens; of booming little lumber ports; the winding Columbia River and the harbor lights of San Francisco.

One could ramble on and on through memory. This book is an effort to bring back some of the salty air of the day of sail, of wooden ships and iron men. As the pen of John Masefield has so aptly scrolled—"I must go down to the sea again, to the lonely sea and the sky, And all I ask is a tall, tall ship and a star to steer her by."

The photos used in *Windjammers of the Pacific Rim* came from many sources. Some were taken by professional photographers of yesteryear; some by old salts who sailed before the mast. Others were found in old steamer trunks and sea chests. In some instances they were reproduced from faded, torn photos, lacking clarity and complete detail. For historical purposes they have been used to afford more complete picture coverage of this virtually forgotten fleet of windjammers.

To one outstanding marine historian much credit must go in the penning of this book. He is the late Dr. John Lyman, professional oceanographer, naval reserve officer and historian. His research data on West Coast sailing ships was published exclusively in the Marine Digest, Seattle Maritime trade weekly, back in the 1940's and this material was most helpful. Formerly of San Diego and later Washington, D.C., he filled key positions with the U.S. Navy Hydrographic Office, the National Science Foundation and the Bureau of Commercial Fisheries. Graduated from the University of California and Scripps Institute of Oceanography, La Jolla, he held a Ph.d. degree for studies of the chemistry of sea water. Dr. Lyman was also a consulting oceanographer.

Table of Contents

Something to make the old shellback's heartbeat quicken—four-masted schooner **S. T. ALEXANDER** showing a unique view of raffee topsails, running foresail and jibs.

R. E. Mackay collection

Nosing into a North Pacific swell—**SCHOONER C. S. HOLMES,** with little freeboard under a full load of lumber. The Holmes later became an Arctic trader commanded by Captain John Backland, and later by his son.   *Courtesy Joe Williamson*

*The winds and waves are always on the side of
the ablest navigators.*

---Edward Gibbon

Part One

The Golden Age Of Sail

THE AGE OF SAIL on the Pacific Coast was an era of pioneering. It was a time when men went down to the sea in ships because the sea lanes were the only lifeline for the mushrooming settlements along the coast. Except for the wooden ships and iron men who braved the dogholes, and treacherous bar entrances, the history of the West Coast would never have been written.

With naught to guide them but the wind, a simple compass, a sextant, the stars and a sixth sense, these hardy mariners suffered a heavy toll in lives and property. Only when the steam powered ship came into the limelight did it begin to crowd the windship off the coastal seas and offshore runs. To fight progress was a losing battle and though nothing had the glamor of the windjammer, even the most zealous of those before the mast had to admit that the extra thrust of an engine was of inestimable value when the wind died while crossing the bar or when the set of the wind and the current carried a vessel ever closer to destruction. Though steam gradually put these winged beauties of yesteryear on the decline, none will forget the doughty men before the mast who depended only on oft-patched canvas to get them from one port to another.

The windjammers built on the Pacific Coast from the mid-19th century were created for the most part to bring lumber to San Francisco from northern California ports and the Pacific Northwest. They usually returned with general cargo and supplies for the little settlements from whence the lumber originated. Some of these wind ships carried lumber to the Antipodes or went to the South Sea islands for cargoes of copra. Numerous others scudded to the Sandwich (Hawaiian Islands), for sugar. Some loaded salmon or cod in Alaska and when there was no fish, sometimes came home to California with a load of ice. There was also a well worn tradelane from British Columbia and Puget Sound to San Francisco, whereby overloaded windjammers arrived with holds overflowing with coal.

The need for Pacific Coast-built sailing vessels came in the wake of the discovery of gold in California in 1849. Tall, swift clipper ships and paddlewheel steamers were coming around from the East Coast bringing thousands of gold-hungry folk to the great West. Other pioneers took the land route—braved the rigors of mountain passes, unfriendly Indians and adverse weather via covered wagon. To keep up with those who

Study in sail—veteran **BARKENTINE MARY WINKELMAN** puts out to sea in 1899 with lumber from Puget Sound ports.

came by sea, their conveyances were affectionately named, prairie schooners.

Preciously little has been told of the Pacific Coast sailing vessels that played such a dominant role in the making of the West. As the tall, timbered shores of the Pacific Northwest beckoned, little mills popped up in hidden bays and coves on Puget Sound, along the winding Columbia River and in small bays and river entrances along the remote shores of Washington, Oregon and northern California. Small shipyards were primitively established alongside the mills where master shipbuilders, who had migrated from the New England states, put their cunning and skill to work. With the barest of essentials, they built some of the finest coastal and offshore windjammers the world has ever known. The timbers for the stout hulls were shaped right on the scene. Predominant was the schooner—spritely, fast and commodious—two-masted, three-masted, four-masted and five-masted. There was also a sprinkling of barks, barkentines, brigs, brigantines and full-rigged ships. The perfection of

the schooner, however, which could take full advantage of the prevelant inshore and offshore winds, which could maneuver in tight spots or in devilish weather situations with a small crew, was the vessel that rightfully predominated.

It was a hard pill to swallow for the windjammer skipper when the steamers took over. Some resigned themselves to progress and learned new ways. For others they would rather have died with their ships than to make the switch.

H. E. Jamison, a former waterfront correspondent, frequently told the story of one of these typical holdouts in the latter day of sail when the last of the sailing ships were lined up in backwater moorages tied up in groups like aged ladies with their knitting, sitting on the porch of an old folks home. This old skipper dreamed of the days when his ship rushed through blue waters at steamer speed under clouds of billowy canvas, the creamy bow wash gurgling a symphony of speed and grace—music to his troubled mind.

16

One day the old shellback was found dead on the deck of his four-masted schooner. Both he and his beloved vessel had outlived their usefulness. Like him, the neglected windjammer had bowed her head in shame while scaley tramps crowded her off the seas. True, many captains and ships have ended their lives together—but that usually has been at sea, after an unsuccessful combat with the elements.

Ships as a rule are company-owned, and when they are no longer profitable they are relegated to the shipbreakers, the shallow backwaters or the torch. It is rare, indeed, that both ship and captain find a snug harbor, drop an anchor to windward and wait to be "cleared" by the Master Mariner. However, this old skipper chose to ignore the march of progress. Neither he, nor his ship, were through, he kept trying to convince himself. Day after day he made the rounds of the shipping offices, char-

A forest of masts at the Port Blakely Mill around the turn of the century. From left—the West Coast SCHOONER BLAKELY, German BARK THALASSA and the downeaster BENJ. F. PACKARD. Note stern ramps for taking on deck loads of lumber. The mill was the world's largest softwood producer in its day. *Webster & Stevens photo.*

Oil skin weather—The four-masted **SCHOONER FEARLESS** puts out to sea under threatening skies. *O. Beaton photo.*

tering houses and brokers. He went from office to office seeking any kind of a cargo. Even garbage would have sufficed.

"Ain't there any lumber moving to South Africa?" he would ask. "We could beat them steam rates a heap." Always the answer would be a sharp "no." Wearily he would row back to his ship by nightfall, drag himself up the Jacob's ladder—trying hard not to notice the opening seams in the vessel's side.

He talked to his ship as though it were a live thing. "Now don't you worry," he'd say, "we'll get something yet."

There came that inevitable day, when he had to admit defeat. He was no longer up to the tremendous effort of rowing to shore and making his rounds. On cold and rainy days, he huddled close to the galley stove to warm his thinning blood. The occasional bright day brought him up on deck for long hours of pacing on the poop, a tattered old sea jacket bundled about him. He would frequently tilt his head aloft to look at the tattered and neglected rigging. His

failing eyes, however, didn't see the rot, but only visions of billowing sail bellied to the wind, the creaking and groaning of the mainbrace and the limber seamen going aloft.

One bitter evening the chill of the wind whipping the water drove him into his cabin. He was cold and there was no fuel. The watchman on a neighboring vessel saw him climb shakily up the shrouds of the mizzenmast to the crosstrees—laboriously unship the topmast and then lower it by block and tackle to the deck. The meditations of his heart were obvious only to him. He was telling his ship that this was the Puget Sound country from whence came the finest spars in the world.

In need of more fuel, the next day he repeated the same operation on another mast. It was too much for him. It was like feeding off the carcass of his best friend. He stumbled into his cabin and died.

In days of yore the difficult crossings of the coastal bars were frequently beset by endless delay and often tragedy. Numerous windjam-

18

mers left their bones to whiten on the sandbars or were snagged by the sharp teeth of hostile rockbound coasts.

Sometimes all went well—like with the schooner *Sadie*, which logged a passage around the turn of the century from San Pedro to Oregon's Umpqua bar, took on a full load of lumber and returned to San Pedro—the entire operation in less than 17 days. Another time she sailed from the Umpqua to San Pedro in three days fourteen hours with 400,000 board feet of lumber. There were indeed many remarkable passages made by these swift windjammers of yesteryear, but at best they were subject to the elements of weather and the pranks of nature which frequently produced a variety of unfortunate incidents.

Basil Knauth, former editor of the San Francisco Maritime Museum's Sea Letter, described the situation as thus:

Time and tide wait for no man—to take a sizable sailing vessel across a river bar on the Oregon Coast in the dead of winter (when prevailing winds and storms always made for that dread of sailormen—a lee shore) was no mean feat. It took expert seamanship, courage and luck. Yet around the turn of the century thousands of crossings were made each year—and many failed. Some vessels were wrecked and some turned back.

Today, freighters, tugs and fishboats venture up and down this coast emboldened with powerful engines, radar and fathometers, plus efficient aids to navigation along the shore. Breakwaters and dredging make the bars less dangerous, but the open sea is still comfortable by comparison.

Picture it! Hundreds of great wooden two-masted, three-masted and four-masted schooners sailing up and down this coast supplying the burgeoning cities of California with lumber to build and grow. No other means of supplying the demand existed. No railroads or highways for trucks had been built in the 1890's or early 1900's. The risks were great,

Hard aground opposite Coquille (Bandon) Lighthouse—**SCHOONER C. A. KLOSE** in 1903. She was later refloated and lost for good March 21, 1905. Her hull came ashore bottom up on North Beach Peninsula, north of the Columbia River five days later.

but the rewards were high.

Now—about crossing the bar, those fearsome shoals that built up and choked the entrance to the rivers and lumber ports along the coast—Humboldt Bay, Umpqua, Coos Bay, Noyo, Coquille, Willapa, Grays Harbor and the Columbia.

Remember, you are on a lee shore in command of a three-masted schooner that has been at sea for a couple of weeks. You have been unable to get a good sight for the last few days. You have no power except your sails. The coast is likely rock-bound. There is a buoy—somewhere, and a lighthouse — somewhere. Your vessel which was designed to carry cargo is light and unwieldy because you have not much to bring from San Diego (West Coast schooners scorned ballast); maybe a piano and supplies for the mill town and logging camps, Flower Girl chewing tobacco, Russian Salve, Snowflake Lard, Kennedy's Medical Discovery, hoarhounds for the children, Noyo axes, blanket-lined canvas coats, etc.

So you stand off and outside the bar waiting for proper conditions to get in. What are these conditions?

The last reported soundings at low water on the bar were nine feet. You draw 12, and every storm changes the location of the best channel and its depth. The most favorable situation is, of course, a fairly smooth sea, an onshore breeze, the last of the flood tide which will help

BRIGANTINE COURTNEY FORD off the West Coast of Vancouver Island about 1897.

SCHOONER ALLEN A., a codfisher, aground at Baranof, Alaska, April 3, 1919. Wreck was purchased by H. Liebes & Co. of San Francisco, refloated and renamed **FOX.** Thereafter she made whaling and fur trading voyages to Point Barrow.

you in at high water, and being within a mile of the bar when these circumstances prevail. At best these conditions exist for a couple of hours a day—they also exist at night, but you don't have a searchlight. Still you might have a desperate fling at it.

Of such were the nightmares that the master of the coastal windjammer of yesteryear constantly faced. At best, it was a hard, exacting life for those who sailed before the mast.

Robert Weinstein, of Los Angeles, well-known maritime historian, sometime back, obtained permission of Mrs. Vera Paul and Mrs. Arthur (Olive) Peterson, to make public the contents of an old letter written by Captain Oliver Peterson of the schooner *Lucy,* dating from the year 1907. Captain Peterson had been

master of the same schooner for 16 years and was one of the best known sailing ship skippers on the coast. His command was a three-masted schooner built at Fairhaven, California, in 1890. On this certain voyage as on numerous others, the vessel was bound for the mill at Gardiner, Oregon, to load lumber for California. The letter read:

My Dear Son & Daughter:

We arrived off the Umpqua bar in 12 days but have been unable to get in. It has been terribly stormy, one blow heavier than the last and a tremendous heavy sea and squalls. Today there is no wind, calm and the sea going down and the barometer going down. That means another southeaster. Oh, I am so tired of this sea life, surely this must be my last venture to sea. I haven't the nerve I had 20 or 25 years ago.

Sunday, December 15, was calm all last night, this is a lovely day and pretty smooth too, wind light from Northeast. Can see the land and I am in hopes to get in tomorrow, weather permitting.

Monday, December 16, Olive dear, we have been sailing round the bar all morning but no tug. It was half water 10 o'clock so there will be no getting in today. Schooner *Louise* here too.

Wednesday, December 18, Olive dear, we have been sailing round the bar all forenoon, but it's pretty rough. The tug didn't come. The *Louise* got in yesterday. We were too far off to get in with the tide, we are here now eight days sailing round, and comes pretty hard on me for this is the hardest part of the trip laying off the bar.

Thursday, December 19. It's blowing a gale from south to southwest.

Friday, strong south wind and rough bar, rainy.

Sunday, December 22. Well dear, we are still sailing round trying to get in but have not as yet. The water is rough and we can't always find the place at high water. When it rains and blows we are glad to get out to sea, clear of land. This, the shortest day of the year and tomorrow winter begins. If it gets worse than it has been lately, I have to stand it anyway, as I am here and can't get away. Doubt if we get in before Christmas. If not we will not have much of a Christmas dinner, but I don't care for dinners if we could only get in.

December 25 — I wish you a Merry Christmas. Yesterday we had dead calm and today it's blowing a gale from the south (hove to), 20 miles north of Umpqua, 28 days and 16 round the bar. Have just had dinner. Didn't have a very select dinner, in fact, we haven't got much stores left. Had the last potato for breakfast. Got plenty of beans and flour, but little beer, but I don't care for dinners if we were only safe in port. I shall not be able to stand another winter.

Lovingly, from Papa

Thursday, December 26—Today is moderate, some westerly squalls and heavy swells. Got observation today. First time in week. 60 miles north of Umpqua.

Saturday, December 28—Well dears, the weather is moderate. Again once more we are abreast Umpqua, but sea rough and the tide as ever, late and early. I don't expect to get in before Monday or Tuesday even with favorable weather.

Tuesday 31st—Last of the year, we are still sailing and drifting around. The worst trip I can remember. If it keeps moderate tonight, we may get in tomorrow if the bar is smooth enough.

Thursday, January 2nd, 1908—Well dear, we are still asail on the ocean. I did expect to get in yesterday, but it started to blow early in the morning and blew us out to sea as a New Year's gift. Short of provisions.

Port Townsend—(Puget Sound) January 10, 1908. My dear Daughter: We arrived here today as we could not get into Umpqua. We had to get somewhere or starve. I am going to send for a new captain. I am not able to take her out and not if they would give her to me. I am going home as soon as the captain gets here. The mate may take her, will recommend him. This has been the worst trip I can remember. It has completely worried me and I think the schooner will load on Puget Sound.

Well dear, I will close with much love.

Lovingly, Oliver Peterson,
Papa

It was just ten days later that Captain Oliver Peterson, 70 years of age and worn out from many hard years at sea, finally did cross the bar. But his crossing was final. He died in San Francisco's Marine Hospital, after going there to consult with the owners of the *Lucy*.

The *Lucy* sailed on without her old skipper and years later was diverted to trading between Papeete and San Francisco under the name of *Raita*. She was wrecked near Clo-oose on Vancouver Island's west coast January 16, 1925 under Captain J. L. Richam, while flying the French flag.

Wrecked at Redondo Beach, Calif., March 11, 1904—**SCHOONER MABEL GRAY.** The 205 ton vessel was built at Fairhaven in 1882 for George D. Gray of San Francisco.

The men of the U.S. Lifesaving Station, Coos Bay, Oregon, are pictured in 1891 with beach cart and lifesaving equipment. These men were responsible for the saving of scores of lives from windjammers cast up on the rugged Oregon beaches.

To the rescue! Dobbins surfboat from Coos Bay station fights mammoth swells enroute to aid troubed lumber schooner before the turn of the century. *Old Coast Guard photo.*

Man's control stops at the shore. Wreck of the **SCHOONER MARCONI** adjacent to the Coos Bay lookout tower. She was cast ashore on March 23, 1909.   *Old U.S. Lifesaving Service photo*

A plaything for the elements—**SCHOONER HARRIET** battered in a gale at Nome, Alaska in 1900—a total loss.
Lomen Bros. photo

Total destruction—wreck of the **SCHOONER ADVENT** on February 16, 1913. After the wind died while she was crossing Coos Bay bar this was the end result. The crew of eight survived. *Rehfeld photo*

In January 1901, the **TWO-MASTED SCHOONER JOSEPH & HENRY** was brutally wrecked on the central Oregon coast near Big Creek, four miles south of Alsea Bay (Waldport). Her entire crew of seven were drowned in irascible surf. From time to time over the past eight decades the ghost of the schooner rises and disappears from the sands at Big Creek. This photo was taken in 1983. The **JOSEPH & HENRY** was built by Matthew Turner at Benicia in 1892.

24

The graceful windjammer **HELENE** is pictured inbound from Hawaii to Grays Harbor to load a cargo of lumber.

Taking a severe punishment in the surf, the **TWO-MASTED SCHOONER BARBARA HERNSTER** is pictured here hard aground near Point Arena, California, January 24, 1901. She was later salvaged and finally wrecked four years later working as an auxiliary schooner in the Bering Sea. She was built at Fairhaven in 1887.

Aground at Point Hudson Light at entrance to Port Townsend Harbor is the **SCHOONER HELENE** in 1918. The vessel was later refloated with only minor damage.

Wreck of the **SCHOONER ONWARD,** stranded near the entrance to the Coquille River, Oregon, February 25, 1905—a total loss.

Two-masted coastal schooner tackles irascible Coquille River bar inbound for Bandon in quest of lumber in early years of this century.

The **SCHOONER IDA SCHNAUER,** while anchored one mile west of Tillamook Bay bar, June 17, 1908 awaiting a tug, was carried ashore near Bayocean, Oregon, dragging her anchors, becoming a total loss. She was built at Port Ludlow in 1875.

Hopelessly trapped in the surf is the **SCHOONER CHARLES H. MERCHANT,** near the mouth of Oregon's Nehalem River August 11, 1902. She was built by Hans Reed at Marshfield, Oregon in 1877 for E. B. Deane & Company, as a lumber packer.

Bound from Seattle to San Francisco, the **SCHOONER OZMO** struck a rock off Cape Blanco. A vessel came to her rescue and towed her to Coos Bay bar. While crossing, however, she struck the south spit and is seen here in her death agonies May 17-18, 1922. The **OZMO** was formerly the **HUGH HOGAN,** one of several shoal-draft schooners built for Humboldt Lumber Company. She was later owned by Captain Louis Knaflich, well known Arctic trader who placed an auxiliary engine in her in 1916.

The **CODFISHERMAN AZALEA**—her oft-patched sails catching the North Pacific breeze—homebound from a successful season in the Bering Sea.

Joe Williamson photo

Laden with lumber for the South Pacific, the Charles Nelson-owned **S. T. ALEXANDER** put out to sea. She left Mukilteo, Washington, on July 19, 1914, and was wrecked at Toku, Tonga, September 28 of the same year.

Named **GEORGE E. BILLINGS** for the manager of the Hall Brothers fleet, this graceful five-masted schooner was built in 1903.

A sight to behold — **BARKENTINE GEORGINA** becalmed. In 1903 she made a run from Callao to Port Townsend in 30 days 12 hours. The old windship ended her days as a fishbarge at Redondo Beach, California, in 1935.

FOUR-MAST TOPSAIL SCHOONER
FRED J. WOOD built by G. H.
Hitchings in 1899 is seen here
with high deck cargo of lumber.
In July, 1902, Capt. Jorgen J.
Jacobsen, master, on a voyage
from Portland to China, was
stabbed to death at sea, and a
Japanese cabin boy was charged
with the crime at Honolulu.

Old print of Port Gamble, on Puget Sound, as it looked in 1869.
This was Pope & Talbot's mill town founded in 1849 where scores
of West Coast windjammers and square riggers from around the
world loaded lumber. The town and mill are still functioning at
this writing.

TWO WINDJAMMERS—one in-
bound off the mouth of the Columbia River, the other laden
down with lumber for the outbound trek to the South Seas.

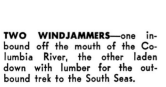

Nosing into a giant swell in the North Pacific—**BARKENTINE PORTLAND.** This veteran vessel was built by John Kruse at North Bend in 1873 and had a full and eventful life.

A fast clip is set by the **THREE-MASTED SCHOONER MAGGIE C. RUSS** in a growing sea in the 1890's. Built by Euphronius Cousins at Eureka in 1881, the Russ was wrecked at San Blas, Mexico, June 11, 1903.

BARKENTINE MAKAH races San Francisco Bay scow schooner in Mariners' Day race on San Francisco Bay in 1884.

One of the formidable lumber mill ports on Puget Sound in days of yore was Mukilteo. Many West Coast windjammers made regular loading calls there. In this photo through courtesy of Pete Hurd, the **OLYMPIC** is pictured loading at the Mukilteo Lumber Company many decades back. The Olympic was the only vessel ever built (East Coast) to have two masts square-rigged and two fore and aft-rigged.

Scene at the Port Blakely Mill Co. about the turn of the century. Stern ramp loading for lumber deckloads can be noted. Two West Coast windjammers are seen at left.

Steam **TUG RICHARD HOLYOKE** towed countless windjammers to and from Cape Flattery.

Commanded by Captain Nielson, the **BARKENTINE MAKAWELI** is seen knifing along through the South Pacific in 1911. Courtesy Capt. E. J. Stull.

Helmsman looks aloft as the **BARKENTINE MAKAWELI** moves through the Pacific a half century ago. E. J. Stull photo.

It took two photos pieced together to get the full effect of this picture. It was taken by Captain E. J. Stull in 1911 when he was a hand aboard the **BARKENTINE MAKAWELI** breezing through the Pacific. He was looking down from the crosstrees of the mizzenmast. A deckload of lumber can be seen. The vessel was bound for the Antipodes from Willapa Harbor.

A large gathering was present at Port Blakely in 1902 for the launching of the **FIVE-MASTER SCHOONER H. K. HALL.** The white-bearded gentleman in foreground is Henry K. Hall for whom the vessel was named.

Busy Port Blakely harbor on Puget Sound is seen in early years of the century. In the foreground is **SCHOONER BLAKELY,** a Northwest lumber packer. On her starboard side is the German **BARK THALASSA.**   Webster & Stevens photo.

One of the typical "highflyers" of the coastal age of sail was the trim two-masted schooner *San Buenaventura*, a vessel which was adopted by Ventura, California. Dated November 18, 1876, Ventura's publication, *Town and Country* reported the following:

"On Wednesday (Nov. 15) forenoon a schooner was discerned approaching our port, flying more bunting than is generally displayed by vessels in the coasting trade. Glasses were brought into requisition, and by their aid it was soon discovered that while the Stars and Stripes were flying at the maintopmast head, the fore displayed a large burgee with the words 'San Buenaventura'. This was a complete surprise, as the new schooner was not considered due until Saturday or Sunday. Nearing the wharf she rounded handsomely and let go her anchor, having made her maiden trip from Umpqua in six days, including 24 hours in which she was becalmed.

"*San Buenaventura* is owned by Messrs. Daly & Rodgers, and was built at Humboldt Bay for that firm by the well known shipwright H.D. Bendixsen. Her length of keel is 105 feet; breadth of beam 30 feet; depth of hold 9 feet giving her a carrying capacity of about 230,000 feet of lumber. Her masts of equal length, measure 90 feet from keelson to masthead; her topmasts 48 feet each and her mainboom 75 feet. She carries a flying and a standing jib, fore staysail and gaff topsails. The vessel is built of the very best Oregon pine, thoroughly treenailed and bolted. While drafted with a view of carrying capacity the element of speed has not been neglected, as her fine lines and clean run plainly indicate. Buried as she is under a deckload of lumber, it is impossible at present to give a description of her interior or deck finish.

"This fine craft is under the command of Captain (Oliver) Peterson, who was master of the old brig '*Crimea*' when she went ashore here last spring. Messrs. Daly & Rodgers thoroughly satisfied with his conduct on that occasion, and that the loss of his vessel was due to her rotten hawsers and light ground tackle, offered him the command of the new craft. May both have a long and successful career."

Daly & Rodgers, the owners of the *San Buenaventura* received a oil painting of their new vessel from the builders, a copy of which is seen elsewhere in the book. As it turned out, the Ventura-based schooner proved to be a vessel of excellent sailing qualities making one fine coastwise passage after another in fair weather and foul. On December 24, 1876 the vessel left Trinidad Bay and the fact was telegraphed to and published in the *Bulletin*. Before the paper containing the news arrived at Ventura, the schooner lay at the wharf, having made the run of 658 miles in three and a half days with 220,000 feet of lumber for her owners Daly and Rogers. The run was made in steamer time, so quickly that her cargo of corn was not yet assembled at Ventura and the vessel was forced to depart in ballast to fetch another cargo of lumber. Her voyage to that date was a record from Trinidad Bay to Ventura.

Captain Peterson, very much attached to his swift steed, entered her in a sailing regatta at San Francisco on July 4, 1877, according to the *Ventura County Star Free Press*. She was the largest of 20 vessels in the bay race. Getting off to a slow start, the smaller craft able to collect the light breeze at the starting gun, she nevertheless came on strong, finishing fourth. She could have easily won the complete laurels had the race been run in open coastal waters. Five days later she set sail for Puget Sound.

Captain Peterson and his command became household words around Ventura County and had he run for mayor he probably would have won. He evidently had great influence over the owners of the vessel, Daly and Rodgers, and they pretty much let him run his domain with little interference. If they had a complaint it was that his vessel always arrived early rather than late, and the skipper loved nothing better than to unfurl all the canvas the vessel could hold. He even thought of inventing some sails never before used. With tongue-in-cheek, one of the early publications in Ventura County chided him about such practices. "He is trying to make the *Free Press*," stated the newssheet on June 29, 1878. "Last week, when Captain Peterson, with schooner *San Buenaventura* heavily loaded, was on his way down, we allowed him nine days (which is good time) to make the trip from Umpqua to this port (Ventura), coupling the announcement with a puff for the Captain's seamanship. What does the ungrateful scamp do but come flying into port Sunday, with everything set and drawing flying jib, gaff topsail, topmast staysail and all, four days in advance of our predictions, making the run in five days. We accept his apology, however, and if Daly and Rodgers can stand it we can. The schooner brought 230,000 feet of lumber for her owners. She will sail this morning for Trinidad Bay for a cargo of redwood lumber for the same parties."

In May of 1880, *Town & Country* reported: "The fine schooner *San Buenaventura*, Captain Peterson, arrived from Port Blakely on Tuesday, with piles for Captain Sudden, and pine lumber for W.J. Walton and Salisbury & Co. Considering the baffling weather and strong southeast winds, the schooner made an excellent trip.

During his absence, Captain Peterson has selected a chief mate for himself, in the person of a beautiful bride, who is at present the guest of Mr. and Mrs. James Daly. The Captain's old friends heartily congratulate him on his marriage, and hope for health, wealth and happiness to bride and groom."

Petersen went on to a long and successful career taking command of the schooner *California* after leaving the *San Buenaventura*. Born in Denmark in 1840, he came to San Francisco on the ship *Florence*.

In 1869 he was mate on the schooner *May Queen*; in 1873 mate on the brig *Tanner* and the following year was named master of the brig *Merchantman*. Shortly thereafter he took command of the brig *Crimea*. Then began his seven year run as skipper of the *San Buenaventura*. Stepping up the ladder to larger schooners, he was master of the barkentine *Catherine Sudden* and schooners *J.B. Leeds* and *Lucy*. His basic route of operations along the Pacific Coast crossing virtually every bar entrance in California, Oregon and Washington placed him in the unusual category of never having a bar-oriented accident in more than two decades. The only vessel he ever lost was the *Crimea*, and he was exonerated of blame when faulty moorings caused his command to go on the rocks.

As for the *San Buenaventura*, she gave an admirable account of herself for nearly 25 years under several different skippers, and never lost her reputation as a vessel of splendid sailing qualities—handsome, almost yacht-like in appearance for a coaster. But as it must to all ships and all men, the schooner came to an untimely end on January 13-14, 1910. In command of Captain James Madison, lumber laden, she got into trouble off the Rogue River on Oregon's southern coast. In iracible seas her seams opened up and water poured in unchecked. The captain ordered the vessel abandoned and though all hands escaped, the schooner drove up on the outcrops off the river entrance and became a total loss. Her last owner was C.P. Overton. Due to the vessel's age, only the minimum amount of insurance was carried on her.

In the winter of 1975, Captain G.F. "Fred" Lindholm, a Puget Sound pilot, received a letter from The International Association of Cape Horners of St. Malo informing him that he had the distinction of being a "mollyhawk". A mollyhawk is a person that had a masters license at the time when sailing ships were going around Cape Horn. Lindholm recalled that his father, the well known Captain O.B. "Hands and Feet" Lindholm was in command

THREE-MASTED SCHOONER EMMA CLAUDINA, was the initial vessel to come under ownership of the Captain William Matson, who built a fabulous empire in shipping and allied industries. Built by Matthew Turner at San Francisco in 1882, Captain Matson bought shares in the vessel carrying general cargo to Hawaii and returning with sugar. The vessel is seen here bucking heavy seas in the Pacific. She was wrecked off Grays Harbor, Washington, November 14, 1906. Matson Navigation Company photo.

of the four-masted barkentine *John Palmer* in 1912 and that he and his brother Wolmer went with him on a voyage that would take them around the world. The *Palmer* departed Port Gamble where the boys had gone to school and loaded lumber in their off hours.

Said Lindholm, "We sailed around Cape Horn to Port Elizabeth in 112 days. At Port Elizabeth we attended school while the vessel was unloading. We lived at the consul's home— what a beautiful place that was.

"From there we sailed across the Indian Ocean in ballast through Basses Straits between Australia and Tasmania to Astoria and Portland in 89 days, a record I believe still stands. Dad used to take a turn at letting us stand on his hand, his arm extended outward while standing upright. He was a powerful man and his authority was never questioned by any man of the sea.

"I remember one outstanding event on that ship. There was a fellow dubbed by father as "Fancy George". George Johnson, a fine sailor, had given us each a $5 gold piece. He used to get all dolled up and wax his mustache hours before going ashore. Once when he returned to the ship after shore leave, he looked like he had been in a real brawl. The wax was gone from his mustache, his clothes were torn and his face bruised. Fancy George was, at that moment, the most unfancy sailor I ever saw.''

The elder Lindholm established a brilliant seagoing career, and son Fred continued the family tradition as a master mariner until becoming a Puget Sound pilot.

Fancy George Johnson went on to get his master's license and was in the four-masted schooner *Polaris*, as first mate, when she broke loose from the steam schooner *Wilmington* and piled up on Duxbury Reef on January 16, 1914 in command of Captain A.S. Hansen. According to a member of the schooner's crew everyone was drunk when the vessel hit the reef and they climbed into the rigging to keep from being washed overboard. Fancy George is alleged to have said while all hands were hanging on for dear life, "Well, let's call it a day boys."

The men from the Coast Guard Lifesaving Station at Bolinas fired a line over the wreck. Fancy George managed to rig a breeches buoy which was the means of saving all 12 hands. The survivors walked from Bolinas to Sausalito, a distance of 30 miles where they were cared for.

What about those commercial schooners built for the lumber trade and ending their active days as codfishing vessels under sail? There was a fair sized fleet which worked the waters of the Bering Sea annually from ports on Puget Sound and San Francisco Bay. One such vessel was the graceful three-masted schooner *Fanny Dutard*, built by the White Shipyard in San Francisco in 1882 as a lumber drougher, boasting exceptional lines and well appointed throughout. That well known coaster made the transition to the fishing industry as early as 1905 when purchased by J. A. Matheson. By the following year she found herself in company with several other sailing vessels that had long served the coastal routes, including the *Carrier Dove*, *Lizzie Colby*, *Maid of Orleans*, *Joseph Russ*, *Fortuna*, *Alice* and *Harold Blekum*. All of the above sailed from Puget Sound ports but their total catch of over a million fish was 400,000 less than the 11 codfishers that put out from San Francisco Bay ports. The following year the Puget Sound fleet came home with a slightly better catch than their California counterparts, and again in 1908. By 1910 the bulk of the codfish sailing vessels were operating to Alaska from Puget Sound, the shorter run being an incentive.

When the schooner *Wawona* joined the fleet in 1914 she brought home an all-time record codfish catch for a single season, 240,000 fish of 1.1 million pounds. But perhaps the most durable and dependable of the entire Pacific Coast fleet was the *Fanny Dutard*, giving a good account of herself each year until sold to J.E. Shields in 1918, for offshore trading. After the war she returned to the codfishery.

For a glimpse of what it was like to be a hand on a codfishing schooner, the comments of a salt named Gus Dagg of Anacortes, who first sailed aboard the *Dutard* in 1924 are presented here:

"Outside of a compass, big iron stove in the galley, a one-lung gas engine for pulling the anchor and three kerosene lanterns (one for the galley, one for the foc's'cle and one for the cabin aft), we were exactly like a ship in the time of Christ. Only in the time of Christ, people had more sense than to go codfishing in the Bering Sea.''

Dagg continued, "At Pier 59 (Seattle) lay what was to me one of the most beautiful sights in the world; a trim, three-masted sailing schooner, with a nest of twelve 16-foot dories on each side." He was referring to the *Fanny Dutard*.

Dagg went on to say, "The last thing before we left Seattle, half a cow was brought aboard and hoisted up to the top of the mainmast. It

Captain S.C. Mitchell, his wife and their children, nurse and the vessel's first officer ride a loading wire to the **SCHOONER IRENE,** moored at Noyo, California in 1916.

was supposed to keep better up there but I think the real reason was to make it hard for some steak-hungry fisherman on the night watch to get himself a feed.

"We got a few meals from the cow the first week out, but that was the last fresh meat, or for that matter, fresh vegetables or fruit, we would see for four or five months. The potatoes usually lasted to about the last month before home. There was always a lot of butter and bacon to go with the hotcakes, fish and beans—that was our staple diet. The big bean pot was always on the table, every meal.

"Water was a big problem and could be used only for drinking and cooking. We washed clothes by hanging them over the jibboom on lines. The constant lifting and dipping of the schooner acted like a washing machine and the clothes came out cleaner and whiter than in any Maytag. The only drawback was that the salt had a tendency to store up in the lower ends of the garment.

"The dories, the years I fished with them, had no power of any kind, and neither had the schooners, except for an old Swedish kerosene engine started with a blowtorch or a wheezy steam donkey. This was used only for pulling the anchor. But half the time the engines would not start, or if a storm came up too quickly, there was no way of picking up the anchor and going to the aid of the dories. Fog was, of course, another big hazard. We had small compasses, but to try to find the speck in the ocean that was the schooner was a gamble—especially considering the way the tides run in the Bering Sea. The dories always tried to stay to windward of the schooner, so as to be able to make it back in case of a storm. We never lost a man on any of the vessels I fished for four years, although some of the other outfits lost people.

"I remember one time when the dories got caught out in a terrible sou'wester. We all made it back to the vessel, except one guy who was too far to leeward to buck it back. Everybody was on the stern watching the poor devil struggling to make it, but then he finally disappeared in the fog. I am glad to say that we picked the guy up 30 hours later, in fair condition.

"We were called out at 2:30 every morning. Breakfast was at 3, consisting of mush, hot cakes, bacon and beans. If you were a couple of minutes late, you didn't get any. Dories were out at 3:30. This was not an easy operation, as it was almost always rough, with a sea running. Everybody was aware that one mistake could cost a man his life. Among the Bluenose fisherman were a couple of old men in their seventies. It was bad enough for us younger guys to make the flying leap necessary to make it aboard the

dories. I always marveled at seeing those old men going over the side like cats. On the sailing fishing schooner your life depended on the quickness of your response to ever-occurring emergencies. There were no life preservers. Neither did we have any toilets. You went over the jibboom and hung onto the stays. It is a testament to the wonderful seaworthiness of those old ships that I can never remember getting my behind wet, even in the most raging storm. A little spray, of course, but no more.

"There was always somebody aboard with a pair of old scissors, trying to make an extra buck cutting hair. The old fisherman had a superstition that it was healthy and beneficial to shave your head and wash it with kerosene. As we young men greatly admired and tried to imitate the old Bluenose fishermen as much as possible, we all did it.

"Cut and bruises were common. There was no medical kit. Something called a fisherman's salve, a wax-like substance which was heated over a candle and dripped red hot into the sore, or hemorrhoid was the treatment, so painful, though surprisingly effective. Most of the guys did not go to the cabin for treatment."

"It was a hard life for the codfisherman and the pay pretty much depended on the catch, but most of those who participated were sorrowful when the traditional schooners were replaced by engined craft."

Probably one of the best known of the codfish schooner skippers was Captain Tom Haugen who lived to see 90. A native of Norway of hearty stock, he never liked his given first name Torsten, and was always known by Tom. Unlike most of the crusty old salts, he didn't begin his seagoing career at sea in sailing ships but first shipped out in 1907 on the steamer *Guert*. After migrating to the United States he dabbled in the tall timber and on railroads in the west. However, nothing satisfied until he went back to sea in 1915 aboard the halibut schooner *Tom and Al*, operated by King and Winge of Seattle. He later shifted to the codfish schooners, *Alice*, *Fanny Dutard*, and *Maweema*, the latter vessel owned by the Alaska Codfish Company of San Francisco. He filled the off season with berths on coastwise steamers and sailing vessels. Oddly enough, it was while he was a passenger on a steamer in the spring of 1924 off Coos Bay that he was forced to slide down a cable to save his life when the vessel suffered shipwreck.

It was that same year he signed as second mate aboard the schooner *Wawona*, owned by Robinson Fisheries Company of Anacortes. It was the beginning of a 24 year association with the vessel. In 1927 he became first mate, and

Two early views of Port Townsend, Washington taken in the 1880's. A cross section of the city and the harbor shows many ornate buildings and a fleet of sailing ships and steamers in Port Townsend Bay. Port Townsend was infamous for its little "Barbary Coast" not too far divorced from that of early day San Francisco. It was believed in the early years that the city would remain the chief seaport in the Puget Sound area but the railroads chose other terminus's favoring the east side of the Sound.

maintained that post until Captain Charles Foss died in 1935, while the schooner was headed for Unimak Pass. Haugen assumed command. There was another death at sea in 1941, when Haugen's first mate and best friend Nick Field died.

The highlight of his career as master of the *Wawona* was the year 1937, when the schooner came home with the all-time record catch for a three-masted codfisher.

The U.S. Army grabbed the *Wawona* during World War II along with the Robinson schooner *Azalea*, and used them as barges. Only the schooner *Charles R. Wilson*, owned by Captain J.E. Shields of Poulsbo, continued to seek cod in the Bering Sea.

Robinson Fisheries had the *Wawona* returned in 1944, and after receiving a refit and new masts she hoisted her sails and went north from Anacortes for cod in the 1946 season. Unfortunately the season was one of the worst on record.

Haugen and his wife spent the following winter living aboard the vessel at Anacortes, but the poor previous fishing season and a deflated market for salted cod spelled the end of a colorful chapter in maritime history. New refrigeration and freezing methods caused Robinson Fisheries to look instead to cod livers and tongues, and the *Wawona* was equipped with cold storage, plumbing and water tanks for processing work. Her last voyage under sail was in 1947. The venture was unsuccessful and the schooner was sold, passing from one hopeful owner to the next until finally she ended up as the property of Save Our Ships, a Seattle maritime preservation group.

39

Hearts of oak are our ships,
Hearts of oak are our men.

---David Garrick

Part Two

Principal Builders Of West Coast Windjammers

The Hall Brothers

THE HALL BROTHERS, Winslow G. and Henry Knox, made shipbuilding history on Puget Sound. They were natives of Cohasset, Massachusetts, a fishing village and summer resort on the southern shore of Boston Bay, not far from the infamous Minots Lodge.

John Lyman, eminent maritime researcher recalls that it was here and at Medford, Massachusetts, that these skilled craftsmen learned shipbuilding first hand from the tops in the trade, and rose to master ship's carpenters.

The Hall Brothers came to San Francisco during the Civil War when the cry of gold had turned the Bay City into a beehive of excitement. Unlike most of the gold-hungry population, however, the Halls went West to practice their chosen occupation of shipbuilding. Henry K. Hall became a leading man at the Mare Island Navy yard for awhile, but the brothers found time between 1863 and 1869 to build three staunch two-masted schooners. Winslow built the *Sarah Louise* and the *California,* while brother Isaac constructed the *Stranger.*

In 1873, Isaac heard the call of the tall timber and turned the theme of "Go West Young Man" into "Go Pacific Northwest Young Man." He took a gang of men to Puget Sound with a contract in his pocket to build a small schooner for San Francisco interests. He found a desirable site at Port Ludlow on the peaceful shores of Hood Canal, an area surrounded by great stands of timber, desirable for building ships. His first effort in Paul Bunyan country was the trim 107-ton, two-masted schooner *Z. B. Heywood.* She was named for one of her new owners and the occasion brought every man, woman and child in the locale to the shipways to witness the launching. Predominant among the crowd were Indians from Puget Sound tribes who examined the "big canoe" with intense curiosity.

This vessel became well known in the lumber trade and established an enviable record until her loss 15 years later at the mouth of the Navarro River in California.

While awaiting another contract, Isaac worked for a time as a journeyman shipwright on the barkentine *S. M. Stetson,* under construction at nearby Port Madison on Bainbridge Island. Later he returned to San Francisco where he persuaded his brother Winslow to enter into a partnership after telling him of the great cost advan-

The Hall Brothers Marine Railway and Shipbuilding Company on Eagle Harbor, Bainbridge Island about 1907. A four-masted schooner is seen on drydock and another at anchor.   *Webster & Stevens photo.*

tages of building ships near the mills. It was thus arranged that Winslow would remain in San Francisco, where he would attend to design work, seek contracts from prospective buyers and arrange for procuring the sails, cordage, fastenings and other materials that could not be obtained in the Northwest.

Isaac soon returned to Puget Sound with another contract from the same group of Californians that had ordered the *Heywood.* Thus, the schooner *Annie Gee* was built in 1874.

Following her completion, an illustrious shipbuilding era was opened for the Halls. Before the year 1874 had run out, the shipyard turned out four additional two-masted schooners and another three schooners in the following year. These ships were received with great praise from the owners, and the yard took another stride forward by building its first three-masted schooner, the *Emma Utter* in 1875, a design that proved highly successful in the haulage of lumber.

In the year 1876, the Hall **Brothers,** now well established and highly respected, built three

more three-masted schooners, and one of these, the *Reporter,* they elected to retain under their exclusive ownership. This was a wise decision as the ship was loaded to capacity time and time again at Puget Sound mill sites. The *Reporter* ran almost continuously until March 13, 1902, when she came to grief near San Francisco's Cliff House enroute from Grays Harbor.

Following virtually in the wake of the *Reporter's* launching came the barkentine *Quickstep,* the yard's largest effort to that date. This vessel was also retained for Hall ownership and more than lived up to her name by once showing her heels to the full-rigged ship *St. Mark* on the return leg of a voyage to the East Coast. The *Quickstep* was a high stepper until the fall of 1905 when she was abandoned in sinking condition off Yaquina Light on the Oregon coast.

In 1877, Hall Brothers turned out five of the most handsome two-masted schooners ever designed—all for Hawaiian interests. Both as island traders and ocean hoppers, these vessels proved their great seaworthiness, and opened new avenues that kept the yard flourishing through the next two lean years in Pacific Coast shipbuilding.

After building the barkentine *Catherine Sudden* for their own account, and the schooner *Luka* for Allen & Robinson of Honolulu in 1878, the Pacific Coast suffered a recession and the yard dabbed about with the conversion of a schooner into a steam-powered craft, and in 1880 built its first steamer from the keel up —the *C. R. Bishop.*

Steam, however, was not yet economically feasible in Pacific Ocean lumber trades and the yard was soon back to its chosen trade—the construction of wooden sailing vessels—their finest being the 470-ton barkentine *Wrestler.*

By the end of 1880, the now famous Hall yard was faced with a big moving job, prompted by the closure of the mill at Port Ludlow. The facility had slowly declined with the death of one of its owners in 1877. Although another mill was begun there at once, a subsidy from other Puget Sound mill owners kept it from

cutting, in order to keep from flooding the lumber market.

The new Hall yard was located alongside the Port Blakely Mill Co. (Renton, Holmes and Company), across Puget Sound from Seattle. This aggressive mill complex eventually became the largest of its kind in the world and shared its success with the adjoining Hall Brothers yard. In its heyday, the lumber yard employed 1,200 workers and cut 400,000 feet of lumber a day. That was three-quarters of a century ago. Many of the new sailing vessels built at the Hall facility were for the mill owners who supplied the lumber, the spars and the masts. The small harbor was often crowded with endless rows of sailing vessels from all over the world, awaiting lumber cargoes.

The third brother, Henry K. Hall, who joined the shipbuilding enterprise in 1875, continued to manage the shipyard operations after the death of Isaac in 1879. He more than proved his ability in the fruitful years that followed.

Winslow Hall died at San Francisco in 1898

Lined up like old ladies at a sewing bee, tall sailing vessels of yesteryear are seen in Eagle Harbor.

Webster & Stevens photo

The productive Port Blakely Mill Company on Bainbridge Island once cut 400,000 board feet of lumber a day. Here, famed shipbuilder Henry K. Hall looks over the mill located next to the Hall Brothers shipyard. Much of the timber for Hall ships was cut at the facility.

and the office was then managed by George E. Billings. Billings had married Maria Hall in 1877, a niece of the shipbuilding Halls. This was his introduction to the business. Despite the fact that his experience with the maritime was nil, he was a good businessman with considerable experience in the stationary and publishing enterprises. He took over Winslow's role at the company's San Francisco office.

In 1902, after building the ship of his dreams —the five-masted schooner *H. K. Hall*—erect, white-bearded Henry K. Hall retired from active management of the yard. The new ship named for him was the second five-master built by the facility. The first was the handsome schooner *Inca,* constructed in 1896.

Henry was succeeded by his son James Hall. The following year—1903—with the completion of the five-masted schooner *George E. Billings,* of 1,260 tons, the largest built by the firm, shipbuilding operations at Port Blakely ceased. The yard moved a few miles northward on Bainbridge Island to Eagle Harbor where the town of Winslow was established in honor

of the late Hall brother. The reorganized firm was named Hall Brothers Marine Railway and Shipbuilding Company, with James Hall as manager. Joining the Halls in the organization were Pope & Talbot and Port Blakely Mill Co., the idea being that the yard would maintain the vessel fleets of the three founding groups.

In 1904, John L. Hubbard replaced James Hall as yard manager and the Hall era ended. The last of the original Hall brothers passed away in 1909 at a time when the sailing ship was in its sunset years.

The new yard, though repairing numerous sailing vessels, turned to building steam-powered ships.

From the founding of the Hall yard at Port Ludlow in 1874, to the closing of the yard at Port Blakely in 1903, some 96 sailing vessels over 100 tons, and 12 steam-powered vessels were constructed.

HESPER

Strange to say that of all the sailing ships constructed by the Hall brothers, none is as well remembered as the bark *Hesper.* Unfortunately her memory was not kept green because of her splendid sailing qualities, but by a mutiny which haunted the ship throughout most of her career. The *Hesper* was described as a two-skysail yard bark and was launched by the Hall yard at Port Blakely in 1882. The *Hesper* and her sistership *Albert* were among the few sailing vessels built on the Pacific Coast to carry figureheads. Most had only scrolled billet heads, so recalls Captain P. A. McDonald, renowned sailing ship master of Santa Monica. He further remembers that the vessel made many fast passages including one of nine and one-half days from the Hawaiian Islands to Cape Flattery. But, she was chiefly famous or rather notorious for that one foul deed—which took place upon the high seas during a passage from Newcastle, N. S. W., to San Francisco.

It was at Newcastle in 1893 that the *Hesper* loaded a cargo of coal. The harbor was bustling with tall square-rigged ships, the shoreside pubs and boarding houses were doing a land office business and the docks were virtually alive with activity.

Even as the *Hesper* was having her hungry holds filled, a sinister plot was being hatched in the fo'c's'le. Among the crew was one known as St. Clair, a rugged bully with a domineering, twisted personality. A big trouble maker and instigator of many nefarious schemes, he had always managed to elude serious penalty by the law.

By contrast, the *Hesper* was in command of a respected master mariner named Captain A. Sodergreen. He ran a tight ship and usually got the most out of his crew. Young for a skipper, he was both alert and strong. On this certain

voyage, his bride of a few months was making the passage as a sort of a belated honeymoon.

The chief mate was named Lucas and the second mate Fitzgerald, a big Irishman, who took great pleasure in bullying the seamen with his meat-like fists.

The man St. Clair, around whom this episode revolved, had learned that the *Hesper* carried $20,000 in cash in the ship's strongbox, and this was the target of his plot. He had wasted little time intimidating the crew and had found at least two avid supporters who were his willing tools. One of his new partners in crime was a greasy, olive-skinned man named Sparff, and the other a beefy Scandinavian called Hanson. With these domineering three, the remainder of the fo'c's'le gang had no choice but to remain passive or neutral. None had any desire to tangle with the tough St. Clair whose methods of getting what he wanted were anything but orthodox. Indeed, they feared reprisal in case the mutiny proved successful.

St. Clair laid his plans carefully. Again and again he briefed Sparff and Hanson, making them repeat his words over and over. The master plan was to kill the ship's officers, capture the ship and sail away for waters where the vessel could be sold or used in a profitable vocation of buccaneering. It would have seemed at this late date that pirateering was over, but St. Clair, nonconformist that he was, had visions of reviving the forbidden practice and perhaps become another Blackbeard. He was well aware of the *Hesper's* reputation for speed. The ship could be his, plus a fat bonus in cash if he could pull off his dastardly plot.

It was the second mate's watch from eight to

A jewel of Victorian architecture the Flavel house in Astoria. Now the property of the Clatsop County Historical Society, the old mansion was built by Captain George Flavel in 1887. He and Captain A. M. Simpson, of North Bend organized the Columbia River bar pilots in the mid 19th century. From the cupola of this house a lookout was kept for windjammers approaching the Columbia River bar, prompting the dispatch of a pilot to bring them to safe haven.

midnight on the appointed night, after the ship was well out to sea. According to plan, Fitzgerald was to be the first one murdered. The breeze was light and the moon partially filtered as the *Hesper* cut through the dark waters. The decks were silent except for the creaking and groaning of the tackle. Most of the canvas was set and the vessel moved along at a fair gait. Suddenly the relative quiet was broken as St. Clair lumbered aft to gain the attention of Fitzgerald.

"Sir," he said in a soft, raspy voice, "I was wonderin' if ye could come for'ard to see some trouble with the riggin'."

"What the hell is it now?" barked the irritated mate.

"Jist follow me," St. Clair insisted.

The two started forward, as the helmsman, grim-faced in the dim light of the binnacle, watched them fade into the darkness. Hiding in the shadows were Sparff and Hanson, the former with a hatchet in his hand. Quicker than the flash on an eye the blunt end of the weapon came down on top of Fitzgerald's head with a sickening thud. Again and again it struck the unsuspecting officer until his body crumpled to the deck. Immediately St. Clair dragged the blood-smeared figure to the scuppers, and then without the slightest hesitation lifted him to the gunwhales and dumped him overboard.

Move number one of the sinister plot had come off as planned.

When it came time to call chief mate Lucas for the midnight watch, a duty usually performed by the second mate, one of the crew was substituted. Lucas became suspicious on hearing the unfamiliar voice and, instead of going out on deck immediately, knocked on the

Outbound with a full load of lumber, the **BARKENTINE JAMES TUFT** spreads her wings in the North Pacific. Built by the Hall Brothers at Port Blakely in 1901, she cost $74,000. The vessel burned as a gambling barge off Long Beach, California August 22, 1935.

H. H. Morrison took this photo of the **BARKENTINE SKAGIT** in the Strait of Juan de Fuca with all sails set, around the turn of the century. Built by Hiram Doncaster at Port Ludlow in 1883 for Puget Sound Commercial Company the vessel was wrecked with the loss of two lives near Clo-oose, B.C. October 25, 1906.

captain's cabin door. In a whisper the two discussed the situation. They were overheard by the captain's wife who was awakened from her sleep.

"Please," she murmured in pleading tones, "don't take any chances, I have just had a premonition that some terrible thing would happen this night."

Captain Sodergreen heeded his wife's warning and placed a gun inside his jacket, and, with Lucas, stole silently out on the deck. They cautiously worked their way amidships until confronted by the dim shadows of three men. Pausing, they glanced about and there in the half light was the blood-stained deck, telltale evidence of foul play. Sensing the danger, the captain's hand slipped inside his jacket and whipped out the pistol. There, against the pinrail crouched low, they saw the frame of a big man that could be none other than St. Clair. He was like a tiger ready to spring. The others hung back, awaiting their leader's move. A scuffle ensued, but at the sight of the gun the mutineers' zest for murder was hastily quelled. The skipper held the pistol firmly against St. Clair's head and ordered him and the others to put their hands on the railing. There was no more fight left in them, only the low murmur of profanity from the ringleader's twisted mouth.

Red faced and enraged over the attempted mutiny, the captain bellowed like a rampaging bull, "All hands on deck!"

The sound reverberated throughout the vessel and half-dressed, hollow-eyed crewmen came stumbling out of the dark recesses to undergo a tongue-lashing supreme. The skipper was determined to clean up every tag end of the thwarted plot. He singled out a few for punishment and only when thoroughly convinced that the others were not directly involved did he dismiss them.

The following day the decks were holystoned removing the last evidence of the brutal murder. The three despots were stashed away in a dingy compartment below for a long voyage of misery in irons and a scant diet of hardtack and water.

A course was set for Papeete, where the implicated men were thrown in the local jail until passage could be arranged for them back to San Francisco.

No West Coast-built sailing vessel was better known than was the **HESPER.** This masterpiece of the Hall Brothers, built in 1882, had her career blemished by a mutiny in 1893. Here she waits for assignment to pick up a load of Puget Sound lumber in the early days.

The trial did not take place until the *Hesper* finally arrived at the Bay City. Newspaper headlines played up the mutiny trial to the hilt, and national attention was centered on the court room when the trial was convened. After the facts were laid on the line, there was no doubt among the jurors that St. Clair was the instigator of the nefarious scheme. He was accordingly sentenced to be hung by the neck until dead, and his accomplices were all given jail terms in proportion to their share of the crime.

Had the mutiny come off as St. Clair planned, it might have been the revival of the nearly obliterated practice of piracy on the high seas. Except for the alertness of the *Hesper's* first officer and the premonition of the captain's wife, the drama would have taken its place next to the mutiny on the *Bounty*.

The episode blackballed the *Hesper*. The story followed the vessel wherever she sailed and frequently it was hard to get seamen to sign

aboard. Despite the admirable qualities of the windjammer, she aged without the usual dignity of a proud sailer, and her career became somewhat checkered due in much part to the superstitious nature of seafaring men.

Some 17 years later, we find the leaky and worn *Hesper* loading at Grays Harbor, preparing to sail for South America in command of Captain Charles Hacket. Hacket, a salty old seadog, had convinced backers to underwrite a treasure hunting voyage to Cocos Island. He claimed to be the last of a long list of adventurers possessing the map of the location of this long sought cache of gold, silver and plate reputedly deposited there by pirates.

The *Hesper* first had an arduous voyage to Chile to discharge a cargo of lumber and then proceeded to Cocos and the excitement of hunting treasure. Despite determined diggings, labor, sweat and toil, the hunt proved no more successful than the *Hesper* mutiny.

And what became of the *Hesper?* Some years afterwards, in the harbor of Antofagasta, the tides ebbed and flowed through her abandoned, ghostlike remains. Her rotted timbers and stumped masts seemed to bewail her jinxed career.

By contrast with the *Hesper's* unfortunate life, there was the three-masted schooner *Fred E. Sander,* a lucky ship. She was built at the Hall yard at Port Blakely in 1887, just five years after the *Hesper* was constructed. This schooner was 157 feet long with a 37-foot beam and of 463 gross tons. She was owned by the Halls throughout the greater share of her active years. In 1917, she was sold to Peruvian owners and was still afloat as late as 1930 under the name *Lionelo.*

The fame of the *Sander* was in her speed, so predominant in Hall-built vessels. As was pointed out earlier, such schooners often outsailed barks and full-rigged ships with almost twice the spread of canvas.

Records clearly show that the *Fred E. Sander* once sailed from her wharf in San Francisco to Schwabacher Dock at Seattle in the remarkable time of 72 hours—without the aid of any tugs. This was accomplished with naught but her canvas and the wind that God supplied to belly her sails. The feat was logged in the year 1902.

Nor was this an exception. The *Sander* made many epic voyages during her career. The 1902 passage, however, placed her in the maritime hall of fame as far as West Coast coasting records were concerned. On this certain voyage, she was in the command of Captain Charlie Roos—a man of wide reputation who really knew how to lay on every stitch of canvas and take full advantage of the prevailing winds. His record voyage not only eclipsed every record set on a coastwise run by a sailing vessel, but was also faster than most of the passenger liners of that day. The *Sander* was competing against some familiar old Downeaster clipper-type sailing vessels like the *Dashing Wave* and *Forest Queen,* which often logged fine 80 to 90-hour voyages with the use of tugs at both ends of the line.

The *Sander,* under the command of Captain George Ekrum, almost duplicated her record in 1912. On August 7 of that year, she sailed from Everett, Washington, to San Pedro, California, with 600,000 board feet of lumber and missed only by a few hours her 1902 northbound record.

The history of sail is a saga, for it was under sail that the world was discovered. A saga telling of venture and strange experiences of a hard, dangerous way of life, rich in famous ships and men, often glorified in romance but, in reality, unrelenting and full of privation.

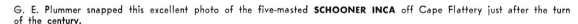

G. E. Plummer snapped this excellent photo of the five-masted **SCHOONER INCA** off Cape Flattery just after the turn of the century.

The three-masted **SCHOONER FRED E. SANDER** was the fastest of the coastwise windjammers once posting an all-time record run under Captain Charlie Roos of 72 hours, San Francisco to Seattle. On August 1, 1911 she set another record being the first ship to reach Point Barrow with 750 tons of supplies, knocking eight days off the previous record. Her master then was Captain George Ekrum. She ended her days as the **LIONELO,** registered at Callao.

CAPTAIN MATTHEW TURNER
Master Shipbuilder

In the ranks of West Coast sailing vessel construction, no name is better remembered than that of Captain Matthew Turner. This invincible man of the sea was born at Geneva, Ohio, in 1825, and found his way out to San Francisco at the height of the Gold Rush in 1850. In many respects he could be called the "granddaddy" of big time commercial wooden shipbuilding on the Pacific Coast.

After a taste of placer mining, he went to sea as both owner and master of sailing vessels. His most successful command was the brig *Nautilus,* which he himself designed. So pleased was he with her sailing qualities that it drove him into a shipbuilding career. He had also studied the sailing qualities of the schooners *Toronto* and *Louis Perry* and the brigs *Timandra* and *Percy Edwards,* all of which he sailed on as officer or master. His mind was never idle, but constantly on the lookout for innovations in accomplishing faster passages at sea under sail.

Gordon P. Jones, Seattle, noted in his Alaska Sportsman article "Cod Bangers to Alaska" that Captain Turner, in making regular runs to Siberia as early as 1859, became aware of the codfish bonanza. In the *Timandra* in 1864, he outfitted the vessel strictly for codfishing, opening up the thriving Pacific cod fishery which later attracted scores of West Coast-built windjammers.

Turner was actually an idol of the Hall brothers. Henry Hall, who learned many lessons from Turner, kept a notebook on the man which is now at the Penobscot Marine Museum at Searsport, Maine. Some excerpts follow:

San Francisco, November 9—Matthew Turner is a popular builder here, and in fact is about the only active one beside the Dickies. He was born, or at least lived at Geneva, Ohio. In the winters, his father would build a boat of some kind. In the summers, father and son would go out on the lake. The young man thus gained his first insight into shipbuilding.

He came here 15 or 20 years ago. He

49

was not satisfied with the models then followed on this coast. In 1868, he made a model of the brig, the *Nautilus,* 173 tons and had the vessel built for him on Humboldt Bay. The old models were full and short forward. He reversed the plan, and made them long and sharp forward, lean and full on the waterline aft. His model was laughed at. They told him his brig would pitch and dive into the water and be always wet. But it did not turn out so. She was a good vessel, very fast and successful, and is alive yet. She is 104 feet on the waterline and 24.9 feet beam, ten foot hold and carries 260 tons.

Mr. Turner built all his vessels on this general principle of a long forebody and a short after body. He began the business of building in the winter of 1870-71, and has been regularly at it ever since. He has introduced many new ideas. In some of his boats and yachts he employs masts which are in one piece from keel to truck. The lower masts and topmast are all in one. He also introduced the Bermudan sail, which Jerau once employed in Brooklyn, New York. It is the fore and aft sail without gaff, being a large triangular sail.

Mr. Turner says that his experience in sailing on the Pacific Ocean showed him the utility of that style of sail. In sudden squalls, the sail can be let go, and brought on deck with great ease, there being no terrible gaff to bring inboard and dispose of. Other builders have not adopted the "Turner Model" and the Bermudan sail, and spars of a single stick. The *St. Paul,* bark rigged, had fore and mainmasts 108 feet long, each in one stick . . . the steam brig *Dora* was rigged with masts, each a single stick.

From the time Turner opened his first yard at San Francisco, including the later move to Benicia, he turned out a total of 228 sailing vessels, and though many were small in size, this record was probably never equalled by any other individual shipbuilder in the American era of sail. He further, in all probability, built more vessels for foreign account than any other American since the Revolution. A large part of his production was for owners in the South Sea Islands, where he had extensive trading interests.

Turner's death in 1909 marked the end of an era and the passing of a remarkable man who had vision, skill and determination all built into a well-rounded personality. So pronounced was his influence on the design of the South

Pictured in 1912, the **BRIGANTINE WILLIAM G. IRWIN** is seen offshore. Built at San Francisco in 1881 as a sugar packet for J. D. Spreckels, she was re-rigged as a three-masted schooner a year after this photo was taken.   *O. Beaton photo*

Packing 900,000 board feet of lumber, the Hay & Wright (Alameda) built **SCHOONER COMMERCE** is seen heading into the Pacific swells in 1913. G. E. Plummer photo.

Seas schooner that, as recently as 1941, a two-master built at Tahiti and sailed under the French flag to San Francisco was named *Benicia* by her native builder who had learned his trade in Turner's old yard.

Another class of commercial sailing vessel, in which Turner specialized, was the Bering Sea pelagic sealing schooner, and he turned out a large number of them until the United States law banned sealing, just before the turn of the century.

The old files of Bowes & Andrews of San Francisco contained many of the outstanding sailing records and fast passages of Turner-built ships:

Barkentine *Benicia*, Newcastle, N.S.W, to Kehei, Hawaii, 35 days.

Schooner *Solano*, Shanghai to Port Townsend, 24 days (April 1902).

Barkentine *Amaranth* (four-masted), Shanghai to Astoria, 23 days, plus four voyages Puget Sound to Taku (Shanghai), under Captain E. C. Bowes in 100, 110, 118 and 123 days, including full round trips back to Puget Sound.

Brigantine *Galilee,* Tahiti to San Francisco in 22 days (in 1891).

Brig *Nautilus*, Turner's prototype vessel, Tahiti to San Francisco, 20 days.

Schooner *Papeete,* San Francisco to Tahiti, 17 days.

Schooner *Emma Claudina,* San Francisco to Hawaii, 8 days 8 hours; Hilo to San Francisco, 9 days, 20 hours.

Brigantine *William G. Irwin,* San Francisco to Kahului, Hawaii, 8 days 17 hours (1881), and from Honolulu to San Francisco, 9 days.

Brigantine *John D. Spreckels,* San Francisco to Kahului, 28 days, including loading and discharging; from Honolulu to San Francisco, 9 days, 20 hours (1891).

Brigantine *Geneva,* Launceston, Tasmania to Newcastle, N. S. W., 2 days.

Schooner *Anna,* Honolulu to San Francisco, 10 days (1886) and 8 round trips, San Francisco to Kahului in 357 days.

Brigantine *W. H. Dimond,* San Francisco to Honolulu, 9 days, 10 hours.

Turner also built a schooner-yacht with racey lines that won three of the first four San Pedro-Honolulu yacht races in the bygones.

Little wonder that this renowned builder became one of the greatest names in American maritime history. His fame was world-wide and his ships a testimony to his skill.

In 1882, Captain Turner built the 195-ton, three-masted schooner *Emma Claudina* for sugar baron John D. Spreckels. Aside from living up to the tradition of the Turner brand for speed and new records, this vessel cornered another small piece of history. She afforded the inspiration for the founding of the Matson Navigation Co., which has flourished to the present day.

Back in 1882, Captain William Matson, then 33 years of age, a Swedish-born, mustachioed, self-adopted San Franciscan, dropped anchor in Hilo, Hawaii, in command of the *Emma Claudina,* and procedded to haul sugar between the Hawaiian Islands and the U. S. mainland. Business was so good that the schooner couldn't begin to handle it all, so skipper Matson decided that he would work his way into the business of sugar hauling and eventually start his own fleet.

Thus, in 1887, we find that Captain William Matson and the Spreckels Brothers were joint owners of the brigantine *Lurline,* of 358 tons, built by Turner at his Benicia yard in 1887 and designed especially for the sugar trade. An eye-catching vessel, she appeared more like a great winged yacht than a commercial sailing vessel. She carried a skysail yard and had all the speed of a racing yacht, once logging a passage of eight days and eight hours between San Francisco and Honolulu.

From this one vessel the Matson fleet grew into the lifeline of the Hawaiian Islands and eventually served all the South Seas, the Antipodes and the Far East.

The passenger liner *Lurline* of today, serving Matson's California-Hawaii trade, would dwarf her predecessor. The liner is 632 feet in length; the original *Lurline* 135 feet. The present *Lurline* is of 18,500 gross tons; the first *Lurline* 358 tons. But at least, on one occasion, the little brigantine bested the passage time of her modern counterpart. In early 1965, the SS *Lurline* limped into San Francisco Bay with engine trouble having required nine days to complete the voyage from Honolulu. This time was equalled by the original *Lurline* many times and bettered on a few occasions. Of course, when the SS *Lurline* is under her full power, she makes the passage in four and a half days.

Both the *Emma Claudina* and the original *Lurline* had long and eventful careers. The former, reverting from the sugar to the lumber trades, was lost by foundering off Grays Harbor on November 14, 1906, her crew of eight being saved. The *Lurline,* on the other hand, was last owned by Captain Charles Nelson and went to the bottom after being rammed by the SS *Panaman* of the American-Hawaiian Line off Salina Cruz, Mexico, on January 11, 1915. Her crew was rescued following the fatal collision.

JOHN D. SPRECKELS

The sugar magnate John D. Spreckels had a Turner vessel constructed and named for him at San Francisco in 1880. She was a 266-ton brigantine, heavily rigged and carrying topmast stunsails for additional speed. The vessel was also fitted to carry passengers, though only 124 feet in length. To her credit were at least three ten-day voyages on the San Francisco-Hawaiian Island run.

In 1905, as larger ships began to take over the island sugar run, the *John D. Spreckels* was converted to a codfishing schooner, swapping the tradewinds for Arctic blasts. She proved successful in the San Francisco-Alaska run until the grim day of March 29, 1913.

On that day a thick pall of fog hung over the

With virtually no freeboard the 183-foot **SCHOONER BLAKELY** is pictured outbound for the Pacific islands. Photo by H. H. Morrison.

Captain Matthew Turner built and retained ownership of the **BARKENTINE BENICIA** in 1899. She was wrecked on the south coast of Haiti under ownership of Whitney-Bodden Company, Mobile, October 10, 1920.

Golden Gate and for several miles northward. The stillness was broken by the ominous call of deep-throated and high-pitched foghorns at various spots between Point Bonita and Point Reyes.

On March 31, the steam schooner *Temple E. Dorr* came in through the strands of fog at the Golden Gate and reported having sighted the derelict schooner *John D. Spreckels* with only a small section of her stern and some of her mizzen and spanker rising above the surface of the ocean. The remainder of the vessel was well in the depths, ready for the final plunge straight to Davy Jones Locker. The *Temple E. Dorr's* master reported searching the area for several hours without the slightest trace of survivors.

The ill-fated schooner, owned by the Alaska Codfish Company, was returning from her Alaskan station with 120,000 codfish salted down in her holds. She was commanded by Captain Charles Prellberg and carried a crew of seven men.

When the word of the schooner's misfortune reached the Bay City, the U. S. Revenue cutter *McCulloch,* at dock in San Francisco, put to sea under full steam, her whistle blasting as she entered the fog banks. She arrived at the scene of the wreck and immediately began making wide sweeps around the derelict, searching for survivors and warning other ships to stand clear of the dangerous menace to navigation.

Meanwhile, San Francisco newspapers were playing up the story of the mystery of the missing crew of the *John D. Spreckels.* There

appeared no logical solution to the incident until finally, on April 3, a message received in San Francisco from Victoria, B. C., reported that the British freighter *Statesman* had picked up the survivors of the schooner after having rammed her in a pea-soup fog. Two of the Spreckels crewmen were trapped inside the vessel following the crash and were carried to a watery death. The schooner went down to her precarious position in less than three minutes, but for some strange reason refused to go to the bottom. Seven other crewmen, including the captain, narrowly escaped with their lives.

Just before the fatal collision, the master of the cod-carrying schooner recalled sighting the massive bow of the freighter looming above him as it broke the veil of fog. Before he could take a deep breath, there was a grinding, splintering impact that virtually severed the schooner. The mighty blow brought an inrush of water like a mountain river, sweeping through the mortal wound. The vessel reeled for a brief moment, those on deck stunned by the suddenness of it all. There was no chance to save anything, no chance to lower a boat, no chance for rescuing those trapped inside. The after end of the schooner rose like an elevator to the height of the bluff bow of the freighter. Barely able to maintain a foothold, the survivors pursued the course of least resistance and leaped to the deck of the *Statesman.*

Captain Prellberg felt that the master of the freighter would have been wiser to have kept the bow of his ship impaled in the fore quarter of the schooner, rather than backing off immediately. As a result the *Spreckels* drank up the sea water like a thirsty dragon and almost immediately was down by the head. With the survivors aboard, and all hope gone for recovering the bodies of the missing, the freighter continued her northward trek, refusing to risk the thick fog that obliterated the entrance to the Golden Gate. For this, and for leaving a dangerous derelict in the steamer paths, Captain Bass of the *Statesman* was later to come under severe criticism.

Captain Prellberg, on the other hand, in telling of those last horrible moments before the collision, claimed that his vessel was keeping carefully to her course. He said however:

"I do not believe the accident could have been avoided. There was a light breeze and we were making about four knots. We knew steamers were in the vicinity by their whistles, but we did not see the *Statesman* until her bow was upon us. She struck us on the starboard bow,

53

just aft of the cathead and cut into us toward the foremast. We were five miles off Point Reyes, heading E.N.E. The captain and the officers of the *Statesman* treated us well and did everything in their power to make us comfortable."

But, all of the blame, the sorrow and tears could not erase the loss of two lives, of a stout schooner and her full load of fish. Until this fatal incident the schooner had plied the Pacific for well over three decades with success.

At the memorial services for the deceased, the minister presiding asked in his prayer that someday man would conquer the fog and make the sea safe for navigation. In many ways that prayer was answered, as just a few precious years later wireless, radio and finally radar came into their own. Though not absolute perfection—as man's achievements never are— these innovations are indeed remarkable and have been the means of saving countless lives and millions of dollars in property. Both at the funeral and in the local newspapers, the words of William Whiting were used in remembrance of those who had perished at sea.

> *Whose arm hath bound the restless wave,*
> *Who bid'st the mighty ocean deep*
> *It's own appointed limits keep;*
> *Oh hear us when we cry to Thee*
> *For those in peril on the sea.*

Meanwhile, out on the briny, a constant vigil was kept over the drifting remains of the ill-fated schooner. Still refusing to go to the bottom and presenting a grave danger to other vessels, the cutter *McCulloch* repeatedly rammed the derelict and used her for target practice, but could not break her hold on life. Finally her remains had to be towed to a beach near Alameda and there were blown up. Her persistent will to live was a tribute to the prowess and skill of Captain Matthew Turner, master shipbuilder.

HANS DITLEV BENDIXSEN— Man With a Dream

Hans Ditlev Bendixsen, a man with a dream that came true, was a Dane and a native of Thisted, Denmark. Born in 1842, this dynamic individual migrated to California while still young and eventually settled in Humboldt County. He was the son of Consul F. C. and Mariane von Mehren Bendixsen, and while a youth in Denmark became an apprentice in a wooden shipbuilding firm at Aalborg. He took to the trade like a duck to water and for two years was a shipwright at Copenhagen.

Desiring a well-rounded insight into vessel performance he elected to go to sea as a ship's carpenter. Eventually his adventures led him to San Francisco where he arrived on a ship from Brazil in the year 1863. Coming ashore he found employment for a few years in Bay City shipyards at four dollars a day, but the pioneer spirit beckoned him farther northward where the timber grew tall. Thus young Hans moved to Eureka with his knowledge and experience and wasted little time getting settled in his trade, all the time with a huge dream in his mind's eye of a day when he would launch out for himself and build sailing ships, firm and stout, like those in his native Denmark.

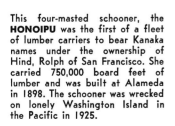

This four-masted schooner, the **HONOIPU** was the first of a fleet of lumber carriers to bear Kanaka names under the ownership of Hind, Rolph of San Francisco. She carried 750,000 board feet of lumber and was built at Alameda in 1898. The schooner was wrecked on lonely Washington Island in the Pacific in 1925.

Hopelessly aground—**SCHOONER CHARLES E. FALK,** 12 miles north of Grays Harbor, near Copalis Rocks, March 31, 1909. Her crew of eight reached shore safely.

Hans Bendixsen was a direct man with determination and a diligent, hard worker. He toiled on the construction of the barkentine *Eureka* and the brig *Nautilus* on Humboldt Bay in 1868 and played a leading role in the building of the schooners *Dashing Wave* and *Luella.* It was on completion of these two vessels that he entered independent shipbuilding at the Street yard in Eureka.

His dream was fast becoming a reality. The firm of Bendixsen and McDonald was formed for the construction of the two-masted, shallow-draft schooner *Fairy Queen,* and in 1870 Bendixsen built the centerboard schooner *Undine.*

His craftsmanship was first class, and though there were several experienced and highly competitive builders in the area, orders began coming to the Dane. He proved equal to the task. His ships were built right and turned out on time. Bendixsen hired only the best workers and demanded perfection. Between the years 1872 and 1874 he turned out six two-masted schooners and two small coastal steamers. Some old records say he built an additional half dozen small schooners between 68 and 80 tons during this period.

Business boomed, and in 1875 this master builder abandoned the inadequate Eureka site and acquired a tract of land on the sandspit north of the entrance to Humboldt Bay. It was across from the port of Eureka and adjoined Humboldt Lighthouse reservation. The yard grew like a mushroom and with it rose the town of Fairhaven. Business flourished for a quarter century through good times and bad, depressions and fires. The same year the shipyard was established Bendixsen had orders for three small Tahitian trading schooners—the *La Gironde, Vini* and *Varao* plus the brig *Paloma* and five two-masted schooners ranging in size from 69 to 224 tons.

The village of Fairhaven soon became a boomtown, taking much of the glitter away from Eureka. Bendixsen became known far and wide, and his pockets began to jingle. In 1876 he turned out 11 two-masted schooners and his first three-masted schooner—the 348-ton *Excelsior.*

A recession in 1877 held shipbuilding down to only one three-masted schooner and some repair jobs. With the slow recovery, Bendixsen tried to keep his dream alive through a partnership arrangement. He joined forces with another reputable master builder, Thos. Peterson, who had a yard on the Mendocino coast. The partnership, however, was short lived, and inasmuch as both had formed their own molds, they soon parted company as friendly enemies.

While endeavoring to acquire new orders for ships, Bendixsen rebuilt the ill-fated paddle wheel tug *Mary Ann* and the schooner *Albert & Edward* after the two vessels were salvaged from Humboldt bar.

Bendixsen established a highly enviable record from 1879 until his retirement in 1901. Amazing was the fact that during this period he had financial interest in two-thirds of the vessels he built. In 22 years, he constructed scores of two-masted schooners, 34 three-masted schooners, 11 four-masted schooners, one three-masted barkentine, three four-masted barkentines, seven steam schooners and one steamer. With the launching of the four-masted schooner *Alvena* on February 21, 1901, the aging Bendixsen decided to retire from active shipbuilding and sold his plant for a quarter million dollars to a San Francisco group who incorporated as the Bendixsen Shipbuilding Co., maintaining the name of the great shipbuilder.

Tired and worn, the Dane, whose dream ended on a harmonious note, died February 12, 1902, almost a year to the day of his retirement. His remains were shipped back to his native Thisted, Denmark, the following spring, and the cycle was completed. Bendixsen's widow erected a monument to her late husband in Thisted and gave money to support the needy of that town in his honor. The shipbuilder during his celebrated career built a total of 113 deep-sea vessels, plus numerous smaller craft.

Bendixsen had tutored many of the shipwrights at his establishment, and most stayed on after the yard was sold in 1901. The die had been cast, and right up through World War I the yard continued to build outstanding schooners and barkentines including a five-master for Charles Nelson. From 1901 to 1917 the yard built five large sailing vessels, the largest being the *Crescent*, one auxiliary sailing vessel, 27 steam schooners and one steamer.

SCHOONER WAWONA

One of the most venerable of all West Coast-built windjammers, the schooner *Wawona,* managed to live on into the space age. Built by Hans Bendixsen in 1897, she was one of the largest, if not the largest, three-masted schooner ever constructed in North America. Designed and built for the firm of Dolbeer & Carsen of San Francisco and Eureka as a lumber carrier, the vessel measures 165 feet in overall length, exclusive of her 30-foot bowsprit. She is registered at 468 gross tons and, like all Bendixsen-built sailing vessels, was put together like a wooden fortress. Her design was similar to many West Coast lumber schooners, slightly spoon-shaped bow lines, pleasant sheer and gradual deadrise. The beam, draft and sail area are such that she maneuvered well without ballast, a necessity for the quick return passages desired in the lumber trades in the Pacific. The *Wawona* is planked with a species of Douglas fir known as Humboldt pine. The durable timber was well dried by the prevailing northwest winds which persist on the Humboldt Peninsula. The schooner's long life is due in large part to the fact that fine, dry material was used in her original construction, and rock salt, which preserved the codfish in her holds

Before and after—on the 50th anniversary of the wreck of the **SCHOONER SOLANO.** She stranded in 1907 on the North North Beach Peninsula, opposite Oysterville, Washington. Matthew Turner built the Solano in 1902. *Chas. Fitzpatrick photo.*

Stern section of the **SCHOONER JOHN D. SPRECKELS** after a collision with the British freighter **STATESMAN** in fog off Point Reyes, California, March 29, 1913. Two of her crewmen perished. Last serving as a codfisher, the Spreckels was built and named for the great sugar baron in 1880.

for so many years, had a hardening affect on the hull's interior.

After a varied career in the lumber trades, the *Wawona* in 1914 was purchased by Robinson Fisheries Co. of Anacortes, Washington. She sailed to the Bering Sea codfishing grounds every year but one, until 1937, for the same owners. During that one year, the *Wawona* was used in the cannery trade.

While on one of her last codfishing voyages, in 1947, the schooner, plagued with old age, encountered considerable trouble. On the homeward passage the winds chopped up Unimak Pass, producing a howling sea which for 11 harrowing days prevented the vessel from getting through the waterway dividing the Bering Sea from the Pacific Ocean. Food supplies were dangerously low and two fishermen were ill when the message for assistance was radioed. A Navy tug was dispatched to her aid and helped bring the vessel to safety.

Another page from the log of the *Wawona*, this in 1935, told the terse news of the passing of Captain Charles Foss, the schooner's master since 1914. He perished when the vessel was at sea, and was buried on reaching Lost Harbor, on lonely Akun Island in the remote eastern Aleutians. Tom Haugen, first mate, assumed command and brought the vessel safely back to

Puget Sound. The following year the *Wawona* made a solemn voyage carrying a tombstone to Captain Foss's gravesite.

In the early 1950's it appeared as if the *Wawona* was about to revive the glorious past when, after many months of idleness, a ship's bos'n, Ralph E. Pedersen, survivor from a freighter which burned off the Washington coast, purchased the windjammer. He endeavored to set up a share-the-expense cruise to the South Seas, and accordingly made alterations in the schooner's accommodations to handle both men and women. When the Coast Guard learned that the new skipper did not have master's papers, the plan came to a screeching halt.

Wealthy Montana cattle rancher W. P. Studdert purchased the *Wawona* in 1953, and it was rumored that he planned to sail her to Siberia with a cargo of cattle. The plan, however, died a slow death. The schooner then spent more than a decade in solitary confinement on Seattle's Lake Union until an ambitious group of ship lovers, who called themselves "Save Our Ships, Inc." (SOS), purchased the vessel from Studdert and began a restoration job to turn her into a museum ship in memory of Puget Sound's salty maritime past.

One of the finest periods in the *Wawona's* early career came when Captain Ralph "Matt"

57

Peasely was her master. This colorful figure became none other than the inspiration for "Cappy Ricks" in the amusing best-selling novels created by Peter B. Kyne. Peasely was skipper of the *Wawona* for five years. It was during this period that he met the future Mrs. Peasely, daughter of Captain James Dalton, prominent in coast shipping and lumbering circles. She was working in a Grays Harbor lumber office, but when the wedding bells rang in 1903, the couple not only became man and wife, but shipmates as well. At her husband's side she sailed aboard sailing schooners more than 250,000 miles in Pacific tradelanes.

The *Wawona* was not only successful as a lumber carrier but rendered admirable service as a codfisher. Like all of the early coastal windjammers, however, the *Wawona* had her unfortunate moments. An almost disastrous fo'c's'le fire at the height of a driving storm in 1917 almost spelled her demise. It started when all hands were called on deck to work ship and a careless crewman left a low burning candle in his bunk. It set fire to the bedding and then to four other bunks. By the time the fire was discovered, smoke was so thick that the blaze was difficult to trace. A bucket brigade was promptly assembled and, after hours of toil and sweat, the flames and choking smoke were quelled. Had the fire reached into the tarred timbers of the schooner she would have become a blazing inferno, and escape by the crew in the cruel storm-whipped seas would have been impossible.

Later the same year, the *Wawona* was caught for days in a dead flat calm off the west coast of Vancouver Island, unable to get inside the Strait of Juan de Fuca. Finally, after drifting off and on, the vessel wound up in the middle of the shipping lanes at the entrance to the waterway in the middle of the night. A salmon troller pulled alongside and informed her skipper that German cruisers were lying in wait just off Tatoosh Island. Inasmuch as the schooner was making no headway, a group of volunteers rowed a dory six miles to Neah Bay to phone for a tug. The call was answered, but when the towing craft was unable to locate the *Wawona* at the reported position, she instead took two other sailing vessels in tow.

The following night, as the watch on the *Wawona* gazed through the murk, he saw a big, dark vessel moving down on them. It showed no lights. He alerted the mate, who thought it

Battered remnants of the four-masted **SCHOONER MARCONI** on the beach below Coos Head after her towline parted on Coos Bay bar March 23, 1909. The crew was rescued but the lumber laden windship was totalled out.

58

SCHOONER KING CYRUS hard aground on Chehalis Point at the entrance to Grays Harbor July 17, 1922. She was inbound to Grays Harbor from Honolulu.

might be the tug approaching. Then, with frightening speed, the towering steel hull of a huge freighter loomed near the schooner on a collision course. At first it was thought to be a German warship. Bells suddenly clanged, lights flashed, and the water heaved like a geyser as the cargo ship went into full astern. Veering sharply, the great steel ship missed the *Wawona* by less than 50 feet.

By daybreak, the uneasy crew of the schooner was greeted by a breeze. The wind soon bellied the slack canvas and the vessel moved briskly all the way into Puget Sound.

Other troubles aboard the *Wawona* included the usual fights among her rough, tough crewmen. The log of 1914, when Captain Charles Foss was master, tells of one man who was placed in irons as a result of an altercation. He was rudely dumped in his bunk and boards were nailed over top to restrain him. Somehow he got one ankle free of the shackles and kicked out the slats. Trying to get out of the top berth in a three-tier set is not an easy task when one's hands are tied. But, the man did it. Unfortunately he fell out head first squarely onto the fo'c's'le deck with a sickening thud. The vessel's master laid the seaman's survival to being a "hard-headed Norwegian."

There was another reckless seaman, who served aboard the *Wawona* in days of yore, who was addicted to alcohol. Every time he got inebriated, he would start throwing all the loose gear overboard. The log tells of a man named Healey who grabbed him, on one occasion, after he had relieved the vessel of belaying pins and other gear. He hastily wrapped a rope around the drunk's boots, threw the other end around a boom and hoisted him up head down until he sobered up.

SCHOONER C. A. THAYER

The only other surviving (intact) pre-century West Coast-built sailing vessel, the schooner *C. A. Thayer*, was also constructed by Hans Bendixsen. She is now a unit of the San Francisco Maritime Museum fleet of ships. Both the *Wawona* and the *Thayer* were built as lumber schooners and both spent the greater share of their years in the codfishing trade between Puget Sound and the Bering Sea.

The E. K. Wood Lumber Company executives went to Fairhaven, California, in 1895 to discuss plans with Bendixsen for a new three-masted schooner which was to be named for a company partner, C. A. Thayer. Little did the men, who discussed the vessel that day, realize

59

that this common workaday windjammer would be one of the last survivors in the era of West Coast sail. Who could have known that her sturdy Humboldt pine hull would withstand the buffeting of both the tropic and Arctic waters and last on into modern times?

Bar ports were the terror of the Pacific Coast sailing vessels, as has been told earlier, and on more than one occasion the stout *C. A. Thayer* rose to the test. In 1908, she stranded at the entrance to Grays Harbor after striking the bar and tearing away her rudder and deadwood. The lifesaving craft from the local station went to the aid of the troubled schooner, standing by until it was certain that all hands were out of danger. When the tibe ebbed, the schooner was left high and dry on the sands, where it appeared that her bones might rot at the whims of mother nature. So certain was the lifesaving crew that the *Thayer* would be a total loss that, as was their custom, they removed one of her liferings and hung it in the boathouse at their station. (On the walls of the structure were the ring buoys of numerous vessels that had come to grief on or around the bar.)

The *Thayer*, however, was different. Her hull remained tight, and tugs, with the aid of a flood tide, eventually got her afloat and towed her to Cosmopolis where she was careened and repaired.

The schooner had another narrow escape in the winter of 1912. Terse messages were received from the wireless stations at Eureka and San Francisco:

"Lumber carrier from Grays Harbor in sinking condition off Humboldt bar, one woman on board. Tug which started to relief of vessel is unable to cross bar in dense fog. Ship is waterlogged. Steamer *President* reports the wreck by wireless to Eureka and proceeded on her way to San Francisco."

The following day, Eureka news sources continued to tell the shipping world about the plight of the troubled schooner, now identified as the *C. A. Thayer*."

"A crew of seven men and a woman are in grave danger aboard American schooner *C. A. Thayer* which lies tonight 20 miles off Humboldt Bay, leaking badly and momentarily in danger of sinking. Owing to the roughess of Humboldt bar, the schooner's calls for help have so far not been answered, as a heavy fog combined with a rising sea makes it extremely perilous for a tug to venture out. The schooner is too far distant for lifesavers to render aid."

The first intimation of the *Thayer's* plight reached Eureka January 14, at 7 p.m., when a wireless message was received from the SS *President* saying that the *Thayer* was settling low in the water and in urgent need of assistance.

The government station earlier reported that a tug was prepared to go to the schooner's relief on receipt of the first news of trouble, but it was found impossible to cross the bar while the fog persisted. The towing craft reported she was standing by in readiness to make a dash for the open sea the moment the fog lifted.

The *Thayer* was nine days out from Grays Harbor, bound for San Pedro with 400,000 board feet of lumber. She had fallen victim to a heavy gale, one of many that had been lashing the coast in the winter of 1912. The buffeting

BRIGANTINE GENEVA at the lumber dock, Raymond, Washington, in 1910. She was one of the last vessels of her rig built in North America. Matthew Turner constructed the GENEVA in 1890 for his California South Seas Navigation Co. (Tahiti packet line). The GENEVA was destroyed by fire in the Gulf of Mexico June 11, 1926. Photo courtesy Capt. E. J. Stull.

In dire distress off Destruction Island, the **BARKENTINE JAMES TUFT** January, 1923. Coming to her aid is the tug **SEA MONARCH,** after the Coast Guard cutter **HAIDA** removed all but two of her 12 man crew. The skysail yarder—waterlogged, was towed into Winslow and repaired.

seas had opened the schooner's seams, and it appeared she was being held afloat only by her cargo of lumber. Grave fears were felt for those aboard. Further the vessel could no longer be properly navigated.

The following day (January 15) further word was received at Table Bluff.

"The schooner *C. A. Thayer,* waterlogged and leaking badly, and with her pumps out of commission, was picked up by the steam schooner *J. B. Stetson* and is being towed south."

Another day passed before the following message was received:

"The schooner *C. A. Thayer* which was sighted in distress off Eureka by the steamer *President* and which for a time was feared lost was towed into San Francisco tonight by the steam schooner *J. B. Stetson.* The *Thayer* was sunk deep in the water owing to the opening of her seams and failure of her pumps, but her cargo of lumber was intact and Captain Fred Scott, his wife and seven crewmen are unharmed. The *Thayer* left Grays Harbor on January 5 and two days later began taking water faster than the pumps could discharge it. The hand pumps failed shortly and the steam pump had to be stopped because nearly all the fresh water on board had

been consumed. A tug spent all day Sunday searching for the *Thayer* but, owing to the thick fog did not sight her. Sunday night the *Stetson* was signalled and took the *Thayer* in tow after putting four men aboard to repair and help man the pumps. The *Thayer* will be towed to Oakland and her cargo discharged."

The rugged schooner had been beckoned by Davy Jones but had braved the wild Pacific and again came out a winner due in much part to Hans Bendixsen's skill as a builder of wooden sailing vessels.

SHIPBUILDERS OF EARLY DAY OREGON

Isolated as was the Oregon coast in the middle of the 19th Century, wooden shipbuilding was nevertheless started there by stalwart pioneer shipwrights, virtually working under the shade of the countless acres of timber.

At Port Orford in 1857, William Tichenor built one of the first seagoing vessels there—the two-masted schooner *Alaska.* The same year, James C. Fitzgerald, Daniel Giles and Thomas Hall turned out a small schooner on the Coquille River. The initial vessel built on Coos Bay was the brig *Blanco* constructed near Captain A. M. Simpson's sawmill at North Bend. And it was Simpson, with his master builder John Kruse, that made Oregon shipbuilding history as far as sailing ships were concerned. Simpson's shipyard which he ran in conjunction with his adjoining sawmill turned out some 58 vessels including the five-masted schooner *Louis* in 1888, first of her rig ever built in the United States.

Whenever the early day Pacific Coast shipbuilding industry is discussed the name of Asa Mead Simpson always comes to the fore. This almost legendary pioneer of the lumber and shipping business permanently established Coos Bay as one of the world's greatest lumber portals. It was his foresight that led him to the wilderness of the bleak but beautiful Oregon shores as far back as 1850. He was a product of the salty Maine coast, born February 26, 1826, at Brunswick. His father was a ship's carpenter spending much of his career in New England shipyards and his family before him were all seafaring folk.

In 1849 the banner news of the California gold rush reached the East Coast and Simpson joined the ship *Birmingham* en route to San Francisco to try his hand at seeking gold. Like thousands of others he returned from the hills of promise empty handed, but far from discouraged. Instead, a new frontier opened. He voyaged northward to the vicinity of Coos Bay and purchased ground for the construction of a lumber mill, the second mill established in the area. The machinery for the firm came from a shipwreck on the treacherous Coos Bay bar.

After the mill began to produce, Simpson branched out into the construction of ships. The Simpson yard started out small till the advent of the *Arago* in 1859, one of the first of the West Coast-built sailing vessels to exceed 100 tons. The *Arago*, a brig, had a highly successful career making much money for her owners. She was in service until 1905 when dismantled.

Simpson, who seldom carried any vessel insurance, was a thrifty individual and had a reputation for collecting odds and ends of supposedly worthless junk here and there and putting it to good use on his ships or in his mill. One of his first endeavors was to purchase, and then salvage, the wreck of the sailing vessel *Potomac* out toward the river entrance (Middle sands Columbia River) from Astoria. The *Arago* actually contained timbers and gear both from two wrecks and from some of the abandoned vessels left to die on the mudflats of San Francisco Bay following the gold rush. Simpson's master builder on the brig *Arago* was a man named McDonald who shared Simpson's money-saving policies. One can imagine that such thinking paid off when the 185 ton, 103 foot vessel was delivered at a total cost of only $13,000. During the interim, Simpson also found time to inaugurate pilot service on the Columbia River bar in partnership with Captain George Flavel of Astoria.

After the completion of the *Arago,* Simpson

BARKENTINE GEORGINA loading lumber at Everett. Note stern ports open and stern ramps for loading through ship's stern and over the poop onto the deck. This vessel once had a run from Callao to Port Townsend in 1903, of 30 days 12 hours. She was wrecked serving as a fishing barge at Redondo Beach, California, in 1935. Courtesy Pete Hurd.

Dangerous and ticklish task—seaman aloft on yardarm tending sail on the **BARKENTINE MAKAWELI.** Capt. E. J. Stull photo.

and to herd logs about the mill. The rather unorthodox tug itself was a former brig, having been built years before of teakwood at Calcutta, India.

As North Bend commenced to grow, more and more ships visited the harbor. The shipyard thrived and scores of sailing vessels were constructed from 1860 to 1903. During that half century a ship was built every year at the Simpson yard.

As Simpson's sunset years drew near he announced that he was ready to curtail his shipbuilding activities and retire. Thus, in 1894, a stately 584 ton barkentine slid down the ways with the name *Omega* gracing her bows. Omega is the Greek word for last, or the end. Though he fully intended that this vessel would be his last and that the mill would be completely in the hands of the younger generation, he just couldn't get comfortable in his old rocking chair and decided to build one more ship. One vessel led to another and the given names of each of those colorful windjammers told their own story. There were the *Repeat, Echo, Addenda* and *Encore.* With the launching of the schooner *Marconi* in 1903, the Simpson yard finally did close and was purchased by Kruse & Banks who continued to maintain an excellent reputation for building wooden vessels, both sail and steam.

The complete Simpson lumber interests were sold out in 1915. The transaction ended over a half century of progress during which time Coos Bay received its rightful place as the soft lumber exporting capital of the world.

Some years prior to the disposal of the Simpson property, the sun finally set on the life of this enterprising shipbuilding and industrial genius, who dwelled in a palatial mansion near the scene of his achievements. His name will long be revered as one of the pioneers of the Pacific Coast. Among his celebrated maritime accomplishments was the first full-rigged sailing vessel built on the Pacific Coast (the *Western Shore*); the first bald-headed schooner (the *Novelty*); first five-masted sailing vessel (the *Louis*). He further brought the first big tugboat to Coos Bay and was indeed the outstanding pioneer of the Oregon lumber industry both in Coos County and the entire Oregon coast. Despite the loss of many of his ships down through the years, vessels on which he carried not one cent of insurance, he rolled with the bad news and came up smiling. He figured over a long period that he gained more

returned to San Francisco and purchased three of the hundreds of abandoned ships that choked the bay. He acquired the *Quadrauts, Tarquina* and *S. R. Jackson* for a pittance and had them sailed back to his Oregon yard. There his yard workers rebuilt them and placed all three in the lumber hauling business between Coos Bay and the city by the Golden Gate.

Simpson then purchased the sizable tug *Fearless,* the first towboat on Coos Bay, which he used for towing windships across the bar

Gallant old **STEAM TUG WANDERER** which towed scores of windjammers out to the Pacific Ocean from her home port of Port Blakely. She is seen here in later years as a unit of the Foss Launch & Tug Company. Turned out at Blakely in 1890 she was finally shoved on the Nisqually mudflats two decades ago.

than he lost by not carrying the insurance. He looked on such things as a gamble and part of the great game of success or failure. He was truly a man of vision and accomplishment.

LOUIS

The sizable Simpson-built, five-masted schooner *Louis* caught the imagination of the shipbuilding world when launched in 1888. Built under the direction of John Kruse, she was somewhat of a mistake. Intended to have been a steamship, the *Louis* was to sail to San Francisco for installation of an engine. In order to get her to the Bay City, she was rigged with five masts temporarily so she could make the voyage under sail. Her unorthodox rig included two masts stepped out of the centerline to afford greater sail spread when running free. The builder, captain and crew had their tongues in their cheeks as the windjammer departed on her initial voyage south. But contrary to fears she sailed so well that the order

for the engines was cancelled by her owners after she was safely in port at San Francisco.

Scores flocked to the waterfront to view this unusual innovation in naval architecture. The *Louis* measured 194 feet in length and was of 831 tons. She was operated by the Simpson Lumber Company throughout her career and became the first of her rig to circumnavigate the globe.

Simpson owned her at the time of her loss on June 19, 1907. The *Louis* was wrecked in thick fog, on the South Farallon, off the Golden Gate. Captain Dyer and his crew were rescued, but the ship's hull was ripped wide open and her cargo of 900,000 feet of railroad ties, loaded at Grays Harbor, turned the ocean into a sea likened to a torn up train track.

WESTERN SHORE

Another formidable vessel turned out by Simpson interests was the ship *Western Shore*, probably the most beautiful sailing vessel ever built on the Pacific Coast and one that could be well termed as a latter-day clipper ship. Almost a true clipper, she was classed as a three-skysail yarder. Built at North Bend in 1874 at a cost of $86,000, the *Western Shore* was large for her day, registering 1,177 tons. An Oregon product all the way, the hull was designed by A. M. Simpson; R. W. Simpson drew the sail plan and John Kruse was master builder. Most of the material that went into the vessel was from Oregon state and she was owned by A. M. Simpson, T. B. Knowles and Captain J. W. McAllep who was also her master.

The *Western Shore* unfortunately had a brief career though her record was nothing short of remarkable. In 1875 she departed San Francis-

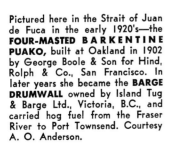

Pictured here in the Strait of Juan de Fuca in the early 1920's—the **FOUR-MASTED BARKENTINE PUAKO,** built at Oakland in 1902 by George Boole & Son for Hind, Rolph & Co., San Francisco. In later years she became the **BARGE DRUMWALL** owned by Island Tug & Barge Ltd., Victoria, B.C., and carried hog fuel from the Fraser River to Port Townsend. Courtesy A. O. Anderson.

Nothing quite so captures the imagination as a windship outbound packed to the gunwhales. **SCHOONER C. S. HOLMES** heads out to sea.

co at the same time as the highly regarded Steamer *Oriflamme,* a large, fast sidewheel vessel owned by the Oregon Steamship Company. Both she and the *Western Shore* were neck and neck as they passed out through the Gold-

en Gate and headed for the Columbia River. The steamer poured on the coal and the sailing vessel piled on the canvas. It was a thrilling spectacle but thought to be no contest. But on that certain occasion there was a brisk following wind the the *Western Shore* by unfurling extra sail overtook the puffing steamer leading her all the way to the mouth of the Columbia—crossed the bar and dropped anchor in Astoria's harbor—in just two days and three hours—well ahead of her rival.

In 1876, the *Western Shore* sailed from Portland, Oregon, to Liverpool in 101 days, and in 1877 from San Francisco to Liverpool in 103 days, returning over the same route in 110 days. Credited to this handsome vessel was a 97-day passage from the Columbia River to Liverpool, and the three fastest consecutive runs under sail on record for this route.

It goes without saying that the Simpson yard hit its peak in 1874 with the construction of the full-rigged ship *Western Shore*, the only vessel of that rig ever built at the yard. She was, actually, Oregon's version of the clipper ship and was just as successful in every way. On her maiden voyage alone she profited Simpson $23,000, which in those years were mighty big bucks. She was a splendid sailing vessel in every category but unfortunately her career was brief. As the vessel was nearing the entrance to San Francisco Bay, laden with 2,200 tons of coal, the shipmaster had been warned not to try a night entry. He did, and the vessel piled up on dreaded Duxbury Reef becoming a total loss, a big blow to an owner who never carried insurance. He did, however, hold a $25,000 policy on the *Western Shore*.

Of the vessel's master, Asa Simpson recalled: "...he drank, and that tells it all. He mistook the lights of a schooner, which appeared and disappeared as she rose and fell with the waves, for the flash-light of the Farallones, and turning stern to, he steered straight for Mount Tamalpais and crashed upon the rocks in less than 20 minutes. When the pilot appeared the next morning, she was a hopeless wreck."

At the time of the accident the so-called "Oregon clipper", was moving at 12 knots under a strong breeze. She struck so hard she ripped out her entire bottom on the port side. Captain Hotchkiss and the crew immediately abandoned ship and were later rescued by the tug *Wizard*.

A short time earlier a previous master of the *Western Shore* lost his life when a spar struck him on the head.

KLIKITAT

The Puget Mill Company, under the stewardship of Pope & Talbot of San Francisco and Port Gamble, built up a big sailing ship fleet to carry its lumber from its vast holdings on Puget Sound. Established at Port Gamble in 1849, the company became one of the largest factors in the export of lumber coast-wise and worldwide. One of their windjammers constructed by the Simpson yard became the "darling of the fleet," the barkentine *Klikitat*. She was assigned to carry lumber from Puget Sound to Pacific islands. John Kruse put all of his skill into the construction of the *Klikitat*, under Simpson's direction. She was delivered in 1881 amid fanfare. Measuring 163 feet in length and of 493 tons, the vessel was beautifully appointed throughout. The barkentine operated with perfection until her demise on Honlii Point on the island of Hawaii on November 11, 1912.

In 1896 while in the command of Captain Cutler, the *Klikitat* prepared to sail from Honolulu for Puget Sound. Three days earlier the Japanese steamship *Kinshiu Maru* of the NYK Line had departed the Hawaiian port for the same destination. Captain Cutler had

Afterdeck of **FOUR-MASTED SCHOONER C. S. HOLMES,** famous Arctic trader, operated between Seattle and the Arctic for many years by the Backland interests. One of the coast's smallest four-masters at 430 tons, she was built to carry lumber, at Port Blakely in 1893 and ended her days as a barge in 1952.

Four-masted schooner **WM. BOWDEN** (in dock in Seattle), was a hard luck vessel plagued with many problems and long voyages. In 1920 it took her 91 days to reach Sydney, N.S.W., from Astoria.

Standing off the coast—riding light, **SCHOONER DAUNTLESS.** She traded both coastwise and offshore during her career.

TWO-MASTED SCHOONER GENERAL BANNING, built by Captain T. H. Peterson at Navarro River, Calif., in 1883. She was last owned at La Paz, Mexico, in 1920.

Tons of lumber and codfish packed in rock salt were once stowed in the bowels of the durable **SCHOONER WAWONA.** The schooner was fashioned for the most part from Humboldt pine, a species of Douglas fir.

Artist's rendering of the graceful Turner-built **BRIGANTINE LUR-LINE,** which appeared on the cover of a recent Matson Navigation Company annual report. The **LUR-LINE** was the first unit of the vast Matson interests. The drawing was done by L. MacQuillard.

The **BARKENTINE NEWSBOY,** named for the first job of he J. J. Smith of San Francisco, is pictured here in an early century photo becalmed on a flat sea.

H. H. Morrison photo

boarded the steamer just prior to her departure and requested the ship's master, Captain Thompson, to carry a letter to his family in Seattle inasmuch as the liner would get there far ahead of the *Klikitat.*

The surprising sequel to the story was that the *Klikitat* sailed into Port Townsend in only nine days and 16 hours after leaving Honolulu. With favorable winds all the way she set a record for the run never equalled by another sailing vessel until another West Coaster—the *Thomas P. Emigh*—logged a run from Honolulu to Cape Flattery in seven days, 22 hours, under Captain M.A. Ipsen—knocking a few hours off the *Klikitat's* record.

The Japanese liner, on the other hand, though slowed slightly by need of drydocking, arrived several hours after the *Klikitat.* Running just slightly under her usual 14 knots speed, none was more surprised than Captain Thompson when he saw the *Klikitat* at anchor in Port Townsend harbor. Needless to say, Captain Cutler delivered his own mail plus a big hug for the members of his family—proud as a peacock over his record passage. Both he and the Pope & Talbot organization never had kind enough words of praise for the excellent qualities of the famous barkentine.

Following is a list of Simpson sailing vessels built at Old Town on Coos Bay, Oregon, compiled by Louis J. Simpson and John William Kruse, and formulated by Stephen Dow Beckham in his book, *The Simpsons of Shore Acres.*

Blanco, brig, 248 tons, built 1858, two-masted
Arago, brig, 185 tons, built 1859, two-masted
Florence Walton, schooner 75 tons, built 1860, two-masted
Mendocino, schooner, 93 tons, built 1861, two-masted
Advance, brig, 210 tons, built 1862, two-masted
Enterprise, schooner, 189 tons, built 1863, two-masted
Hannah Louise, schooner, 83 tons, built 1863, two-masted
Isabella, schooner, 184 tons, built 1864, two-masted
Juventa, schooner, 191 tons, built 1865, two-masted
Occident, barkentine, 297 tons, built 1865, three-masted
Melancthon, barkentine, 289 tons, built 1867, three-masted
Bunkalation, schooner, 100 tons, built 1868, two-masted
Web Foot, schooner, 361 tons, built 1869, three-masted

Gotoma, schooner, 198 tons, built 1872, two-masted
Oregonian, schooner, 246 tons, built 1872, three-masted
Western Shore, full-rigged ship, 1,177 tons, built 1874, three-masted
Tam O'Shanter, barkentine, 592 tons, built 1875, three-masted
Portland, barkentine, 493 tons, built 1876,- three-masted
North Bend, barkentine, 376 tons, built 1877
Trustee, schooner, 280 tons, built 1878, three masted
Klikitat, schooner, 493 tons, built 1879, three-masted
Tropic Bird, schooner-barkentine, 347 tons, built 1880, three-masted
James A. Garfield, schooner, 316 tons, built 1881, three-masted
Dare, schooner, 259 tons, built 1882, three-masted
Beda, power schooner, built 1883, three-masted
Novelty, schooner, 592 tons, built 1886, four-masted
Louis, schooner, 831 tons, built 1889, five-masted
Gardiner City, barkentine, 475 tons, built 1889, three-masted
Volante, schooner, 125 tons, built 1890-91, two-masted (G.L. Hobbs also listed as builder)
Willis R. Hume, barkentine, 665 tons, built 1890, three-masted
Arago, barkentine, 498 tons, built 1891, four-masted
Nonoha, schooner, built 1892, two-masted

Tranquil in the early morning, tall ships are pictured lined up at the Port Blakely Mill on Bainbridge Island, west of Seattle around the turn of the century. They included the **FOUR-MASTED SCHOONERS JAMES ROLPH** and **BALBOA,** the **BARKENTINE WILLIE R. HUME** and the **BARK LOW WOOD.** The mill could produce 400,000 board feet of lumber a day.

Perhaps the oldest soft wood lumber mill on the west coast still in operation is the one at Port Gamble, a Pope & Talbot facility dating from 1853. Tall ships were still loading lumber near the turn of the century as can be seen in this historic photo.

Omega, barkentine, 692 tons, built 1894, four-masted

Addenda, barkentine, 692 tons, built 1895, four masted

Echo, barkentine, 707 tons, built 1896, four-masted

Repeat, schooner, 455 tons, built 1897, four-masted

Encore, barkentine, 651 tons, built 1897, four-masted

Admiral, schooner, 683 tons, built 1899, four-masted

Churchill, schooner, 655 tons, built 1900, four-masted

Alumna, schooner, 696 tons, built 1901, four-masted

Marconi, schooner, 693 tons, built 1902, four-masted

Alpha, schooner, 300 tons, built 1903, three-masted

In addition, the yard turned out several steam tugs, some of which were maintained for services connected with ship assistance or log towing associated with the Simpson Mill. They were the *Hunter, Astoria, Novelty, Cruiser, Traveler, Ranger, Signal, Columbia, Brunswick,* and *Mandalay.*

Like a winged seabird, the 359 ton **BRIGANTINE LURLINE** the first of several Matson ships to carry the name crossed a skysail yard and carried 640 tons of sugar in the Hawaii-California trade. Built in 1887, the swift sugar packet met a tragic end following a collision off Salina Cruz, Mexico, January 11, 1915 ending a brilliant career. Matson Navigation Company photo.

71

This Webster & Stevens photo is credited with preserving a part of history that might well have faded from memory. The Hall Brothers shipyard at Port Blakely looking toward the Port Blakely Mill Company. Scores of tall ships fill the harbor before the turn of the century. Note the town with its boardwalks. A fire later destroyed most of what is pictured on the fringes of the harbor. The 1888 conflagration was a blow from which the town never fully recovered. The mill was rebuilt but the prominence that once attracted President Hayes as a visitor never returned and by 1914 the operation was dismantled according to researcher Gordon Jones. In its heyday, the town boasted stores, churches, a public hall, 75 room hotel and a 80,000 acre mill tract and was served by 35 miles of rail line with four engines hauling logs and lumber on 100 cars. In 1881, the shipbuilding Hall brothers moved their renowned shipyard from Port Ludlow to Port Blakely and the mill and the yard worked together in beneficial harmony.

The Hall Brothers shipyard at Port Blakely showing a wooden sailing schooner under construction and another at its right showing only the ribs. Several fine vessels were turned out at the yard which moved from Port Ludlow to Port Blakely in 1881. Webster & Stevens photo.

1902 photo of a classic group aboard the new **SCHOONER MABLE GALE** under construction at the Hall Brothers shipyard at Port Blakely. Among those on the deck of the vessel is bewiskered Henry K. Hall, one of the three brothers that founded the yard (seated at the left in the front row.)

Probably one of the most overlooked of the prominent master shipbuilders of west coast sailing vessels was Euphronius Cousins, who in reality was the first well known shipbuilder in Humboldt County, California. At Eureka, he launched his first vessel, the *Ocean Express* in 1865. His background was shipbuilding and ship captains. He came to California in 1865 from Maine where he was a shipbuilder in Ellsworth, Maine. His father was Phineas Cousins, also a shipbuilder. He had three brothers who served as shipwrights or ship captains. However, reports the grandson of Euphronius, Howard M. Cousins of Northridge, California, he did not funnel all his activities into shipbuilding as did Humboldt's other great shipbuilder Hans Bendixsen. He owned lumber mills as well, many of which were top producers in Humboldt County. From time to time, his brothers Heman and Captain Edwin Cousins were associated with him in his lumber enterprises.

Howard Cousins has revealed that contrary to general belief, the two-masted schooner, *Dashing Wave*, sometimes credited as a product of Hans Bendixsen, was actually the work of Euphronius Cousins in 1867. According to him, Bendixsen arrived in California in 1863, worked in San Francisco for several years learning the trade and then came to Eureka, where he gained much knowledge about shipbuilding from the Cousins. At that time, Euphronius became associated with Joe Russ, a prominent Humboldt business man, and at their Gunther's Island mill in Humboldt Bay, it was decided to build a shipyard. In 1869 Cousins

Scene of activity—the Port Blakely Mill Company. The mill, founded by Captain William Renton became the largest of its kind on Puget Sound and supplied millions of board feet of lumber for an endless fleet of sailing vessels that loaded at the company facilities. Captain Renton, seeking pilings for a customer in Boston went ashore to develop the lumber business at Blakely, and by 1864 was cutting 50,000 feet of lumber a day. As business increased so did the output of lumber. Loading at pierside is the **SQUARE-RIGGER MERCURY,** owned by Renton Holmes & Co., a former Havre packet dating from 1851 and registered at Port Townsend.

sold his ways to MacDonald and Bendixsen.

In 1900 Euphronius, then out of the lumbering business due to failing health, recovered enough to gather a group of Humboldters together and move to Aberdeen, Washington to build ships for the Eel River Valley Mill and Lumber Company. At that time he was the local agent of Bureau Veritas, which kept him in touch with the latest techniques in shipbuilding. Unfortunately Cousins died on June 9, 1901 in Aberdeen, and W.H. McWhinney carried on the shipbuilding effort.

Vessels credited to Euphronius Cousins include the following:
Humboldt built: *Ocean Express*, renamed; *Hesperian*, 1865; *May Queen*, 1866; *Dashing Wave*, 1867; *Laura May*, 1868; *Mary E. Russ*, 1875; *Maggie Russ*, 1881; *Joseph Russ*, 1881; *Ruby Cousins*, 1882; *Lillebonne*, 1883.
Aberdeen built: *Coronado*, 1900; *F.N. Slade*, 1900; *Eldorado*, 1901.

Asa Meade Simpson, founder of the Simpson Lumber Company and shipbuilding operations at Coos Bay, controlled his business firms from 1850-1914. He was born in Brunswick, Maine in 1826. Seen here are the Simpson docks, the **FOUR-MASTED SCHOONER MANILA** being towed out by the company **TUG HUNTER.**

Old Town on Coos Bay, the site of the Simpson sawmill and shipyard, as it appeared in the 1880's.

BARKENTINE IRMGARD, built by the Hall Brothers yard at Port Blakely in 1889 was a fast sailing vessel once logging an eight day, twenty hour run from San Francisco (April 1903) to Honolulu. The 670 ton vessel was wrecked in the Fiji Islands in 1920.

BARKENTINE JOHN SMITH is pictured here off the Columbia River in decades past. She was constructed at the Hall yard in Blakely Harbor in 1882 and was sold to Peruvian owners in 1913, last appearing in the register in 1922.

John Kruse, master shipbuilder and superintendent of operations at the Simpson mill and shipyard on Coos Bay. Joining the firm in 1865, he supervised construction of 28 vessels at Old Town.

A Great Ship asks deep waters.
                                    ---George Herbert

Part Three

Borrowings from the Logbooks

W. H. TALBOT

In APRIL OF 1910 the schooner *W. H. Talbot* was crossing the Pacific from Newcastle, N.S.W. to San Francisco in command of Captain Andrew Knudsen. The skipper was the father of Agatha and Sylvia Knudsen, 16 and 19, respectively, who were making the voyage with him.

In mid-Pacific, Captain Knudsen became gravely ill and no longer was able to assume command. About the time he was confined to his cabin, the Pacific grew irrascible as if intent on hammering the schooner into submission in his absence. Shipping giant seas, the vessel took an unmerciful beating. The crewmen were wet to the skin, tired and worn from endeavoring to keep the ship into the wind. No hot food could be cooked and sleep was virtually out of the question. The winds snapped the jib-boom and sprung the mainmast and it appeared for awhile as though the vessel was doomed.

The girls were apprehensive, but they were brave, having much of their father's spirit in their love for the sea. They had tended the skipper in his sickness but they knew he was far too ill to attempt coming on deck to resume command. The young ladies were also aware that the short-handed crew had been worked to the point of exhaustion handling the vessel while urgently needed repairs had gone unheeded.

The situation appeared almost hopeless, when Sylvia appeared on deck, much to the surprise of the crew. She was garbed in her dad's sou'wester, oil skins and sea boots. The men thought for awhile that she had taken leave of her senses. But no, this brave girl insisted on relieving the man at the wheel so he could be of use in helping repair the vessel's rigging. And, sister Agatha not to be outdone alternated with her sister, handling the helm around the clock.

For several days the brave, diligent girls tended the wheel and at the mate's guidance kept the tempest-tossed schooner on course. The extra help afforded the shot in the arm needed to spur the crew onward.

The *Talbot* eventually arrived at San Francisco; Captain Knudsen recovered and the two girls became the heroines of the San Francisco waterfront as well as the apples of their daddy's eye. The storm-battered schooner got a face-lifting at a local shipyard and went on to many years of hard trading until broken up on the Chinese coast in 1924.

There's just clearance for the booms above the high deckload of lumber on the **SCHOONER ANDY MAHONY** (about 1905). John Lindstrom built her in 1902 for Olson & Mahony of San Francisco. *O. Beaton photo*

MINDANAO

Recollections of the four-masted bald-headed schooner *Mindanao* built at Aberdeen, Washington, in 1902 as the *Andy Mahony,* are vivid in the mind of one of her former crewmen— Bert Cappelin of Lund, Sweden.

In April 1925 the *Mindanao* was chartered from her owners to load lumber in Vancouver, B. C., for Suva, Fiji. A few weeks of hard work put the vessel back in reasonable condition. Canvas was broken out of the sail locker, blocks and hoops checked and running gear rove. The sails, one after the other, were bent and furled. The decks and paint work were in bad condition so out came the chipping tools, brushes and holystones—and the labor began.

The *Mindanao* departed from Vancouver after an elongated loading period. She dropped the towline off Cape Flattery on June 11. After about three weeks at sea the ocean fell almost dead flat. About six bells one evening, Cappelin recalled that the mate suddenly shouted, "Fire! Fire!"

All hands except the helmsman came tumbling out on deck. Fire at sea has always been the dread of any blue water men. From the lazarette hatch on the poop issued plumes of smoke. The entrance way was hastily sealed and a parley ensued as to how best to remedy the situation. Inside were several oil drums and if the fire reached those drums it would be out of control. The skipper after pondering the situation ordered the men to hack openings in the deck planking and they immediately set to work making eight neatly cut vents. It was now the midnight hour. Without stopping to rest, a bucket brigade was formed and sea water was poured into the openings in an almost steady flow.

In the interim, the ship's boat was taken up atop the deckload and boom tackles were rigged in the fore and main riggings to lower it away in case the schooner gave indication of blowing up.

There was nothing but endless acres of lonely sea in every direction and the thought of

Seeking cargo—**FOUR-MASTED SCHOONER BLAKELY** returns from Pacific voyage.

TUG WYADDA tows lumber laden four-master to sea from Puget Sound.

abandoning was anything but pleasant. The ship's boat by this time was stocked with blankets and provisions, and a red lantern of distress was hung at the crosstrees in the vain hope that they might be sighted by another vessel.

Smoke continued pouring out the vent holes despite the hundreds of gallons of water that had been poured through constantly. Around the clock till six the following morning the bucket brigade persisted. At this hour it was decided that the hatch should be opened. Great billows of smoke rolled out. One of the crew with a wet rag wrapped about his face volunteered to go below to locate the cause. Down he went into the recesses, coughing, gagging and staggering about among the canvas, blocks, and rope until he finally found the location of the fire. The lazarette had been blackened and the skipper's quarters above were badly damaged. The blaze, however, had not reached the nearby oil drums sitting in about three feet of seawater, which alone saved the schooner from certain destruction.

Several other crewmen hastily went below to help squelch the fire and after a concerted effort with axes, shovels and buckets the crisis was over and the mop-up job begun.

Cappelin recalled that the greatful master, following the dousing of the stubborn blaze, insisted that all hands turn in while he alone for several hours took the wheel and tended to the needs of the schooner.

The following day everything was made as shipshape as possible. Then, as if the jinx were prevailing, the vessel again fell into a flat, windless sea. But it was short lived and soon a breeze picked up which carried the *Mindanao* to her anchorage at Suva Roads, 56 days out from Vancouver. The schooner's party anxiously greeted the green, lush slopes of the South

Sea island. As the vessel swung on her hook, a whale boat pulled by eight husky islanders came alongside. One of them, a pilot, came aboard and immediately took the schooner in between the reefs to a safer anchorage. The difficult voyage had ended and the skipper gave his men freedom to live it up in the village before preparing to discharge the lumber cargo and return to the states with a load of copra.

ZAMPA

Another West Coast windjammer, the three-masted schooner *Zampa* built at Port Madison, in 1887 was a prime example of a vessel that defied destruction.

We find this 385 ton schooner fighting a fierce gale off the Columbia River on July 17, 1904. Aboard was Captain Kellenberger, his wife, and a crew of nine. The howling storm was pounding the craft, slopping green water onto the decks. Suddenly the mate on watch noted the erratic behavior of the vessel. The helmsman who had been struggling to hold a proper course found the wheel spinning free. A look over the side showed the rudder had been dislodged and was drifting away in the turbulence. Indeed, the schooner was almost uncontrollable. Some more canvas was hoisted in an effort to claw away from the beckoning shore but she was drawn like a magnate toward Point Leadbetter, near the entrance to Willapa Harbor. A hole opened up in the murk and the roaring, rumbling surf erupted all about. Jostled about like a piece of driftwood, the vessel was thrown unceremoniously into the churning cauldron much to the fear of the crewmen who were struggling just to keep their feet. A series of voluminous breakers then raised their hoary heads and literally picked up the *Zampa* and flung her high upon the sands beyond the drift line. Much to the amazement of her company, the schooner remained erect and appeared to have suffered little structural damage. Nor were there injuries among the crew.

The horse-drawn lifesaving equipment and the oilskin clad surfmen from the Klipsan Lifesaving Station were soon on the scene to aid the survivors.

When the storm finally abated and the tide ebbed, the *Zampa* was fully 300 feet from the water and her chances of ever gaining full floatation again were extremely remote. For months she rested upright on the sands—virtually free from serious damage but with no place to go. A guard was kept aboard to protect from vandalism while plans for salvage were carefully worked out. The area was notorious for the permanent imprisonment of trapped ships once afoul of its sandy barriers. The salvagers had everything to gain and little to lose and despite the odds against them took up the challenge. Using a variety of equipment as well as beasts of burden, they dug a trench around the vessel's hull and formed a basin leading toward the ocean. Using tidal variations to dig and to winch, the vessel was moved a few feet each day—some days none at all. Utilizing anchors and additional winches the schooner was eventually worked back into the breakers, her bowsprit pointing due west. The weather remained moderate and the seas calm.

Held in position by anchors, the first big flood tide was awaited to attempt the refloating of the *Zampa*.

A tug was summoned and a long hawser run out between the two craft. It was a touch and go proposition, but the elements favored the ordeal and the schooner, both to the amazement of the North Beach Peninsula folk and the West Coast maritime world as well, was free once again. The beachdwellers cheered the successful effort but lamented the loss of the spoils of the wreck—a vocation that had proved highly profitable in the vicinity. The tug coddled her charge until she was again in deep water entirely free of the clutching sands.

The *Zampa* was towed to safety and continued a charmed career until her final demise in 1926, three miles north of Honolulu.

ADMIRAL

Where the mouth of the Columbia River meets the thundering Pacific, exists a battleground of nature, long a challenge to man. At first the enemy made great inroads against his human opponent, but in recent years man has brought this graveyard of ships under control.

Back when nature was still the aggressor, the 683 ton, four-masted schooner *Admiral*, commanded by Captain Joseph Bender, was beating off the mouth of the Columbia. It was a morning in mid-January of 1912 and from

Powerful Puget Sound **TUG GOLIATH** shepherds a three and four-masted schooner out of the Strait of Juan de Fuca as windjammer crews unfurl canvas and ready to cast off hawsers.

Ashore near Dungeness, Washington **SCHOONER RESOLUTE** was later pulled free, her deckload restowed and the voyage resumed.

shoreside nothing was visible but the gray walls of rain and leaden clouds which seemed to almost touch the water. A mighty southwest gale from the direction that whips the bar into its wildest frenzy was blowing out its lungs and sending great geysers of water scudding over the south jetty. Somewhere out there beneath that wall of gray, the *Admiral* had been driven off course and faced destruction.

Word reached the Point Adams Lifesaving Station at 8:45 a.m. on January 13 that a vessel was in peril. The report came by phone from another lifesaving station via wireless from a tanker that had sighted the floundering schooner.

As Captain O. S. Wicklund, in charge of the station, was taking down the details, the phone suddenly went dead. The strong blasts of wind had knocked down the telephone wires. From the scant information, he summoned his crew and voiced the old slogan of the surfmen:

"You have to go out, but you don't have to come back."

Captain Wicklund knew only that the troubled ship was somewhere south of the jetty . . . but where? He didn't dare launch a surfboat in the mounting breakers without know-

ing the exact location. Even if he had known, chances of surmounting the surf were negligible. There was more than one way to approach the problem, however, and Captain Wicklund was nobody's fool. He'd been in rescue work too long to twiddle his thumbs.

At the shore end of the jetty near Fort Stevens was a locomotive, a small narrow-gauge contraption that had been used to haul rock over the jetty trestle for extension and repair work. It would afford the best means of getting out on the jetty in an endeavor to locate the wreck. With the wires down there was no way to alert the fort to have an engineer fire up the engine's boiler so Captain Wicklund ordered his men to stand by with the beach cart, horses and breeches buoy apparatus while he went ahead on foot to secure the engine.

The wind blew so hard that he could barely stand up, but he drove himself across the sandy peninsula for three tormenting miles—something inside spurring him onward. It was the thought that souls could be perishing. Visions of the schooner smashed to kindling against the mighty boulders of the jetty haunted him and he could see in his mind's eye terrible struggles for survival. His thoughts made him forget the driving rain and stinging sand. Finally he gained the fort and immediately got prompt action from willing helpers.

"It's a case of life or death—every minute counts," he told the commanding officer at the fort.

The weather was thick as wool and one could only see a few feet ahead. There was also the despairing thought that the breakers crashing against the jetty may have torn out part of the trestle. Despite the risk, the engineer and fireman showed no hesitancy and soon had the little iron horse puffing down the trestle toward the jetty. Captain Wicklund craned his head from the cab straining his eyes through the haze. Occasionally the distant sound of a fog-horn would rise over the roar of the tempest and again the shrill call of the engine would blast forth. The locomotive reduced its speed, the man at the controls ready to pull on the brakes should a break be sighted in the wooden trestle.

The rain drove down in torrents on the heels of 75-mile-an-hour winds. Still there was no sign of a vessel in distress. Maybe it had foundered with all hands was the fearful thought that crossed Wicklund's mind.

The engine passed the three-mile mark and was now going at little more than a crawl as breakers leaped up the side of the great, black rocks and bathed the engine in spume. Then, like an apparition, the beam of the locomotive revealed a dim outline on the tracks dead ahead.

"Brakes!" Wicklund snapped, and the engine came to a screeching halt. He leaped from the cab and fought his way forward until he recognized a human figure approaching, half walking, half crawling. As he approached, Wicklund recognized that the figure was wearing a tattered and torn uniform of a ship's officer and under one arm had a small infant wrapped in a

sweater and blanket. Exhausted, the man handed the baby to Captain Wicklund, who in turn removed his oil skins and wrapped them about the babe whose body was blue from the cold.

The mumbling ship's officer finally gasped, "Jetty gone!" Pointing his trembling finger, he blurted again, "Jetty gone—three more coming."

Assuring the man that he understood him, Wicklund finally got him into the engine cab while the train operator held the baby near the boiler fire for warmth.

Soon the engineer had the locomotive moving forward once again under a very slow bell. The wretched ship's officer was trying to tell his rescuers that the baby boy belonged to the ill-fated ship's captain whose wife was somewhere on the trestle. Before he could get the words out, the engineer pulled on the emergency brakes once again and the engine screeched to a stop in front of a figure almost as white as the fog-filled atmosphere. Again Captain Wicklund leaped from the cab only to find a thinly clad woman dragging herself along the ties. Wisking her up in his arms he deposited her on the floor of the engine cab where she lapsed into unconsciousness.

A few feet farther down the track the master of the wreck was sighted, his clothes almost torn from his body. He had been half shoving his wife down the track until his strength had all but waned. Next the ship's cook was discovered several paces behind the captain but he was in slightly better condition.

Soon all were packed into the tiny cab like sardines in a can, the well ones trying to get circulation back into the suffering by rubbing their hands and legs. The cook tried to get some gin from a flask down the throat of the

The **MARY WINKELMAN** is towed in after a collision with a tanker.

Faded old photograph of **TWO-MASTED SCHOONER C. T. HILL** aground July 30, 1912, at the entrance to Oregon's Nehaelm River. In a novel salvage effort some months later she was refloated and lasted until 1916.

At anchor at a Puget Sound port, **BARKENTINE MARY WINKELMAN** is seen minus part of her bowsprit. She collided with the **TANKER LA PURISIMA** in the Strait of Juan de Fuca April 23, 1923. Built at Seabeck, Washington, in 1881 the vessel ended her days on a reef near Pago Pago November 13, 1923.

young mother. She gasped and choked and suddenly sat up like a ramrod. "My baby," she cried, "Where's my baby?"

"Here he is," confided Captain Wicklund, placing the bundle in her arms. As tears flowed from her sunken eyes down her sallow cheeks, she trembled, but a warm glow masked her face when she was assured that the infant was still alive.

The locomotive by this time was moving in reverse with increasing speed. When the fort was reached the survivors were taken to the base hospital and given preferential care.

Meanwhile the lifesaving crew had arrived with the beach cart, breeches buoy and line-throwing equipment. They loaded the gear onto a flat car which in turn was hooked up to the locomotive. Soon the engine was again clanking out over the jetty trestle in search of more survivors. Caution was exercised, as they now knew that a break existed in the trestle somewhere beyond where the earlier rescue had been made. Suddenly the engine came to an abrupt halt and just in the nick of time. There before it was a break in the trestle almost 200 feet wide. A few more feet and the train would have dropped into the deep fissure. Faintly discerned on the other side was a group of bedraggled sailors huddled together to keep warm. Between the breach in the trestle massive acclivities of water boiled and hissed across the inundated black boulders with the sound of thunder.

Without the slightest hesitation, the lifesavers rigged up the breeches buoy and, with their Lyle gun, shot a line to the survivors on the other side. Before long, the men were being hauled across the break one by one until all seven gained the assuring outstretched arms of the rescuers. After all were packed into the engine cab or onto the flatcar, the murk lifted just enough to allow a view of the wreck which had driven over the jetty rocks.

The master of the ill-fated schooner *Admiral* told of the final hours while approaching the end of an 8,000-mile voyage from Valparaiso. They were headed for Grays Harbor, but the intervening storm terminated the voyage short of the goal—running afoul of the vagaries of the Columbia River entrance. They came to grief, several miles off course, at 8 a.m. on the 13th day of January. The seas swept the schooner right up to the top of the jetty rocks and through the trestle work in an ear-shattering drama of water, rock and timber. Miraculous was the escape of the ship's company—the most serious injury being suffered by the steward whose feet were crushed in the wreck. The schooner itself was later carried right over top of the sea-washed jetty into the ship channel. The bar tug *Wallula,* commanded by Captain Nolan, sighted the derelict and attempted to put a line aboard and tow her across the bar. Risking death, three of the tug's crew got aboard and made a line fast. Just as the tow started, the schooner began to heel over and the terrified men crawled out on her side to await rescue. In pulsating seas, a small boat was launched from the *Wallula* to pick them up. As the *Admiral* flipped bottom up, one of her anchors broke loose and shackled her to the bar floor. The pounding seas eventually caused the cable to snap and the wreck was dashed up on Peacock Spit and totally demolished.

The alertness of Captain Wicklund, his life-saving crew and the volunteers from Fort Stevens put a happy ending to an otherwise harrowing experience by the *Admiral's* company.

EQUATOR

Saved from the sandspit at Everett, Washington, where the tides had long licked at her decaying hull, the remains of the former schooner *Equator* have become the property of a preservation group called Equator Inc.

Though spending much of her latter life as a Puget Sound tugboat, the vessel became famous for two outstanding adventures in her early years. She began life as a pert, two-masted trading schooner, properly named *Equator,* for her or leserving the South Sea islands. Within a year of her commissioning she rode out the devastating hurricane of 1889 that reaped havoc in the South Seas, doing untold property damage and destroying six major warships. Secondly, she was once chartered by the renowned Robert Louis Stevenson, author and poet.

Built by the Wightman Brothers at San Francisco in 1888, the schooner was excellently put together and tastefully fitted out by master craftsmen. This was borne out by her ability to escape total destruction in the 1889 hurricane. The *Equator* and the British warship *Calliope* were the only vessels within a radius of 200 miles of Apia to escape. Towering waves were mounted by phenomenal winds said to have reached a velocity of 200 miles-an-hour. Every standing thing on the islands in the path of the hurricane was leveled and large formidable war vessels—three American and three German—were literally blown like matchsticks up on tropical beaches, some for miles inland. Hundreds of lives were snuffed out and property damage reached astronomical figures.

None would have dreamed that such a tiny craft, slightly over 80 feet in length, could have survived such an act of God, but she did, and the episode was the start of a charmed career.

In June 1888 Robert Louis Stevenson, a tall, lean man with friendly eyes and pleasing personality, along with his wife, his mother and stepson, sailed from San Francisco in the schooner-yacht *Casco,* one of the most celebrated vessels of her day from the standpoint of comfort and sailing qualities. He chartered her on what was intended to be a voyage for his failing health. As it turned out, he spent the re-

On March 22, 1916 the waterlogged **SCHOONER OAKLAND** was carried ashore on Manzanita (Nehalem) Beach, Oregon. She remained stranded until January 23, 1918 when successfully refloated and repaired. She foundered off Cape Mendocino, Calif., June 24, 1924. In the photo, the Oakland is aground near Manzanita, with Mt. Neah-Kah-Nie in background.

The Port Blakely Mill Company ran the **SCHOONER BAINBRIDGE** from 1900 till 1923 when she was sold to L. A. Scott, Mobile. She was lost at Nags Head, N. C., in 1929.

additional housing over her open decks.

Cary-Davis Tug & Barge Company, founded by the late Captain George R. Cary and Captain Lindley Davis, purchased the *Equator* in 1915 and a few years later removed her steam engine in favor of a diesel plant. Her longtime home port of San Francisco was traded for Seattle.

This defiant little vessel got into some real trouble in 1923 when she stranded while crossing the treacherous and remote Quillayute River bar on the Washington coast. The accident happened while the *Equator* was towing a log crib to sea in company with the tug *Dolly C.* Both vessels hit the shoals—the latter managing to get free but the other stuckfast, her hull filling up with sand. With the incoming tide she was down in 20 feet of water, the seas flowing through her confines. To all intents and purposes she would have remained there a total loss. Her age was against her but the underwriters authorized the long gamble. They dispatched some experts to the area to make a survey. Whether by challenge or intrigue, the effort was undertaken. The wrecked tug was filled with empty oil drums, hundreds of them, until the reserve buoyancy lifted her off the sandy trap. A salvage tug then darted in, made a hawser fast and pulled the half sunken craft, submarine-fashion, to shallower water. There winches and anchors got her to a place where she could be temporarily patched and repaired.

She was then dragged back into deeper water and towed to Seattle for a brand new lease on life.

From sail to steam, and from steam to diesel, the aging lady kept abreast of the times. She performed admirably up-Sound, down-Sound and cross-Sound. By 1941 the old vessel had worn out another engine and was ready for a third. Despite her 70 years, the *Equator* kept running. In 1956, under operation of Puget Sound Tug & Barge Company, this worn out craft was given her retirement papers. The port captain for the Seattle towing firm said: "She's outlived her usefulness."

BARK HESPER, marked by a mutiny, had the reputation of a hell ship. She's seen here off Tatoosh Island six decades ago. H. H. Morrison photo.

A symphony of beauty—The four-masted **SCHOONER R. W. BARTLETT** returns from a Pacific crossing. Built for Wright, Bowne & Co. by Hans Bendixsen at Fairhaven in 1899, she was last afloat under the Peruvian flag as the Cuatro Hermanos.

And so with the passing parade of time they took everything but the heart out of the stout little vessel. Denuded of all equipment, one day without fanfare she was quietly towed to the sandspit at Everett, north of Seattle. Her oaken framed hull was shoved aground on the spit alongside other decaying vessels and hardly a tear was shed at her passing. She lay idle on the spit for several years before maritime historically-minded civic groups of the port city became interested in restoring her as a living memorial to the past.

One of the saltiest of the old West Coast square riggers was the **BARK TIDAL WAVE.** She was built at Port Madison, Washington, in 1869 by W. H. Bryant for Meigs, Gawley, San Francisco, for $50,000. She was a fast sailer in the coastwise trade, once making the run from Port Madison to San Francisco in five days, and in 1877 five round trips in five months under Captain Edward B. Reynolds.

Hawaii-bound — **SCHOONER MARY E. FOSTER** in 1901. The vessel was in the lumber trade between the Northwest and the Pacific islands for her entire career. She was built at Port Blakely by the Hall Brothers in 1898.

Artist's rendering of the five-masted, 1,443 ton **SCHOONER CRESCENT** built by the Bendixsen Shipbuilding Co. at Fairhaven for the Charles Nelson Co. She was the largest sailing vessel built on the West Coast till the advent of the World War I sailing vessels. Captain Theodore Olson was master of the handsome schooner throughout her entire career. She was abandoned at sea in 1918 after catching fire. Value of ship and cargo was $400,000.

SCHOONER HELENE with lumber for Hawaii puts out to sea in 1900 from Puget Sound. She was almost a total loss when stranding in the Hawaiian Islands in 1918 but escaped to finish a long career.

The golden age of sail comes back to life with scenes such as this—**SCHOONER ROBERT R. HIND.** Built in 1899 by Hay & Wright for Hind, Rolph & Company, she was broken up 25 years later in Australia. One of her best known skippers, Captain E. O. Erikson, died while the ship was in the mid-Pacific in 1907.

This pert little three-master named **QUEEN** was a worthy member of the coastwise lumber fleet. Only 124 feet long and hauling 350,000 board feet, the vessel was built by C. G. White at San Francisco in 1882 and was sold to Mexican interests in 1912.

"AURORA."
→ CAPT· ALFF S. HANSEN· ←

BARKENTINE AURORA built at Everett, Washington in 1901 by the Everett Shipbuilding Co. for Charles Nelson & Co. From a painting by Laidlaw & Harris, Sydney, N.S.W.   *Courtesy of R. E. Mackay photo collection.*

At left—rugged **TWO-MASTED SCHOONER MAID OF ORLEANS** in Lake Union, Seattle, about 1935. The **MAID OF ORLEANS** which became famous in the South Seas and in the Arctic was built by the Dickie Bros. at San Francisco in 1882 and was still afloat eight decades later. *Harry A. Kirwin photo.*

TWO-MASTED SCHOONER ALICE hard aground at Turtle Bay on Mexico's West Coast at an unknown date. She was built by Sebastian Ligouri in 1863 at Eden Landing on San Francisco Bay, near where the San Mateo Bridge is now located.

The **ALEX T. BROWN** was one of five similar schooners built by Thomas C. Reed at Ballard, Washington for Globe Navigation Company, in 1903. She was wrecked May 29, 1917 after leaving Fremantle for Manila.

Tug comes alongside to assist the **ROBERT SEARLES** before the turn of the century. Built in 1888 she was abandoned in a gale off the Hawaiian Islands August 24, 1913, one of her crew being drowned. The derelict was towed into Kahului harbor and converted to a coal barge.

The rather ignominious guano trade attracted the **BRIGANTINE COURTNEY FORD** before the turn of the century. This vessel was later converted to a schooner and lost in Alaska in 1902.

Rare sight—tugs were often scarce off Cape Flattery in the rip-roaring days of sail. This one picked up a handsome fee by towing in three windships at the same time—a three and four-masted schooner and a barkentine. The year was about 1900.

A cargo of logs fills the deck of the **SCHOONER COLUMBIA.** She was built by G. H. Hitchings at Hoquiam in 1899 and was sold to British owners in 1928.

Four-masted **BARKENTINE AURORA,** 221 feet long and of 1,211 tons, carried 1.35 million board feet of lumber. She is pictured in 1902 operating for the Charles Nelson Company. The vessel was converted to a schooner in 1920 and ended her days as a California fishing barge. Her former master, Captain P. J. R. Mathieson, described the Aurora as "fine, well kept and comfortable."

Discharging lumber from Willapa Harbor at Brisbane—**BARKENTINE MAKAWELI** 1911.   *Capt. E. J. Stull photo*

Burned out hull of **AUXILIARY SCHOONER ARGUS** which caught fire off Destruction Island June 13, 1906. She was the first big West Coast schooner powered with a gas auxiliary, and was commanded by Captain W. J. Moloney who carried his wife and child aboard. All hands escaped the fire and the hull was towed to Port Gamble—a total loss, but later rebuilt as a barge.

Berthed at Raymond, Washington, in 1911, the **BARKENTINE MAKAWELI** is pictured loading lumber for the Antipodes. Photo courtesy Capt. E. J. Stull, retired master mariner, who once served on the vessel.

At the Schwabacher Wharf in Seattle in 1910, **TUG TYEE** ties up after towing a windjammer in from Cape Flattery. Courtesy Capt. E. J. Stull

Peaceful setting—the three-master **JOHN G. NORTH** waits at anchorage. She burned while serving as a floating tuna cannery off Cape San Lucas, Mexico May 14, 1919 after years of sailing coastwise and to the South Pacific, carrying for the most part lumber and copra.

This photo is believed to be the **FIVE-MASTED SCHOONER CRESCENT** at Mukilteo waiting to load lumber. Built on Humboldt Bay in 1904, she was lost en route to San Francisco from the Antipodes after catching on fire in the mid-Pacific June 1, 1918. Captain Olson, his wife and 12 crewmen sailed in an open boat 1,400 miles to San Francisco after abandoning ship. Photo courtesy Pete Hurd.

U.S. Lifesaving Station at Baada Point on Neah Bay in 1910. The motor lifeboats on the ways went to the aid of numerous tempest-tossed windjammers around the entrance to the Strait of Juan de Fuca. *Old Coast Guard photo*

Launching day for the barkentine **JANE L. STANFORD** at the Bendixsen yard at Fairhaven. The year was 1892. She was the largest sailing vessel built in California up till that year. Initial master was Captain J. A. Johnson. Captain P. A. McDonald who loaned this photo, was also a former master of the vessel.

SCHOONER ZAMPA stranded at Leadbetter Point at the south entrance to Willapa (Shoalwater) Bay, July 17, 1904, after losing her rudder in a gale off the mouth of the Columbia River. Captain Kellenberger, his wife and crew reached shore safely.

Veteran TWO-MASTED SAILING SCHOONER ECLIPSE at anchor in Port Townsend Bay just before the turn of the century. The 234 ton vessel, built at New York in 1852, was crushed in the ice at Cape Romanoff, Alaska in 1900 in the service of the La Connor Trading and Transportation Company.

Hard aground on Chehalis Point at the entrance to Grays Harbor —SCHOONER KING CYRUS—July 17, 1922. The 717 ton vessel inbound from Honolulu became a total loss.

Typical of the smaller West Coast built windships was the **CASCO** which did much trading in the South Seas and later became a sealer. Fast, sleek and yachtlike, Robert Louis Stevenson, once chartered her for a South Seas cruise with his family. Seen here are deck and cabin scenes aboard the vessel.

Vintage Winter & Pond photo showing steamers and two-masted schooners discharging cargo at Dyea, Alaska in 1897.

The four-masted **SCHOONER MARY E. FOSTER** was the second vessel to bear the name—the first being a two-master. She was once skippered by Capt. Ralph E. "Matt" Peasley, and was built for the lumber haul to the Hawaiian Islands in 1898.

Breasting lazy swells off the Pacific Coast, the lumber-laden **SCHOONER KITSAP** with practically no freeboard, moves toward the islands.

SCHOONER DAUNTLESS off Grays Harbor. This vessel survived a major collision with the steamer St. Helens off Fort Bragg October 13, 1912.

SCHOONER CAROLINE tows to sea from Grays Harbor. Built at a cost of $37,500 in 1902, her first owner was Joseph Knowland of San Francisco who named all of his ships for girls.

TWO-MASTED SCHOONER BRILLIANT anchored in wind-whipped seas off the northern California coast reputedly in the 1870's. One of the luckier doghole schooners, more then once she was given no chance of survival. She operated for the Mendocino Lumber Company. Some historians believed the above was the **SCHOONER EQUATOR** in the great Samoan hurricane of 1889, but further research disclaimed that theory.

On Coos Bay, **SCHOONER ADMIRAL,** a fine creation of the Simpson yard. She was wrecked on the Columbia River South Jetty January 12, 1913.

Bone in her teeth—**TUG TATOOSH,** Puget Sound Tug Boat Co., moves out for a windjammer tow.

One of the most powerful tugs on the coast in the early days was the Canadian **STEAM TUG LORNE** which aided in many rescues and towed numerous sailing vessels from Canadian ports out to the open Pacific.

BARK ALBERT, 682 tons, outbound with lumber in 1912. This beautiful vessel built by Hall Brothers in 1890 was wrecked on a voyage from Timaru, N.Z. to San Francisco, eight miles north of Point Reyes, California on the morning of April 2, 1919. The master drowned but the crew reached shore safely. The Albert was built for the Island sugar trade and was engaged as a sugar packet until World War I.   *O. Beaton photo*

Four-masted **SCHOONER BAINBRIDGE,** a Hall Brothers product of the 1900 era, inbound for cargo.

BARKENTINE AMAZON, 1,167 tons, sister to the **AMARANTH,** was among the largest West Coast built sailing vessels. The Amazon was built by Matthew Turner in 1902. In 1916 A. F. Thane purchased her for $55,000 and sold her a year later to J. M. Scott, Mobile, for $160,000. She burned at sea, July 4, 1925.

The famous marine photographer G. E. Plummer took this photo of the five-masted **SCHOONER INCA** off Cape Flattery in 1913. The Inca was built in 1896 at Port Blakely.

Puffing black smoke, **TUG TYEE** tows in schooner from Cape Flattery. To left, British square rigger is seen under tow. Both were inbound for a load of lumber at Puget Sound ports.

Gathering in the breeze, West Coast windjammer tacks offshore.

A flat sea, and little breeze barely billows the canvas of this barkentine.

O. M. Beaton, prominent marine photographer of yesteryear, took this photo, believed to be the **FOUR-MASTED SCHOONER ROBERT SEARLES** laden with lumber off the Columbia River in 1912.

Artist's rendering of the full rigged ship **WESTERN SHORE,** a three-skysail yarder, claimed by many to have been the most beautiful sailing vessel built on the West Coast. Constructed at North Bend, Oregon in 1874, her master builder was John Kruse.

Asa Mead Simpson, lumber tycoon, shipbuilder, empire builder of Oregon's Coos Bay country.

STEAM TUG GOLIAH tows two West Coast windjammers down the Strait of Juan de Fuca about 1912.

This rare photo taken at Chuckanut Bay, Puget Sound, in 1890 shows a line of veteran square riggers at anchorage waiting turns to take on cargoes of coal.

Hans Ditlev Bendixsen, the famous builder of sailing vessels on Humboldt Bay, California.

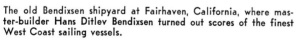

The old Bendixsen shipyard at Fairhaven, California, where master-builder Hans Ditlev Bendixsen turned out scores of the finest West Coast sailing vessels.

Matthew Turner-built sailing vessels were designed to carry the ultimate in sail for fast passages to Hawaii in the sugar trade. Here the **JOHN D. SPRECKELS** spreads her extra wings.

BAR TUG "TATOOSH", ASTORIA, OREG.

At entrance to the Columbia River bar, **TUG TATOOSH**, of Astoria, drops lines from lumber-laden barkentine, around the turn of the century.

Inaugural trip of the **STEAM TUG TACOMA**, a powerful unit used in the towing of windships at the turn of the century. Her bones lie under the old ferry slip at Winslow on Bainbridge Island.

The Columbia River bar **TUG WALLULA** made a great name for herself in marine annals both as a tow craft for sailing vessels and for salvage work. A West Coast schooner laden with lumber is seen in the background.

The **CHARLES R. WILSON** ended her days as a breakwater at Powell River, B.C. about 1947. Here she's seen in greener years. Built at Fairhaven, Calif., in 1891 she served as both a lumber ship and a codfisher. Her last voyage to the Bering Sea for cod was made in the 1940's.

Grace personified — five - masted schooner off the Strait of Juan de Fuca in 1912. She is the **SNOW & BURGESS,** built on the East Coast as a square rigger and converted on the West Coast to a five masted schooner shortly after the turn of the century. O. Beaton photo.

SCHOONER J. H. LUNSMANN rolling over on her beam ends after a collision with the steamer **FRANCIS LEGGETT** near Black Point, San Francisco harbor, July 12, 1913.

Six sailing vessels are pictured loading at the Port Blakely Mill Company around the turn of the century. Second and third from the left are the **FOUR-MASTED SCHOONER BLAKELY,** the **BARKENTINE NEWSBOY** and at the center the large German **BARK LILBEK.** Webster & Stevens photo.

Captain William Renton, one of the most successful pioneer lumber barons on Puget Sound. Nova Scotian by birth, his father Adam H. Renton was a shipmaster. William also went to sea when only 11 years of age, and by 23 was master of his own ship. He came to California in 1850 and made his way north to Puget Sound eventually getting into the lumber business and in numerous civic activities. His Port Blakely Mill gained world attention even attracting the President of the United States, President Rutherford B. Hayes as a visitor.

FOUR-MASTED BARKENTINE JOHN PALMER once skippered by the colorful Captain O.B. "Hands and Feet" Lindholm, father of Puget Sound pilot Captain Fred Lindholm. In 1912 Lindholm took the lumber-laden vessel from Port Gamble, Washington to Cape Elizabeth, South Africa in 112 days. On the return voyage from the African port in ballast through the Indian Ocean and across the Pacific to Astoria and Portland it required only 89 days which could be a record for that type of vessel. The vessel ended her days as the French **SCHOONER YVONNE.**

Hall Brothers Marine Railway & Shipbuilding Company at Winslow in Eagle Harbor, Bainbridge Island, Washington during the era of sail. Nearest the camera was the British **SAILING VESSEL GANGES.** At center is the **FOUR-MASTED SCHOONER KITSAP** and the **STEAMER MONTICELLO.** In the background is the yard showing the shipbuilding shed and the drydock with many vessels awaiting repairs.

55346

113

*How like the prodical doth she return, with
over-weathered ribs and ragged sails, lean, rent
and beggar'd by the strumpet wind!*
                                                    ---Wm. Shakespeare

Part Four

Successful and Unsuccessful Windjammers

WILLIAM NOTTINGHAM

OTHER THAN SEAGULLS, visitors are few to the wretched remains of the old four-masted schooner *William Nottingham,* lying abandoned on the mudflats at the mouth of the Nisqually River in upper Puget Sound.

The colorful old windjammer, a 1902 product of a Ballard, Washington shipyard was built for the Globe Navigation Co. She ended her days with stumped masts in the role of a cable barge for the Puget Sound Power and Light Company. Having outlived her usefulness she was lastly acquired by the Foss Launch & Tug Company who promptly ran her aground as part of a breakwater.

Her ghostly remains tell of the glorious past when she spread her sails before the wind on world voyages including some reputable roundings of timeless Cape Horn.

During her career the *Nottingham* served under both the Norwegian and American flags.

In the summer of 1906 in her fourth year of service she was preparing to weigh anchor at Port Townsend harbor. Laden with a load of fir logs the vessel was destined for Boston. The voyage promised to be a challenge, as many of the logs were over 100 feet in length. The schooner was short-handed and to fill out her complement some rather unorthodox recruiting of crewmen was undertaken. After some underhanded negotiations, crimps came out to the vessel in the dark of night and delivered some inebriated and drugged human forms. They were dumped in a heap on the deck, products of Port Townsend's Little Barbary Coast. Among the unwilling recruits was one extra large sailor. No sooner had the crimps received their blood money than the knock out drops began to wear off this individual. Shaking off the stupor before the anchor could be hoisted, he stoutly refused to sign any papers. The skipper was just as determined that he was going to remain aboard. An argument ensued between the two and the words flew hot and heavy. The air turned blue with profanity. Fists were clenched. The unwilling hand had no intentions of rounding the Horn on a windjammer with a cargo of logs. He'd rather swim the frigid waters of the bay than to sail before the mast on such a vessel.

The ship's crew closed in as the two men stared daggers at each other. Suddenly, like one having taken leave of his senses, the big fellow leaped at the captain wield-

STEAMER GOVERNOR stands by as the SCHOONER J. H. LUNS-MANN rolls over and goes down after a collision with the STEAMER FRANCIS LEGGETT, San Francisco Bay, 1913. Twelve man crew of the schooner was rescued. The 1,090 ton vessel was built at the White yard at Everett, Washington, 11 years earlier.

ing a rusty knife removed from inside his shirt. Before the skipper could strike out with his fists, the knife plunged into his back, once, twice, three times. His legs became weak and he sank to the deck in a pool of blood.

The mate grabbed a belaying pin and brought it down on the attacker's head. Down he went prostrate on the deck.

A doctor was immediately summoned to treat the wounded captain, and the knifer was placed in irons until the town sheriff arrived to haul him off to the city jail. He offered no resistance, pleased to trade a cell for the dank fo'c's'le of the windjammer.

The unfortunate episode seemed to cast an evil spell on the voyage before it got started. The schooner finally was towed out of the harbor by the venerable old steam tug *Wanderer*. The bandaged master was on restricted duty.

The Fall of the year was ripe as the *Nottingham* reached the southern latitudes. She was leaking badly having been mauled by heavy seas. Under the burden of the heaving acclivities the men were frequently at the pumps. Food and supplies ran low and the frigid winds cut to the marrow. The men were miserable and exhausted, the clothes they wore almost frozen to their bodies as icy gale after gale lashed the schooner.

Then one leaden day the lookout shouted down from the crosstrees, "Iceberg to port."

Graceful as a yacht—SCHOONER ENDEAVOR. She was wrecked with the loss of one of her crew on Ongea Reef in the Fiji Islands September 10, 1912. Three years earlier she was seriously damaged when rammed by the STEAMER IROQUOIS off Marrowstone Point, in Puget Sound.

The chilling words echoed across the decks as the solitary ship raced on before the wind. The ice had drifted up from the south as it so frequently does, and a sailing vessel is virtually helpless against its force. Many windships were victims of icebergs in days of yore and were usually reported lost without trace.

It was like playing Russian roulette with the growing menace as night came on in its sinister black cloak. The vessel's plight was that of a blind man on the edge of a precipice. Suddenly, with a terrifying jolt, the schooner crashed head on into a tall island of ice. The crew was thrown to the deck. The foreyard came crashing down in the midst of the struggling humanity. Tons of ice cascaded down from the top of the berg onto the deck causing the vessel's stern to rise from the water. She was down so low by the head that it appeared that she was actually being swallowed by a great frozen beast. There appeared no escape. It seemed but a matter of time till the weight of the ice would crush the fo'c's'le head and submerge the entire forward section and ultimately the ship, cargo and crew.

The men who had thus far miraculously escaped serious injury hastened to the skipper's

order to get the boat stocked with every possible item for survival. An escape in a sea of ice in an open boat was a virtual impossibility. Even if the craft survived, the men stood to freeze to death. The sustaining of life was almost completely dependent on the longevity of the schooner on which they stood. The irascible seas were assaulting the deckload of logs, cascading off onto the fallen ice, slushing up the poop. As the battle between sea and ice continued the crewmen were almost helpless. They just hung on as best they could wherever they could find protection. Whenever there was a lull they would claw their way forward to try to shove away more ice. Some were almost washed overboard in their sudden retreats. The pumps were operating constantly to give the vessel more buoyancy.

The ordeal continued. By day the ice island appeared to spread out for miles but by now the fo'c's'le head had been virtually cleared; the vessel began to edge around the rim of the floe. Like a fly escaping from a spider web the *Nottingham* somehow managed to free herself, drifting away from the blue mass just as another avalanche came tumbling down. All the time the steam pumps and hand pumps were going to ease the sloshing bilge water.

Sail was crowded on to make good the escape

The **SCHOONER ALBERT MEYER** sails hanging almost limp as she rolls in long, oily swells in the North Pacific.

All sails set—**SCHOONER NOKOMIS,** Captain Jens Jensen, gathers wind off Cape Flattery. This vessel was wrecked on isolated Clipperton Island in the Pacific February 28, 1914 outbound for Payta, Peru.

BARKENTINE GARDINER CITY spreads her wings around the turn of the century. She was built for A. M. Simpson at North Bend in 1889 as a schooner but was re-rigged as a barkentine in 1895. After being dismasted off the California coast during World War I, she was re-rigged again as a four-masted schooner and re-named **KITSAP**. She was sunk in a collision with the **STEAMER WAI-LELE** in Kauai Channel, Hawaii, March 21, 1919.

and the westerlies this time aided the cause by ballooning the canvas. The vessel pushed on, dodging between ice fields in this game of chance. For another three days and nights a zig-zag course was pursued. Somewhere beyond the horizon lay the Falklands. The vessel sailed on around the Horn with never an idle moment at the pumps. Battered, beaten, but unbowed the schooner outwitted the brutal elements and at the command of her skipper sailed on and on until the warmth of the South Atlantic replaced the frigid Antarctic blasts.

It was well into December when the leaking vessel and her gaunt crew reached Sandy Hook. They picked up a tug which towed her all the way into Boston, her lengthy timbers still lashed above and below deck. The epic voyage at last was over and all hands breathed a great sigh of relief. It was one of the largest loads of logs ever carried from the West to East Coast in those early years.

The *Nottingham* was placed in drydock for repairs and her rigging overhauled. The owners had lined up a case oil cargo for Australia but when the schooner tied up at New York virtually all of the crew jumped ship lacking an appetite for another rounding of the Horn. Only the mates, against their better judgment, stayed on and the skipper was grateful for their loyalty. A new crew was signed on.

The voyage from New York to Sydney fortunately came off without serious consequence and by comparison with the previous passage was a breeze, that is, if a long passage in a small windjammer can be classified as such.

The *Nottingham* was not again in the news until October of 1911, after leaving Astoria on a voyage to Callao. She was dismasted and waterlogged in a gale off the Columbia River. This time it appeared that she was finished for sure. Her crew escaped in high seas and was picked up from a small boat by the schooner *David Evans*.

But again the schooner refused to die. She was later found abandoned by the bar tug *Wallula* and taken in tow as a prize. After salvage money was paid, the *Nottingham* was taken to drydock, overhauled and re-rigged for another generation of service. She was never conquered despite the worst Mother Nature could dish out.

A former master of the *William Nottingham*, Captain C. T. Larsen, who in later years skippered the University of Washington oceanographic laboratory ship *Catalyst,* recalled that the *Nottingham* was jinxed.

"I'll never forget a voyage I made in the *Nottingham* in 1917," he recalled. "The vessel had been purchased by Norwegian interests for $60,000. We loaded in Tacoma for Durban, South Africa, and towed to sea in January. The jinx seemed to follow us from the time we squared away off Cape Flattery. The ship sprang a leak and we had a terrible voyage. We

117

had good pumps, but not enough fuel to operate them for a long period, so we headed for Tahiti sailing into the harbor at Papeete where we dropped anchor and decided to make a survey of the hull.

"However, there were no docks in Papeete and repairs seemed out of the question. When we were on the verge of despair with the prospect of remaining indefinitely in the South Seas, an idea popped into my head. Why not get the pearl divers of Papeete to repair the bottom of the *Nottingham?*"

And that is just what they did. The skipper hired a dozen pearl divers to swim under the vessel to find the leaks and repair them. They found three butts wide open. Later they went down with caulking irons in one hand, mallets in the other and oakum in their mouths and soon had the seams caulked as tight as a bottle. They then tacked lead over the seams to hold the oakum in.

"We were ready for sea again," Captain Larsen recalled, "but our troubles were not over. Every man of the crew, with the exception of the two mates, deserted the ship. They fled into the groves of breadfruit trees beyond Papeete and attempted to right a lopsided social structure where there were ten women to every man. France had conscripted for the war effort all of the men in the French South Sea islands.

"Well, we got the men back all right," the captain continued. "I offered the French gendarmes $30 each for my men if they were brought back to the ship. They dragged them out of the woods and we were delayed only a few days. A gasboat towed us out of the lagoon and we set sail for South Africa."

NOKOMIS

That these rugged West Coast windjammers could and would go anywhere is indicative of a voyage once logged by the four-masted schooner *Nokomis.*

From the recollections of Captain M. M. Jensen comes data on the voyage of the *Nokomis* in 1899 and 1900, when the late Seattle mariner served aboard her as an AB. Captain Jensen signed aboard the vessel at Port Townsend in

Full and bye—**SCHOONER ETHEL ZANE** on a calm sea in 1912. Built by Peter Matthews at Eureka in 1891, she was abandoned in a South Seas typhoon in 1918, her crew of nine being miraculously saved.

late March of 1899. The *Nokomis* shifted to Port Blakely to load lumber for San Francisco and afterward loaded salt for the remote fishing village of Nikolayevsk on Siberia's remote Amur River.

The passage to the mouth of the Amur, which flows into the Okhotsk Sea, was completed in due time; there the *Nokomis* took on a Castris Bay pilot and began the 150 mile voyage up the treacherous winding river under sail, something the Siberians said could never be done.

Time after time the schooner straddled the shoals and it appeared that with each stranding the end of the voyage had arrived. But the rugged vessel kedged off each barrier and under shortened canvas would bite off one slow mile after another. There was nothing short of a Siberian holiday when the residents of Nikolayevsk saw the battered schooner make the final bend in the river before dropping anchor at the settlement.

There, while the cargo was unloaded, the weary crew absorbed the Siberian hospitality with zest, giving little thought to the return leg of the voyage.

Then, the most unusual part of the adventure was undertaken and perhaps never duplicated by another sailing vessel. The treacherous river currents and the narrow stretches made it next to mandatory that the vessel go back down the river stern first, dragging an anchor behind her and with a square sail

rigged down over and under the stern into the water, two braces leading forward from the sail to the chocks amidships. The pressure of the tide against the sail kept the schooner in the strongest current and the deepest and safest water, as she drifted down stream with the current. The pilot had an apprentice with him who heaved the lead at the stern.

Nor was this unorthodox way of navigation without its humerous aspects. Sometimes the apprentice would miscalculate in throwing the lead and land it in the sail under the stern. The apprentice would then shout:

"Two and a half fathoms."

Like a flash the pilot would shriek the order to let go all the anchors and the schooner would be brought to a dead stop. Such maneuvers inspired verse:

"Said the mate of a sailboat unique
To the cap'n, 'What port shall we sique?'
Said the cap'n 'We'll dock 'er
In Davy Jones locker;
This blasted old tub's sprung a
lique.' "

From dead stop, however, the *Nokomis* would recover her dignity along with the pilot and his aid, and the voyage would resume once again. The schooner finally reached the Okhotsk Sea without serious damage. As if glad to be in open water under full sail once again, the vessel made a remarkable passage from the Strait of Hakodate to Cape Flattery in just 21 days.

Sideway launching of the barkentine **JAMES JOHNSON** at Moran Bros. shipyard at Seattle, March 19, 1901. *T. E. Peiser photo, courtesy R. E. MacKay.*

The late Captain Matthew Turner, master mariner and master shipbuilder par excellence, was one of the all-time greats in West Coast maritime annals. This photo was taken at Benicia, California in 1908 when he was in his sunset years. *Swadley photo, courtesy Wm. J. Mitchell, Oakland, Calif.*

After colliding with the **SS MAUNA KEA** off Diamond Head, Honolulu, April 26, 1923, the **SCHOONER MARY E. FOSTER** is seen here after being beached at Waikiki. Wreck was pulled free, three days later, her lumber discharged and the hull sold for $100—a total constructive loss.

"We had a rattling good leading wind all the way," recalled Captain Jensen.

As for the *Nokomis,* which spent most of her years under the Hall Brothers ownership, we find her on January 17, 1914, sailing from Astoria for Paita, Peru. Due to heavy seas in the North Pacific she was towed disabled into Port Townsend. Sailing again on February 2, she was wrecked on Clipperton Island 26 days later and the crew was castaway in lonely isolation. Some of the men, fearing they would not be found, put to sea in an open boat, setting a course for Acapulco, Mexico. After several weeks of hardship they reached Mexico safely and eventually the USS *Cleveland* put into Clipperton to rescue the others.

The unfortunate sequel to this story is that the *Nokomis'* master, Captain Jens Jensen (no relation to Captain M. M. Jensen), was then given command of the passenger steam schooner *Francis H. Leggett.* In September of the same year the *Leggett* foundered off the Oregon coast with the loss of 65 persons, Captain Jensen being among the missing.

COURTNEY FORD

Lying forlornly among the great dunes of sand-swept Glen Island in the remote Bering Sea area of Alaska, 35 miles northwest of False Pass near Izembeck Bay lies the wreck of the former schooner *Courtney Ford.* Tattered and torn, yet remarkably preserved after more than 60 years of driving snows, ice, wind and sand, the ghostly remains have long been surrounded by an air of mystery.

The strangest thing about the wreck is that it rests more than a mile and a half from the island beach, landlocked and irretrievably lost. Nobody seems to know how the vessel got so far inland. Some say the island has eroded at one end and built up on the other due to shifting, drifting sands. Others say earthquakes have altered the island.

Salient facts are that the 400 ton vessel was on a voyage to the northern reaches of Alaska when on September 7, 1902 she crashed ashore on the insular dot known on the charts as Glen Island. The crew, all save one, put out in a small boat for assistance, leaving one man behind to keep an eye on the vessel in the hope that she might be salvaged. Before help arrived, however, months passed and the lone watchman endured indescribable hardship. The food supply ran out, the weather was sub zero and alone he succumbed to the elements within the confines of the battered wreck.

Hull design of the **NEWSBOY,** dating from 1882, is vastly different from similar vessels built two decades later on the West Coast. She's seen here with a load of lumber about 1900.

MAKAWELI, another of the Hind, Rolph fleet. This barkentine was once picked up off Cape Flattery, all sails gone and one crewman dead. She began her life at Oakland in 1902, built by W. A. Boole & Son, but ended a rather troublesome career as the FISHING BARGE RAINBOW a quarter century later.

Those who had escaped in the boat finally reached civilization.

The *Courtney Ford* which has defied time, even today, in ghostly cloak lies hopelessly landlocked half protruding from the sands of the uninhabited island. She was built as a brigantine at Benicia, California, by Captain Matthew Turner in 1883.

WILBERT L. SMITH

One of the West Coast-built fore 'n' afters that was a victim of circumstances during the first World War was the four-masted schooner *Wilbert L. Smith*. She, like the *William Nottingham*, was built by Thomas Reed by and for the Globe Navigation Company at Ballard, Washington, in 1902.

Her master was the late Captain A. S. Ross who established an enviable record on the high seas. Ross took the *Smith* from Puget Sound to Kobe and Osaka, made ten voyages in her to Callao, one to Antofagasta, one to Mexico, one to Hilo, two to San Francisco, a half dozen to San Pedro and one to San Diego—all in creditable time.

"We made a passage of 23 days from Kobe to Cape Flattery," the late Captain Ross once said. "This was a voyage that never has been equalled by a sailing vessel."

This same skipper also logged a 35 day passage from Callao to Cape Flattery, perhaps another record, and during the ten voyages from

Dead in the water—lofty FOUR-MASTED BARKENTINE JOHN C. MEYER. Built at Tacoma by Robert Banks at the Hardy Shipbuilding Company in 1902, the Meyer was wrecked at Machias, Maine, November 28, 1925.

Callao to Cape Flattery he covered the distance in the *Smith* in an average of 42 days.

Captain Ross was justly proud of these records. After purchase of the Globe fleet by Port Blakely Mill Company in 1914, Captain Ross left the vessel at Seattle. She was later sold to French interests and loaded with general cargo for France. The schooner narrowly escaped the submarine menace but, while in the coal trades during the fever pitch of the war, was destroyed in European waters by an explosion resulting from spontaneous combustion.

ETHEL ZANE

A typical example of the rugged hardships endured by those who sailed before the mast occurred in the summer of 1918. The four-masted schooner *Ethel Zane* had departed San Francisco on June 3. She carried a small crew of eight and was in command of an aging white-bearded skipper, Captain Charles Backus, who had spent virtually his entire life at sea. The schooner was old and had been laid up for years in San Francisco Bay. The urgent war-

time need for ships had demanded most anything that would float and the *Ethel Zane* was no exception. She was hastily refitted, and a crew of sailing ship men recruited. The overhaul of the vessel was by no means complete and her operators had her loaded with lumber and general cargo and out to sea in great haste.

Everything seemed to go well at first. The skipper, and the mate, Charles W. Nelson, another experienced sailing ship man, were highly respected by those before the mast. Good sailing weather was experienced on the transpacific crossing, that is until the wooden four-poster was struck with all the fury that a South Pacific typhoon can generate. That was on July 18.

Within an hour, pounded by mountainous seas and the full kick of the wind, the schooner's masts cracked like jackstraws and the deck was a welter of tangled rigging. The seams opened under the almost merciless onslaught and the bilge was soon full of water. The pumps became virtually useless, unable to handle the overwhelming inflow. The schooner settled lower and lower into the convulsive seas. Massive walls of water swept the decks curling and hissing, snubbing their noses on the raised poop and exploding like dynamite.

The men hung on to anything strong enough to keep them from being washed overboard. The schooner was completely at the mercy of the typhoon. The howling of the elements was so raucous that words were carried away inaudible. In desperation the men attempted to lower away a small boat, but before they could man the craft, it was swamped and badly damaged.

The *Zane* was now so low in the water that she was kept afloat only by her cargo of lumber.

Minutes turned to agonizing hours and faces became masked in the yellow pall preceding death. Exhausted and soaked to the skin, stomachs empty, eyes staring, they awaited the end. Somehow the will to live prevailed yet a little longer and by instinct the crew lashed themselves to the splintered masts and prayed.

The dejected skipper, his clothes half ripped from his body, his silver hair caked with salt and his beard laying tight against his chest, was a pitiful sight. He was at an age when he should have been in a comfortable rocking chair spinning yarns to his grandchildren. The

first mate was quiet and grim; second mate Walberg had broken under the strain and was delirious, screaming and laughing; the four ABs and the cook, almost used up physically, no longer winced when their bodies were struck by the cascading seas sweeping the deck.

Only one among the crew appeared endowed with super strength—a talent given to few when standing under the shadow of death. His name was Johan Ericksen who had shipped aboard as donkeyman. Strong and ruggedly built, he was among the youngest members of

Close hauled—**SCHOONER NOKOMIS** catches wind about 1905.

Defying the elements—**SCHOONER SOLANO** fights losing battle. The wreck is seen here in 1949. She grounded in 1907.

If only she could speak what a story the **SOLANO** wreck could tell. She lies forlornly on the North Beach Peninsula near Ocean Park. This photo was taken about 1950. The schooner was wrecked February 5, 1907.

the crew. Filled with courage and determination he clung desperately, as did the others, but seemed to absorb his punishment like a superman. In those moments of desperation Ericksen remembered that in the pocket of his brine-soaked pants was a waterproof metal match container which held a dozen or so matches. Lashed to the deck below him was a barrel of kerosene still intact. Nearby, inside the cabin entrance, was a fire axe and draped over the back of the crazed second mate was a blanket. These three items were to become of the utmost importance in this seemingly hopeless situation.

The waterlogged vessel pitched and rolled without cessation. Lashed to their posts, through another night, an endless day, still another night and a day, the gaunt men were all in a stupor, more dead than alive. All this time Ericksen's weary eyes scanned the endless ex-

panse as if he expected Jesus to come walking upon the waters, as of old. Eyes bloodshot and hollow, tongue swollen, he somehow managed to keep his vigil.

The others had long ago given up all hope. He too was about to falter when came that long remembered Sunday night. Fighting to stave off unconsciousness he peered once more into the inky fury. Was it only a vision in his tormented brain? He squinted and strained but surely he saw the faint glimmer of a green light, rising and falling. With his remaining strength he loosened his bonds, climbed back to the deck, struggling and staggering until he gained the cabin entrance. Every step was filled with agonizing pain, but his hands finally fell on the fire axe. Then groping his way in the dark he waded across the water-covered deck, shakily raised the axe and brought it down atop the cask, splitting it open. Bolstered by his success he peeled the blanket from the prostrate mate and soaked it in the kerosene.

Returning to his post on the broken mast he

The wreck of the **SCHOONER SOLANO** (1907) was set on fire by careless clam diggers who got over zealous with their beach fire in 1910. The remains of the vessel are still visible on North Beach Peninsula, opposite the Oysterville beach approach. Courtesy Art Appleton.

tied the blanket down and then with his numbed hands began the tortuous task of trying to set the blanket afire against the incessant wind. The matches one after another were snuffed out. Finally one caught hold and the blanket erupted into a great orange ball. Ericksen pushed it as high as his endurance would allow in the hope that those behind the green light might see the signal of distress.

The blaze soon subsided and the gaunt souls were again in the dark. The light seemed to revive the men momentarily and they tried in vain to render a semblance of help as the Norwegian peeled off his shirt for another signal attempt. Repeating the same process the shirt was soon consumed by fire.

The green light was seen occasionally but it faded away, and the grim survivors feared their signal had gone unsighted. When about to abandon their last glimmer of hope they witnessed a blue flare streaking through the black sky to the south. From their parched lips and swollen tongues they croaked, daring to hope that help might come. Hope was all they had left.

Once again they worked to get a rag to burn but broke down with sobs of defeat when their last match was blown out.

No more did they see the green light—no more flares. Despair and misery took over.

Before sleep claimed him, the dauntless Ericksen hours later sighted the green light once again. He believed it only a mirage until his bloodshot eyes detected the faint glimmer of a red glow. With agonizing effort he tried to revive his shipmates by telling them that a ship was tacking off to the south. Later in the night another flare was sighted but the exhausted men had no means of answering. Instead they lapsed into deep comas.

The distant vessel, that had observed the burning material, circled the area throughout the night. She was the full-rigged ship *Arapahoe,* loaded with case oil, bound for Manila from San Francisco. By dawn of the next day the tall ship stood off the battered hulk of the *Ethel Zane.* The sea was still very rough and gray leaden clouds hung about like dirty laundry.

Captain Hans Wilhelmsen, master of the *Arapahoe,* ordered a boat over the side to go to the rescue. He in turn would sail the ship from the windward to the leeward side of the wreck to aid the rescue craft. In charge of the mate, the volunteer crew in a daring feat of seamanship guided their open boat through the troubled seas and somehow managed to snatch the survivors from the wreck. The *Zane's* crew were so far spent that they were hardly aware of the rescue. Miraculously all recovered, though one of their number was in serious condition even after the *Arapahoe* reached Manila.

It was indeed a providential combination of incidents that saved the men of the *Ethel Zane.*

BALBOA

The four-masted schooner *Balboa* was approaching the entrance to Grays Harbor bar on the evening of November 30, 1913. She was inbound from Callao, Peru, where she had discharged a full cargo of lumber. Aberdeen was but a short distance away and the sailors were anxious to terminate the voyage.

The schooner rode high, being in ballast, and wallowed in heavy seas. As darkness approached, the schooner's master elected to await daylight in order to cross the treacherous bar

Small fry West Coast built sealing schooners in homeport at Victoria, B.C. during the sealing days before the turn of the century.

Remnants of the **GRACE ROBERTS** wreck as viewed in 1955 on the North Beach Peninsula. She was built at Port Orchard, Washington, in 1868 and wrecked 19 years later. When new the vessel cost $30,000. She was wrecked December 8, 1887.

It was a sad ending to the career of the **THOMAS P. EMIGH** which began her life at Tacoma in 1901 and is seen here a total wreck at Redondo Beach, California, April 20, 1932, serving as a fishing barge. She held the all-time sailing record of 7 days 22 hours, Honolulu to Cape Flattery, in 1909.

Immediately the lifesaving crew had its Dobbins lifeboat launched and underway. The oarsmen pulled toward the bar entrance but found it so rough that there was no hope of reaching the schooner from the outside. As luck would have it, the tug *Daring* happened to be within hailing distance when they were reconnoitering the bar. The always-existing common bond of men aiding those in peril on the sea prompted the operator of the tug to respond immediately. The vessel pulled alongside the pitching surfboat and obligingly towed it down the channel and around inside the north spit next to the jetty. There a private launch was engaged to take the lifeboat in tow through a gap in the jetty rocks and into a "sink" on the north side of the spit on the inshore side of the wreck.

The canting schooner was cradled against the spit with the breakers beating against her with thundering crescendo. The sails were furled but most of the deck gear had been torn from its fastenings. The men scurried about the slanting deck like ants on a disturbed anthill.

The lifesaving crew experienced great difficulty as they strained at the oars in an effort to reach the wave-swept wreck. The sharp sea and swift current that set toward the jetty compounded the effort. Peril was further augmented by the fact that, while maneuvering to get near the schooner, they were forced to lie

to the sheltered harbor. The hook was dropped in seven fathoms just outside the narrow bar entrance. During the night some atmospheric disturbance offshore set a heavy sea running, and the currents started dragging the 777 ton vessel toward the north spit. The master became concerned and all hands were accordingly summoned.

By 4:30 a.m. on December 1 the cable to starboard, holding the schooner's heavier anchor, parted and the vessel was quickly carried onto the sands 300 yards off the north jetty. She was immediately sighted by the lookout in the tower at the Grays Harbor Lifesaving Station, four miles southeast of where the *Balboa* lay trapped.

Her back broken, the 386-ton **BARKENTINE CATHERINE SUDDEN** pounds to pieces near Cape Nome, Alaska, on the bleak shores of the Bering Sea, September 7-8, 1900. She was one of three sailing ships lost in the gale. The **SUDDEN** was built by the Hall yard at Port Ludlow in 1878 for J. J. Smith, and made several fast passages in her time. At the time of her loss she was valued at $50,-000. Her last skipper was Captain "Crazy" Killman.

Lying forlornly on the mudflats of the Nisqually River in upper Puget Sound are the remains of the former **FOUR-MASTED SCHOONER WM. NOTTINGHAM.** After a colorful career under sail that started at Ballard, Wash., in 1902 for the Globe Navigation Company, she ended her days as a telephone cable repair barge, and was then dumped on the mudflats as a breakwater.

part of the time in the trough of the sea at great risk of being capsized. At last they got near enough to catch a line thrown down from the *Balboa's* poop. They carefully worked down to the vessel between the heavy runs of seas and threw a heaving line on board. Shouting above the thundering breakers, they told those on the wreck to make the lines fast about their bodies and one at a time jump into the maelstrom.

The smashing, crashing breakers did little to soothe the minds of those aboard the schooner. The thought of jumping into the irascible turbulence struck them with fear. They, however, did as directed, knowing that to stay might mean certain death. With his eyes shut, the first to go hit the water with a splash and gasped and struggled as the men in the surfboat hauled in on his line. Like a gaffed fish he was pulled to the side of the boat and into its confines.

Three others were rescued in like manner.

To the rescue—Dobbins lifesaving craft goes to the aid of a sailing vessel in distress off Oregon Coast about 1910.

Spray flying—Dobbins lifesaving craft breasts big swell off Oregon Coast in days of yore.
Old Coast Guard photo

Then a heavy run of breakers raced down on the lifeboat, filled and nearly capsized it. As the waves beat upon and over the boat, the strain put upon the line that ran to the schooner snapped the connecting rope and the boat was swept away helpless. The sea was steadily making with a rising tide. Realizing that to regain the lost position would be a matter of the greatest difficulty, the boat keeper directed his men to pull into smooth water and land the four survivors. Five still remained on the wreck.

The grave danger to the surfboat operating in the crashing surf finally brought about a decision to complete the rescue with the breeches buoy. It seemed feasible to work the buoy from the end of the jetty. The tug *Traveler* was contacted to take members of the lifesaving crew with all possible dispatch to the lifesaving station to retrieve the necessary rescue apparatus. On the return of the tug, the lifesaving crew and breeches buoy were transferred to a railroad flat car connected to a small steam engine waiting to carry them out and over the jetty.

(The railroad was used during the building work on the jetty.) By the time the engine was ready to start, however, the sea had moderated and the confused lifesaving crew again elected to take to their boat.

They braved the surf without mishap, but when they reached the side of the wreck they found that sea conditions were just as insurmountable as before. Fact is, the current was even stronger, sweeping them repeatedly toward the jetty rocks. After a determined hour's struggle they succeeded in getting close to the schooner and could see three of the five survivors with ropes wrapped about them ready to jump overboard in anticipation of rescue.

The boat crew, wet, worn and nearly exhausted, pursued their task like robots and while some remained at the oars the others braced themselves to receive the lifelines. There was no hesitation on the part of the shipwrecked seafarers. They feared that at any moment the wreck would break up beneath their feet. They accordingly plunged into the

Adventures and drama filled the logbooks of the venerable **TWO-MASTED SCHOONER MAID OF ORLEANS.** From blackbirding in the South Seas to breaking through the Arctic ice, the pert little vessel operated from 1882 until the 1960's, ending her days as a lowly barge.

Discharging lumber from the deck of the **FOUR-MASTED SCHOONER TAURUS** in 1921. The vessel made a 36-day run from Mukilteo to Waimea under Captain Svending. Handling lumber is AB Gus Karlson who donated this photo. The crew took two weeks to unload, and the vessel returned to the coast in ballast. Karlson spent a half century at sea in sail and steam.

wild surf and were steadily pulled to the surf-boat and helped inside.

Finally only two men remained on the *Balboa*. Despite the oscillating rescue craft, heaving lines were thrown toward the wreck. They were retrieved on the second try. The last to jump was the *Balboa's* master who was hauled out of the maelstrom still very much alive.

Without pausing for so much as an extra breath, the lifesaving crew took up their oars and began a dramatic pull through four miles of frenzied water against contrary current and tide. Without once resting, displaying superhuman strength and endurance they passed through the break in the jetty and beat the water all the way to the dock on the north side of the harbor entrance.

Too exhausted to return to their station, the lifeboat crew and the rescued men were taken aboard the waiting tug *Traveler*. Stripped of their soaked garments and given generous portions of coffee and brandy, they were tucked into the tug's bunks and there slept like babes for many hours.

The *Balboa* was no match for the relentless surf and was soon pounded to pieces until she was only a memory.

THE UNSINKABLE MAID OF ORLEANS

Eighty-five years of service is a long time for a human, let alone a ship. One of the most unusual and colorful of all the sailing vessels built on the Pacific Coast was the *Maid of Orleans*.

Constructed by the Dickie Brothers of San Francisco in 1882, the schooner left a trail of

At work mending sail—crew of **BARKENTINE MAKAWELI**, 1911, in mid-Pacific.

Towing out to sea, signal flags flying.

log books filled with enough drama and intrigue to provide for several novels of the sea. She long traded to the beckoning South Sea isles, shouldered the worst the frozen Arctic could throw at her, blackbirded, became a rum runner, carried dynamite, poached fish, hauled valuable furs, logs and lumber throughout the Pacific.

Her builders, two Scotsmen, James and John Dickie, who turned out forty-five sailing vessels in their day, built the two-masted schooner *Maid of Orleans* with great care, fashioning her hull of Oregon pine.

Under her initial owner J. J. McKinnon of San Francisco the *Maid of Orleans* for years operated in the South Sea trades, sometimes

Four-masted **SCHOONER ALERT** cutting a smooth course off the entrance to the Columbia River. This vessel built at Hoquiam in 1902 was lost near Niuafou in the Tongas in 1923, the crew of eight reaching shore safely.

The **WM. H. SMITH** of 566 tons was built by the Hall Brothers at Port Blakely for their own account in 1899. Her active years ended in 1937 under the Union Fish Co. of San Francisco.

A big swell almost hides the **SQUARE RIGGER BATTLE ABBEY** being towed across the Columbia River bar in the days of yore.

Columbia River bar **TUG TATOOSH** off Astoria, Oregon, towing in schooner from the bar, bound for Portland, about 1909.

Powerful windjammer-towing tug of yesteryear—**STEAM POW-ERED GOLIAH** skirting along in Elliott Bay, Seattle.

transporting black bodies from the Solomon Islands to the sugar plantations of Queensland. Her adventures, however, were seldom considered illegal as blackbirding was often permissible in those cruel, pre-century years. Such practices were frequent throughout the Pacific, and the white men often used forceful means to take unwilling slaves against their will for the mines in Bolivia and Peru or to copra and sugar plantations throughout the Pacific.

At sixty dollars a head, the crew of the *Maid of Orleans* found it a profitable venture when there was no lumber to bring from the West Coast or copra to transport to the mainland. Though it was considered proper to return the natives once the task had been completed, many died of disease, ran away or were traded from one place to another. Relatively few got back to the place of origin.

Often South Sea islanders joyfully became crew members when vacancies occurred; some even would stowaway. Seldom, however, would they volunteer to work at a distant plantation.

Frequently, the chief of a pagan tribe would hand over several of his tribesmen as laborers just for a watch, a knife or a mirror. If protests arose, a Mickey Finn or a little muscle was applied.

Shortly after the turn of the century the *Maid of Orleans*, slightly worse for wear, turned from South Sea islands to join the cod fishing fleet out of Puget Sound, running opposite such windjammers as the *Fanny Dutard, Lizzie Colby, Alice, Joseph Russ,* and power schooners *Harold Blekum* and *Fortuna*. Annually the vessels sailed to the Bering Sea where the cod flourished.

The *Maid of Orleans* operated under ownership of the Pacific Coast Codfish Company in 1906 and four years later passed to the Seattle Alaska Fish Company which later became the Western Codfish Company.

Captain J. E. Shields, president of the Pacific Coast Codfish Company, sold his interest in the *Maid of Orleans* in 1924 to Captain Christian Klengenberg who is said to be the first white man to penetrate to Victoria Land, 1,200 miles from the North Pole.

Lines dropped, tugboat crewman watches two West Coast three-mast schooners hoist sail and head down the Pacific Coast with lumber, just after the turn of the century.

Towing to sea in 1912, lumber-laden four-masters. **MARY E. FOS-TER** is lead schooner. O. Beaton photo.

Ruth Greene Bailey, in writing in Harbor and Shipping, notes that Alaska had 47 canneries and British Columbia 59 canneries in the first decade of this century and all totalled they handled three million cases of fish per year.

Klengenberg, having long followed the pursuits of the famous little schooner, purchased her for his arduous voyages to the far north. He was a hardy Dane, used to the rigors of the Arctic—often labeled, "Klengenberg of the Arctic." He was not only adventurous, but his actions were sometimes questionable. Married to an Eskimo woman, he raised several half-breed children. On one occasion he shot his first officer, reputedly in self-defense, but was so on edge over the incident that he kept his gun by his side constantly should any of the other members of the crew get out of line. It is said that he used only his wife and children to sail his command after crewmen refused to ship out with a "trigger-happy skipper." Once, up against a heavy ice flow, almost single handed he freed his vessel.

Klengenberg first became familiar with the *Maid of Orleans* in the Bering Sea in 1906. It was love at first sight and he wasn't satisfied until he owned her.

The *Maid of Orleans* became synonymous with the Northland, making annual voyages to the Arctic from 1924 until 1928 mostly out of Vancouver, B. C. She was fitted with a small diesel engine for emergencies.

The aging Klengenberg sold the vessel to the Hudson's Bay Company in 1928, and in 1929 and 1930 she made further trips to the Arctic. On the latter voyage, just before departure from Vancouver, Captain W. H. Gillen, her master, died after stumbling at dockside, falling into the water and striking his head on a log. There were no witnesses and, inasmuch as the body was not found until four weeks later, foul play was hinted. Gillen had skippered trading and sealing schooners on the B. C. coast for three decades prior to his death.

Captain Fred Coe, who replaced Captain Gillen, had formerly served as mate on the ill-fated "Ghost Ship of the North," the *Baychimo.*

When Hudson's Bay purchased the *Maid of Orleans* they changed her name to *Old Maid No. 2,* jokingly in honor of one of the offspring of a company executive who never married. The vessel traded at Cambridge Bay for furs, a short distance from the North Pole.

Competing with steamers—**FOUR-MASTED SCHOONER HELENE** takes a load of coal at Seattle. The vessel was launched in 1900.

A few years later the *Old Maid* was relegated to backwater moorages and eventually was purchased inexpensively for service as a rum runner. The *Old Maid No. 2* then sailed off for Mexico, sneaking a little of the illicit stuff into the darkened dogholes off the California coast under the veil of night. Her logbooks remained a secret during this period, but she played it to the hilt until the rum bonanza trickled away. Only then did she return to Seattle under the ownership of Albert Routai who put her back in acceptable pursuit—trading with the Eskimos of the Far North.

Trouble struck on February 26, 1926, in a heavy snow storm when she ran aground on Sarah Island in Finlayson Channel. The 15 man crew and two women took to the boat and rowed to Boat Bluff Lighthouse.

Still not ready to give up, the vessel held her own against the elements until Captain W. Paul Armour of Prince Rupert was given the task of salvaging the venerable schooner. When he arrived on the scene he found the local Indians had been there before him and stripped away everything that wasn't bolted down. By arrangement, after the vessel was refloated, the salvor's claim was set at $3,750 and the court ordered the vessel sold at not less than $5,000 to satisfy that claim. The rest of the proceeds went to pay wage claims by the crew.

After an overhaul at the Prince Rupert Shipyards, Gibson Brothers, Vancouver Island logging firm, purchased the vessel, took out her masts, installed two old Bolinder engines and

Remains of the **SCHOONER COURTNEY FORD.** One volunteer stayed with the wreck in 1902 while the others went for help in the ship's boat. The loner froze to death in the northern blasts that swept over Glen Island.

A half century of rugged winters did not erase the scroll work under the bowsprit of the **COURTNEY FORD**—carved at her building in 1883.

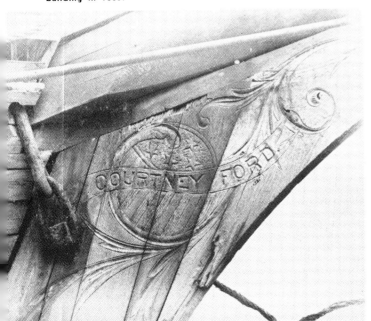

An invader on isolated Glen Island in recent years eyes the remains of the old **COURTNEY FORD.**

converted her into a fishpacker under the name *Joan G.* The Gibsons, who had eyed the craft even before the salvage job was completed, paid $5,000 for the vessel. The *Joan G.'s* first job in her new role was as a dynamite carrier. Inasmuch as a strike was hampering American flag Alaska-bound ships at Seattle, the power schooner was pressed into the haulage of dynamite, urgently needed in Juneau. At a dollar a case, she carried 5,000 cases. The next trip she carried 10,000 cases doubling the price that was paid for the vessel. She then pulled log rafts along the West Coast of Vancouver Island and packed herring and pilchard. Later, a second engine was installed to increase her power and the *Joan G.* ran successfully till World War II when she was often chartered by the Canadian Navy.

Captain Bill Dolmage purchased the vessel in 1954 from the Gibson Brothers and began to dismantle her, inasmuch as her useful days ap-

peared at an end—age 72—hull still in sound condition. The Canadian Fishing Company Ltd. then purchased her as a herring fish barge, and she was used to pack fish from the Queen Charlottes to the Gulf Islands for several more years. Her house was removed in the interim to serve as a living quarters for a boom man on Howe Sound.

By 1965, the barge *Joan G.* was floating in ignomy in a backwater moorage and finally was purchased by Robert Savage as a shingle boat barge at a cost of $400. Several months later she was abandoned at Cockatrice Bay, Broughton Island, nine miles from Alert Bay. The heavy snowfall of the previous winter and some leaks in her hull caused the vessel to partially sink. As far as is known this was the last port of call for the tired, 85-year-old craft. Even though her life cycle took her from riches to rags she deserves a name in the maritime hall of fame. Instead of rusting out, she just plain wore out.

At anchor in Elliott Bay, Seattle—**SCHOONER WM. NOTTINGHAM,** a dependable four-poster of the age of sail.

Loading lumber at Nanaimo, B. C. for Callao—the 2,022 ton **AUXILIARY SCHOONER DANNEMARIE** was built for the French government and launched at the Foundation yard in Tacoma, June 11, 1918.

The **FOUR-MASTED SCHOONER POLARIS** parted the towline of the steam schooner **WILMINGTON** on January 16, 1914 and was swept up on dreaded Duxbury Reef not far from San Francisco Bay. Though her master and crew of 12 were rescued the vessel was a total loss. She was last owned by the Charles Nelson Company. Built in 1902 her career was short.

C.S. Holmes

A four-masted schooner, the *C.S. Holmes,* her master Captain John Backland, and his son made interesting news on Puget Sound and in Alaskan waters for many years. Built as a lumber schooner by the famed Hall Brothers yard at Port Blakeley in 1893, the vessel was purchased by Backland in 1913 in San Francisco and brought north for Arctic trading under The Midnight Sun Trading Company.

Nobody knew the northland better than Captain Backland, a seasoned Arctic navigator. He had established trading posts as far north as Point Barrow and loaded his newly acquired *C.S. Holmes* with just about every item imaginable—guns, ammunition, lumber, groceries, hardware, but never any whiskey. He well knew the effect it had on the Eskimos. Government goods were often carried for Alaska mission stations and one of the largest was at Wainwright. He would return with valuable freight to Puget Sound annually, cargo that included furs, ivory and whalebone, which always found ready buyers.

For a quarter century, the *Holmes* and her skipper found themselves on the Marine page of the *Seattle Times* and the *Post Intelligencer,* whenever departure time came in March and on return in the fall. Sometimes in the off season, the *Holmes* was chartered out for a voyage with lumber to Australia or to South America. She was always back in time for the Alaska trading expedition.

A man of high principles, Captain Backland was unlike most of his breed, a teetotaler, and a highly respected member of the Presbyterian Church. He traditionally mustered his crew aft on the Sabbath. As they stood in the waste, he read aloud from the Bible on the poop deck. All hands respected his efforts and after the final Amen, returned to their stations. Whenever possible he would depart Elliott Bay under sail without the aid of a tug, casting off from Arlington Dock. His vessel had no auxiliary power, but did carry two 24 foot power boats for lifting freight off the beach or assisting the schooner if in a difficult position in the northland.

According to marine historian Doug Egan, the *C.S. Holmes* once sailed from the San Francisco Lightship to Puget Sound's Meadow Point, near Ballard in only five days which may be some kind of an unofficial record for commercial sailing vessels.

Backland's son, John Jr., after graduation from the University of Washington sailed as mate aboard his father's schooner, and after the senior Backland passed away the son took over as skipper of the *Holmes.* As a Navy commander during World War II he served as an ice pilot in Alaskan waters. Unfortunately, the schooner was drafted by the Army and was cut down to a barge. In 1952, she foundered off the British Columbia coast.

Dismasted in a gale off Cape Flattery in February 1911, the **FOUR-MASTED SCHOONER WILLIS A. HOLDEN,** only a single mast standing is towed into Puget Sound for repairs. The vessel was afloat until 1931.

136

*To everything there is a season, and a time to
every purpose under the heaven.*

---Ecclesiastes

Part Five

The Latter Day Sailing Vessels

THE AGE OF BUILDING wooden sailing vessels on the Pacific Coast waned after 1910. Except for the World War I period it would have remained dead, but the press for cargo-carrying vessels of any description caused a last ditch revival for the inexpensive windship.

Many of the sailing vessels of the 1916-1920 era were built of unseasoned timber and fitted with inferior equipment. The average age of these vessels was less than seven years at the termination of their usefulness. Many were built for foreign flag operation and shortly ended up idle in distant ports. Others saw but brief service under the American flag and were quickly relegated to backwater moorages. During their few years at sea there was a constant series of breakdowns. Some of these tall ships were totally lost within a few months of their completion.

Indeed, the end of World War I and the almost complete transition to steam sounded the death knell for this breed of ship, though a few did manage to eke out an existence in post-war years against stiff competition from standard freighters. Windship owners were forced to pick up the crumbs, so to speak, which at best afforded only a meager return. It was a most peculiar fleet of windjammers that wrote finis after seven decades of winged beauties having reigned supreme in West Coast maritime trades. Not representative, in most cases, of their predecessors, they were awkward four and five-masted schooners with a generous sprinkling of barkentines. Some were converted from Ferris type wooden steamer hulls. These windjammers were fashioned in several yards in British Columbia, Washington, Oregon and California.

The press for hasty completion of these vessels caused many to be fitted with malfunctioning auxiliaries and with unorthodox bald-headed rigs. There were a few, however, that were built with care and skill by some of the old shipwrights that refused to turn out inferior products. On more than one occasion the slowness and care in fashioning these windjammers by skilled ship's carpenters earned them a dressing down in the name of fast production.

The brief and hectic careers of some units of this fleet upheld the old adage, that haste makes waste. Such vessels did little that placed coin in the pockets of their owners after the war became history. The facts are that many of them were given away to alleviate moorage costs while scores of others were set ablaze to recover what scrap metal they contained.

Marine historian John Lyman recalls that the wooden sailing vessel building boom on the Pacific Coast began in a small way early in 1916. The lumber producers on the coast found all the foreign tramp steamers, and subsidized French sailing vessels, had withdrawn from the lumber trade to Australia and the Orient to more profitable work nearer the war zone.

Meanwhile the new Panama Canal provided a means of trapping the East Coast market. Late in 1915, the late Martin C. Erismann of Seattle drew up plans for a bald - headed, five - mast schooner, powered with oil engines, and prepared figures showing that with vessels of this type, lumber could be laid down in New York at a total cost of $6.81 per thousand feet.

Erismann's plans and calculations were widely circulated along the West Coast and although he was unable to find backers for his design, three similar vessels were under construction by the middle of the year, the *City of Portland* at St. Helens, Oregon; the *Columbia River* at Grays Harbor, and the *Else* at Tacoma. At the same time the *Flagstaff*, originally intended for a five-masted barkentine, was laid down at Oakland.

During this same period shipowners of neutral Scandinavia, particularly Norway, were beginning to earn immense profits. The Norwegian government introduced a tax of 46 per cent on net earnings and simultaneously prohibited granting Norwegian registry to any but new vessels. The obvious result was a frantic scramble by Norwegian shipowners to place orders in any shipyards not already engaged in war construction. Through the firm of A. O. Anderson & Co. in New York they tied up the output of all steel shipyards in the United States for the next two years, and then took notice of the expanding wooden shipbuilding industry of the Pacific Coast. They immedi-

FIVE-MASTED BARKENTINE FOREST PRIDE at Seattle, 1922.

BARKENTINE FOREST PRIDE tows out of Grays Harbor with lumber in the 1920's. She was one of the lofty end-time windjammers once logging 2,222 miles in nine days.

ately snapped up the *Else* and *Flagstaff* and placed orders for duplicate vessels. New yards were founded and old ones rehabilitated on the strength of the Norwegian orders placed through Anderson & Co., and in a few instances Norwegian working capital was secured. A shipbuilding bonanza thus was in the embryo stage about to blossom into full bloom.

Ships were in demand in all world trades, and the German submarine menace made the price of merchant ships treble. As activity increased, the shipowners of the United States began to realize that they had a full-fledged boom on their hands. Charters for two years could be obtained for a vessel six months before it was completed, and there was a rush by Gulf and Atlantic Coast shipowners to West Coast shipyards. Canada also felt the impact and four yards in British Columbia began turning out auxiliary schooners for Great Lakes interests and then for French owners.

In February, 1917, as the full involvement of the United States became imminent in the war, wooden sailing vessel construction for the Norwegian interests took a broadside. The United States Shipping Board was given jurisdiction over transfers of American vessels to foreign registry. As a result, the Norwegian owners

Reproduced from a painting of the **FIVE-MASTED BARKENTINE FOREST PRIDE,** John Plitz, master. She was built along with her sister ships **FOREST DREAM** and **FOREST FRIEND** at the Grays Harbor Motorship Corp., and completed in 1919. The Pride's last voyage under sail was made in 1927.

were not able to place their vessels under Norwegian registry, but had to set up American corporations to operate them. Not until 1919 or 1920 were they able, in most instances to obtain permission to make the transfers.

After the United States entered the war, in April 1917, the nation's allies were permitted to build ships in American shipyards, and the French government ordered several diesel auxiliary schooners and 40 steam auxiliary five-masted schooners in Oregon and Washington shipyards. These were all delivered by December, 1918.

On August 3, 1917, the Shipping Board requisitioned all steel ships under construction in the United States, and in granting priorities for private construction, thereafter restricted use of steam propelling machinery. This left wooden sailing vessels, with or without auxiliary oil engines, practically the only possibility for new construction for private ownership, as full powered motorships were considered not quite yet out of the experimental stage.

The Emergency Fleet Corporation also made use of the wooden shipbuilding facilities of the nation, contracting for some 700 wooden steamers of 3,500 to 4,000 deadweight tons. Most were standard types of which the Ferris and Hough designs were the most common; but several yards used their own plans.

It should be said that these vessels were not part of the long range program for reviving the American merchant marine that Congress

SIX-MASTED SCHOONER FORT LARAMIE loading lumber at Longview, Washington, in the 1920's.

Five-masted schooner **LEVI W. OSTRANDER** is seen here after being sold to German interests in 1924 and renamed the **TSENG TAI.** She was built at the Seaborn yard in Tacoma and had a stormy career on the high seas including being boarded by Chinese pirates.

Sailing on a sea of sand— **SCHOONER NORTH BEND** homebound from Australia ran aground on Peacock Spit at the entrance to the Columbia River January 5, 1928. Woodfield photo.

Unemployed windjammers, in the wake of depression lay idle in Seattle's Lake Union—no wind for their sails.

had in mind when it set up the Shipping Board in 1916, but were built for the war emergency, and at the Armistice in November, 1918, most of the contracts not yet completed were cancelled. Some of the hulls were converted to barges, but on the Pacific Coast several were rigged as six-masted schooners or five-masted barkentines and served as sailing vessels.

During 1919, the wartime sailing ship boom for the most part played itself out. The sailers completed during that year had been contracted for a year or even two years previously, and no new orders were forthcoming in 1920. The yards fast became idle and yard workers were retired in droves. Except for the conversion of a few wooden steamer hulls, a work relief project in British Columbia, the construction of the five-masted windjammer *Vigilant,* at Hoquiam, and the launching of the schooner *Undaunted* at Portland (in 1921), it was the end of an era. Few yards majoring in the construction of wooden ships were able to survive the ensuing depression, and those which had sprung up like mushrooms in 1917 and 1918 had disappeared even more rapidly by 1922.

Contrary to most of the hastily built World War I sailing vessels, one of the last turned out to be the best.

VIGILANT

The *Vigilant,* one of the last commercial windjammers built on the Pacific Coast, was a graceful five-masted schooner. She was constructed at the George F. Matthews (Matthews Shipbuilding Company) yard at Hoquiam, Washington, in 1920 for the E. K. Wood Lumber Company.

Not only did the 240 foot *Vigilant* become famous, but the yard where she was created was already known world-wide for many fine sailing ships built in earlier years. George F. Matthews in 1906 took over the Hoquiam shipyard of Hitchings & Joyce which had been established originally by his father, Peter Mat-

Astoria TUG ARROW NO. 3 towing **SCHOONER NORTH BEND** off Astoria in the 1920's. Photo courtesy John E. Davis.

With two million board feet of lumber packed below and on deck the **FIVE-MASTED AUXILIARY BALD-HEADED SCHOONER CITY OF PORTLAND** put to sea for McCormick lumber interests—destination Australia—1916.

thews. It had been operated for the previous eight years by George H. Hitchings and John Joyce.

On the *Vigilant's* initial voyage as a five-top-master she departed Grays Harbor for Sydney in April 1920, returning via Newcastle and Honolulu to Puget Sound. Her second voyage was from Port Angeles to Adelaide with lumber, returning with 2,540 tons of coal for San Francisco. Her third voyage was from Bellingham to Callao, and in June 1922 on her return, the *Vigilant* went into the coasting trade.

On May 29, 1923, leaking badly, she was towed into San Pedro by the steam schooner *Cascade,* 35 days out of Port Angeles. She had struck a submerged object 40 miles off Ventura.

Repaired, the schooner sailed for Bellingham and loaded out for Callao, returning to Puget Sound in June 1924, only to be laid up for lack of business. In 1926, the City Mill Company of Honolulu acquired an interest in the *Vigilant* and put her back into service carrying lumber from Puget Sound to Hawaii. In this trade she established an enviable record.

The first assigned master of the *Vigilant* was none other than the earlier mentioned Captain Matt Peasley, portrayed in the "Cappy Ricks" series of novels by Peter B. Kyne. He was followed by an equally prominent wind-jammer skipper, Captain Charles Mellberg.

The schooner's logbook in 1932 shows the vessel had just arrived from Hawaii in company with the four-masted schooner *Commodore,* also in the islands trade. These two vessels sometimes raced between the two destinations and the press always played up the contest in colorful terms. The larger *Vigilant* with more sail spread was considered the faster though the *Commodore* was always competitive and a fine latter day sailer. (See Appendix D)

The *Vigilant* on one voyage in 1932 made a quick return run of 13 days to Cape Flattery, from Honolulu. There a tug took her in tow to Bellingham where she prepared to take on another cargo of lumber.

In 1936 she was given a new set of masts: 110 foot lowers with 60 foot topmasts. In 1940, she brought a good price when purchased by the Canadian Transport Company. After being renamed *City of Alberni* and hoisting the Canadian flag, the vessel took on another adventurous skipper, Captain John D. Vosper. He was a veteran seafarer, having served on numerous sailing ships, freighters and passenger liners. Vosper fell in love, hook, line and sinker, with the *City of Alberni.* She was refurbished and loaded out with 1,650,000 feet of British Columbia lumber for Sydney, Australia, in the early summer of 1940. The voyage required 71 days from Cape Flattery to Sydney Heads, but the ship was delayed another week off the latter point by adverse weather. Dark clouds gathered to the southward and just at nightfall they encountered a driving, southerly gale. Before the schooner could be reefed down and hove to, the wind tore the sails and damaged the rigging. It took them another eight days, with contrary winds and calms, before the vessel again made the Heads and got a tow to her anchorage. Vosper said he never knew the southerly current off New South Wales to set so strong.

After unloading at Snail's Bay, the *Alberni* was lined up for a cargo of sugar from Latoka, Fiji, to Vancouver. On arrival at the outer entrance to the Fijian port, another problem was encountered. The course through the narrow gap between the reefs was about northeast. With the prevailing trades about east southeast, one could narrowly make it when close-

142

hauled with little or nothing to spare. No tug was available and all aids to navigation were inoperative due to war-time restrictions. It was a very ticklish job getting the big windjammer inside the harbor with nothing to rely on but wind, but Vosper was a clever navigator. After sweating out the ordeal he got the vessel inside the quiet bay only to find the natives removing the covers from the navigation markers.

Aided to the sugar dock by a native launch, the *Alberni* took on 1,500 tons of bagged sugar and sailed for Vancouver, arriving 51 days later.

Captain Vosper commanded the *City of Alberni* for three and a half years, but at the end of that period was forced to terminate a passage to Durban, South Africa. The vessel took a severe punishment in a storm at latitude 41 degrees S and had to put into Valparaiso, leaking badly. After a survey, it was decided to permanently curtail the voyage, there being no facilities for properly repairing the vessel in Chile.

Captain Vosper and the crew were paid off, and the schooner was sold to Chilean owners and renamed *Condor*. A suit was then brought against the former owners over the uncompleted voyage of the *City of Alberni*. Justice Sidney Smith, who once shipped before the mast, heard the case with great personal interest. The suit was against the Canadian Transport Company, Vancouver, B. C., owners of the vessel, by Hunt Leuchars Hepburn Ltd. of Durban, involving $55,000 on the cargo of lumber. The judge decided that the Durban firm was entitled to recover compensation from the ship's owners but commensurate to the price obtained for the cargo when the *City of Alberni* was abandoned at Valparaiso.

As late as January 1946, the *Condor* sailed from Valparaiso for Piraeus, Greece, with rice. En route, the schooner was damaged by rough seas and much of her cargo was water-soaked. This necessitated putting into Montevideo. What could be salvaged of the cargo was sold at that port. The *Condor* was repaired and fitted with a new set of sails before departing to load at Bahia Blanca. During this passage the schooner caught fire and was towed back to port, a total constructive loss.

Wooden sailing vessels under construction at the Puget Sound Bridge and Dredging Co., Seattle in 1917. The one nearing completion is the four-masted auxiliary **SCHOONER PORTLAND**. She later burned at sea. Other ships building are the **BARLEUX** and **REMITTENT**.

NORTH BEND

Kruse & Banks of North Bend, Oregon, turned out three fine sailing vessels, among the latter day fore 'n' afters. Between 1919 and 1921 they produced the six-masted schooner *Fort Laramie,* the five-masted schooner *K. V. Kruse* and the four-masted schooner *North Bend.* The *Laramie* was later burned for scrap on Puget Sound and the *Kruse,* as a barge, was lost in January of 1941 in Hecate Straits, British Columbia, after breaking away from the tug *La Pointe.* The *North Bend,* smallest of the three, outlived the others and had by far the most colorful career.

Most people have a strong desire to cling to life. Like humans, ships sometimes possess the same qualities.

The four-masted schooner *North Bend* stood off the mouth of the Columbia River in ballast, inbound from Australia where she had delivered a full load of lumber. Her charter had expired and she had come home to find more cargo, in those, the last, difficult years for the commercial windship.

The date was January 5, 1928. She hovered off the river mouth awaiting the pilot ship. Captain Theodore Hanson, a seasoned windjammer skipper who had crossed the bar many times, grew impatient when the boat failed to make an appearance. He was well aware of the

Six-masted **SCHOONER HELEN B. STERLING** was originally intended to be a steamer but was completed at the Peninsula Shipbuilding yard at Portland as a schooner, originally named Oregon Fir, for Grant-Smith-Porter & Co. of the Rose City. Sailing the Pacific until 1932 she was broken up at Sydney, NSW.

temperamental qualities of the bar in this battleground of nature where the great river flexed its muscles against the inrushing Pacific. He had experienced its vagaries on many occasions. He knew its tides, currents, and shifting ridges of sand and most particularly the dangers faced by ships dependent only on sail in gaining entrance.

But none could deny the favorable wind behind his tall ship, and he decided to risk it and sail her across the bar.

His strident commands echoed down the wooden decks and the sea-weary crew, anxious to set foot on terra firma, worked like bees about a honeycomb as they ministered to the maze of ropes and lines which controlled the canvas on the schooner's four lofty masts. The vessel sprang to life. Like the graceful thing she was, she plunged into the swells as the wind filled her sails. Soon her taff rail log recorded a 12-knot clip.

She was skirting dreaded Peacock Spit when, with the same unpredictable suddenness that had doomed scores of ships before her, the wind suddenly died and the schooner wallowed like a dead thing. The currents gripped her hull and moved her toward the spit. Sails hung limp, crying for more wind. But there was no wind. The schooner drifted closer and closer to the graveyard of ships.

Captain Hanson frantically ordered distress signals sent up. Both anchors were dropped. The currents, however, prevailed and the ship was in the throes of a dilemna. Her hooks refused to hold. Late afternoon had arrived and

In 1936, the lofty World War I era **WINDJAMMER MONITOR** was converted to a fish reduction ship for the Interstate Fish Reduction Corp., at Seattle. Turned out by the Benicia Shipbuilding Co. in 1919, she last used her sails in 1927. Walter Miller photo.

the hours ticked on toward the dreaded winter darkness. The ship, was now hovering over the dreaded shoal waters lying, directly off the spit. Still no assistance was in sight.

Then, with heart-breaking suddenness, a heavy fog dropped its mantle over the schooner. The crew froze in their tracks when the vibrant roar of surf shattered their ear drums. It was but a matter of time till the vessel struck. With a violent thump, a shoal of sand came up under the *North Bend's* keel and she reeled and rocked like a drunken woman. Again and again she bumped the spit as the great swells lifted her stern, scudded her length, and dropped her again to the bar floor.

All night long the schooner withstood all that the bar swells could dish out. Her stout

End of the line—**FIVE-MASTED SCHOONER BIANCA** aground west of Clallam Bay, Washington. The bulky, latter day sailer was bound for Puget Sound from Alaska with a full load of canned salmon. She was a total loss.

During the World War I era—deck scene aboard a four-masted schooner at a Seattle pier. Asahel Curtis photo.

timbers were being put to the supreme test. Captain Hanson and his men had exhausted their every effort to get the ship off and were disposed to await the break of day.

Morning came at last, and rescue craft removed the crew without mishap. Plans were then formulated to refloat the wounded but unbowed windjammer from the spit. The Coast Guard cutter *Snohomish* and the rugged little tug *Arrow No. 3,* out of Astoria, managed to get a line on her after several futile tries. As hundreds of spectators looked on from Cape Disappointment, the tug put out her every ounce of horsepower, and finally with the in-

coming tide managed to get the schooner free. Under the strain, however, the towing cable parted and the schooner was dashed on the spit even higher than before. Now, all efforts at salvage had to be abandoned, and it appeared that the *North Bend,* almost fully exposed at slack tide, would leave her carcass to whiten and decay in this graveyard of shifting sand.

The lighthouse keepers could look down on the ship from Cape Disappointment Lighthouse high atop the bold bluff—watching her death agonies at the mercy of wind, tide and surf.

One day, the guardians of the light, who had kept a weather eye on the wreck, noted that

TUG SEA MONARCH, powerful towing craft, often towed coastal windjammers in and out of major coast ports. She is seen here on her trial runs.

Skipper's cabin on the **SCHOONER WAWONA**—Captain Matt Peasley once slept here.

At berth on the Seattle waterfront, ready for maiden voyage, the Norwegian flag **FOUR-MASTED SCHOONER RISOR** was built at the Puget Sound Bridge & Dredging Company yard in Seattle in 1917.

On Lake Union in Seattle during the depression years, groups of unemployed sailing vessels were moored side by side. From left, **SCHOONER K. V. KRUSE, BARKENTINE CONQUEROR, SCHOONERS MARGARET F. STERLING, FOREST PRIDE** and **C. A. THAYER.**

her position had somewhat changed. No longer was she broadside to the full force of the surf. Her wooden prow was pointing inland. The lashing surf, hurrying her destruction, was now at her stern and working for and not against her. As the rising tides surged in, they swirled about her hull, scooping sand away and creating a small salten sea all about the vessel. As the days passed, the 200 foot windjammer actually began to move inland in a channel of water she herself had helped create. Inch by inch, foot by foot, the intrepid schooner began feeling her way through what had been part of a great sandspit.

The *North Bend's* decks were a shambles of rigging, and wind-blown sand had filtered every nook and cranny. But the important thing was that the vessel had an unexplained zeal for life. She was heading in an easterly direction away from the incessant, pounding breakers that had attempted to devour her. All hands had left her to die, but die she would not. Captain Hanson and the underwriters had written the schooner off the books as a total loss.

With each breaking dawn, the vessel moved forward in her little canal, as if some ghostly hand was guiding her. Salvagers had removed rigging and loose gear, figuring that her days

This vessel completed at Rolph, California, at the end of World War I, was originally intended to have been a five-masted barkentine. With the need for such ships having diminished she was fitted out as the **STEAM SCHOONER THOMAS ROLPH.** Later she was resold and renamed **VIKING.**

SCHOONER VIGILANT being towed out to the Pacific by the TUG ACTIVE, bound for Honolulu.

entry into the quiet waters of Bakers Bay, well away from the breakers at the opposite side of the spit. She completed her voyage through what had once been an impenetrable barrier until she was safe inside the mouth of the Columbia River entrance. There on February 11, 1929, 13 months after being rudely tossed up on the sands, the imprisoned vessel, with limited help of the human variety, made good her escape. Tugs awaited her and she was ushered off to the repair yard. Newspapers and periodicals far and wide told of her success. She had done something that all the genius of human salvagers had been unable to do. So impressed was Robert Ripley that he featured the episode in his *"Believe It or Not."*

The *North Bend* was taken to Youngs Bay near Astoria, and underwent hull repairs. The age of sail, however, had virtually ended. Best use for the vessel was as a barge. Her hatches were thus enlarged and she was reduced to the lowly role of a lumber barge. Her owners had a fond respect for her, however, as did others who knew of her lasting qualities.

The scar she had formed in the sandspit has long since healed itself, covering up the traces of that uncanny voyage.

In October, 1940, the *North Bend* changed owners. With a full consignment of lumber she cleared from Reedsport, Oregon, for San Francisco, under tow. Off Coos Bay, in the throes of an October storm, she took such a terrible beating that lumber slopped from her deck and she had to be cut loose from the tug.

Again the tired old ship arose to the occasion. With great graybacks hissing and curling all about her and every fitting turning in its socket, the vessel gallantly rode out the storm. Then suddenly she struck Guano Rock. A crew of four were still aboard.

The schooner was hung up on the obstruction like a coat hanger—a struggling thing at the termination of an endurance test. Her crew was removed with some difficulty and the vessel was left to die.

But so the story goes, they later got her to the beach north of Cape Arago. There she was so badly beaten as to be considered no longer of commercial value. It is alleged that even then she refused to give up the ghost. In turn she had to be towed out to deep water where her seacocks were opened up allowing her to sink in deep water. Another account says her remains were burned on the beach.

had ended. This so weakened the tall masts that they began to tumble. Still undaunted, the schooner moved ever forward, motivated by a desire to live again—to spread her canvas and sail to open water. She had traveled almost a half mile in her self-created inlet which was making a breach squarely through the dreaded spit.

Scores of local citizenry, who had followed the strange antics of the derelict for many weeks, now gathered to watch her triumphant

MALAHAT

One of the typical black sheep of the latter day sailing vessels was the *Malahat,* a rather ungainly five-masted schooner which later ended up as a rum toter. In fact she was the queen of the Canadian rum runners.

Built at Victoria, B. C., by Cameron Genoa Mills Shipbuilders Ltd., in 1917 for Canadian Steamships Company of Montreal, she was one of several 245-foot-long Mable Brown class sailing vessels.

The ship emergency during the war period pushed her to a loading berth as soon as she was delivered, even before her twin auxiliary Bolinder diesel engines had been installed. She was forced to make her initial voyage without the engines and performed reasonably well under sail. But the *Malahat* is remembered mostly for her rum role.

Back in the days when Archie McGillis was owner and skipper of the *Malahat,* she was not only the pride of the liquor fleet but a genuine thorn in the side of the United States Coast Guard.

Acting as a mother ship, she made about two trips per year stacked to the gunwhales with whiskey. In the dark of night, mosquito boats came out to the fringe of the three-mile limit to meet her and load up. The lucrative role was reduced to a single voyage per year when bootleggers in the United States grew more experienced at faking honest bottles and brands which the *Malahat* handled.

Printers in California and other coast states were counterfeiting the labels of guaranteed liquor, and glaziers were producing duplicate bottles for the brands. But even when the trade was slow, the *Malahat* was disposing of 120,000 cases annually.

Though the movements of the *Malahat* were

Such a photo speaks for itself— **FIVE-MASTED SCHOONER VIGILANT,** bound for Honolulu from Bellingham with lumber in the 1930's.

Funeral pyre—discarded **SCHOONER THISTLE**—burned for her scrap by Neider & Marcus at Richmond Beach, north of Seattle July 30, 1936. Her last voyage under sail was for Charles Nelson Company in 1928.

On May 19, 1919, a devastating $400,000 fire swept Grays Harbor Motorship yard at Aberdeen, where latter day windjammers were under construction.

—Jones photo

Ready to have the torch touched to her—stern section of the **CONQUEROR**, north of Picnic Point.

Built by Rolph yard at Humboldt Bay in 1918, the **BARKENTINE CONQUEROR** is seen here being burned for scrap on the Arvid Franzen property north of Picnic Point on Puget Sound in 1947.

SCHOONER JANET CARRUTHERS hard aground January 22, 1919.

Canadian flag SCHOONER JANET CARRUTHERS on the beach north of Grays Harbor in 1919. She ran aground when her skipper confused Grays Harbor Light with the one at North Head. Six crewmen were lost escaping in a boat. Salvage efforts were almost successful, but were halted when pumping operations began polluting the clam beaches.

not publicized, the underworld had a secret network of information that eluded the ever watchful eye of the law.

Liquor shipments were taken out of wooden cases and sewed in burlap sacking, a dozen bottles to the parcel. It was more easily handled this way in small slingloads and also economized on space. Furthermore it was much more easily given the deep six should the rum runners fall under the probing searchlights of government vessels.

The *Malahat* always managed to stay just outside the three-mile limit as she cruised down the Pacific Coast to make appointed rendezvous with the mosquito craft sneaking out from remote sectors along the coast under the cloak of night. All sorts of dodges and decoy tricks were resorted to by the skipper and crew of the *Malahat* to avoid a misdemeanor with the law. On more than one occasion many bags of sand were dropped in shallow water and

marked to look like a rum cache on the ocean floor. By the time the Coast Guard had dragged for the non-existent liquor the *Malahat* had sailed quietly away to an undetected position. She plodded along her way, never faltering and never blundering—due in much part to the cunning of her skipper, a small, dark personality who did far more thinking than talking.

As a bootleg ship, according to Canadian authorities, the *Malahat* was breaking no laws but the effect of the liquor on the U. S. market caused crime to flourish. Uncle Sam spent millions of dollars to prevent bootlegging, but as fast as the Customs officials confiscated the liquor, the faster it came in via the rum runners.

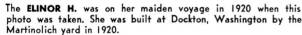

The ELINOR H. was on her maiden voyage in 1920 when this photo was taken. She was built at Dockton, Washington by the Martinolich yard in 1920.

The French flag **AUXILIARY SCHOONER SUZANNE**, berthed at the Skandia Oil Engine Works at Oakland Calif. She was built at Aberdeen, Washington in 1918 and was sold two years later to British interests.　　—*R. E. McKay collection*

Where many of the rum ships made a slip and got caught, the *Malahat* was always a proper lady, manned by seasoned seafarers who knew how to handle both sail and power in amazing fashion. This was much to the chagrin of the patrol vessels which tried repeatedly to catch the ship on a navigation error in forbidden waters. It never happened.

When laws where changed and prohibition was abolished, the *Malahat* was forced to turn honest to eke out an existence. Just when it appeared that her days were numbered, Gibson Brothers, a British Columbia logging firm, purchased her to carry logs from the Queen Charlotte Islands, and the West Coast of Vancouver Island.

On March 25, 1944, the *Malahat* was reported foundering in a North Pacific gale. Her cargo of logs swept from her decks was spread over miles of ocean surface. The logs below deck kept her afloat until tugs managed to beach her at a port of no return.

JANET CARRUTHERS

A short but active life was accorded the schooner *Janet Carruthers*. This 1,466 ton, five-masted, bald-headed schooner was 240 feet in length and was launched by the Wallace Shipyards Ltd., of North Vancouver, B. C., in 1917.

Less than two years later, she came to grief four miles north of Grays Harbor bar, ending a rather frustrating existence.

On her maiden voyage from Vancouver, B. C., with lumber for Adelaide, the vessel got off to a bad start. In addition to her spread of canvas she had been powered with auxiliary Bolinder oil engines, driving twin screws. However, she put into Honolulu with cracked cylinders and a broken shaft. The skipper and crew were so thoroughly disgusted with the performance of the engines that the owners granted permission for the screws to be disconnected, and the vessel for as long as she operated, was a full-fledged windjammer.

By the time she had reached Apia, adverse

152

weather and heavy seas left her in a badly disabled condition. Temporary repairs were made and the vessel put to sea once again. By the time the *Carruthers* neared the Australian coast her condition had so deteriorated that she was almost a wreck. Her deck was a shambles and her rigging twisted and torn. The tug that towed her into Adelaide was awarded $10,000 salvage money on the premise of preventing the schooner's foundering.

After a prolonged voyage back across the Pacific, the *Carruthers* departed Puget Sound on January 20, 1919, for Astoria, to load out for Shanghai. After towing out to Cape Flattery the vessel dropped her line and hoisted sail. Less than two days later, just at nightfall, the skipper, who had been fighting changing winds, reasoned that he was off the entrance to the Columbia River. Mistaking Grays Harbor Light for North Head, the windjammer slammed into the beach four miles north of the Grays Harbor bar. Coming to a jarring halt amid the breakers, the crew was filled with fear. The assumption that the schooner might immediately break up prompted the lowering of a boat. Hardly had it hit the water than a giant breaker caught it broadside and flipped it over. The men were rudely cast into the vortex. Struggling frantically, lungs filling with sand and water, huge combers sucked them down before lifelines could reach them. All six perished.

The suddenness of it all terrified the others and no more attempts were made to leave the schooner.

At daybreak the lifesaving crew was on the scene. The tide had ebbed. All were safely evacuated. The *Carruthers,* however, had assumed a definite port list and began digging her own grave as breakers slammed into her incessantly.

By March, the underwriters paid the insurance but in turn sold the wreck for $11,000. The new owners immediately began pumping oil from her tanks in a desperate effort to refloat her. After but a few days work, the Washington State Fisheries Commission got wind of it and moved in with a vengeance. The beach was a prime clam area and the oil was polluting the beds.

The salvagers immediately had a libel slapped on them, and their endeavors came screeching to a halt. They tried in vain to get around the order, but within a few weeks the sea's assault began breaking the schooner apart. She became a total loss and was eventually swallowed by the hungry sands.

The *Janet Carruthers* had seen less than two years of service, all of it hectic. Her owners, the Canadian West Coast Navigation Company, originally paid $150,000 for the vessel but had little to show for their investment. The company owned six similar windjammers, none of which had lengthy careers.

An artist's drawing of the little port of Seattle which was just beginning to spread its wings, dependent almost wholly on sailing vessels for its trade and prosperity in the 1880's.
Joe Williamson

Typical of the latter day wooden shipbuilding yards on the west coast was the McEachern Ship Company of Astoria, Oregon. Though it wasn't by any means the largest producer, it played a definite role in the production of wooden-hulled vessels shortly after World War I broke out in Europe. A worldwide shortage of shipping due to early war losses, plus the reality of greatly increased sea transportation called in many of the old shipwrights that had labored years earlier in the construction of wooden-hulled windjammers. Existing facilities for steel shipbuilding were as yet inadequate, so the wooden fleet had its last big hurrah. Yards popped up all the way from California on into British Columbia, and many of the old yards in abandonment were brought back to life.

The existing Wilson Shipbuilding Company at Astoria expanded, and two new yards, G.F. Rogers Shipbuilding Company and the McEachern Ship Company were founded. J.A. McEachern of Seattle secured a contract to build eight four-masted auxiliary schooners for A.O. Anderson and Company, Norwegian ship-brokers, who soon after purchased controlling interest in the very shipyard which McEachern had established at Astoria. The yard, built at the foot of Seventh Street on Youngs Bay on April 1, 1916, employed 300 workers and boasted five slipways. Things were booming in Oregon's premier seaport city.

Purchasing stock in the firm were G.M. Standifer and James Clarkson, well known in the shipbuilding industry. They succeeded in getting their share of the cooperative name, McEachern-Standifer-Clarkson Company. They, however wooed away by other investments, sold their interest and the firm took back its original title.

There was a huge turnout of Astorians and others who came to witness the launching of the initial vessel at the local yard. The event took place on October 28, 1916, and the feature attraction was the trim, four-masted, bald-headed schooner *City of Astoria*. For reasons unknown, the registers eventually carried her name only as *Astoria*. She was a fine wooden windjammer in every way, except to the chagrin of the traditional old shellbacks however, she was fitted with two auxiliary 240 horsepower Scandia semi deisel engines and twin screws. Measuring 229 feet in length with a gross tonnage of 1,611, she had a beam of 44 feet and a depth just short of 19 feet. Capable of carrying a good payload, the vessel could accomodate 1.75 million board feet of lumber.

The yard received national kudos in the shipbuilding industry for their fine product, far superior to many of the wooden vessels of the

BARKENTINE ANNIE M. ROLPH, a four-masted vessel built in 1918 by the Rolph Shipbuilding Company in Rolph, California. The 1393 ton vessel became a fish barge in her latter years.

World War I era. Lloyds of London agreed by giving the vessel the top insurance rating.

So proud were Astorians of the new schooner, that the two local newssheets filled their front pages with the news; the Mayor proclaimed a holiday with a parade, speeches, street dances and banquets, the whole bit. More than 5,000 attended the events and the populace reasoned the city had launched into a venture that was certain to create more industry and more jobs.

A little unexpected excitement occurred after Gertrude McEachern, the shipbuilder's daughter, launched the *City of Astoria*, with the traditional bubbly. The line attached to a drag anchor parted as the schooner hit the water and, as if chafing at the bitt to get free, she drifted toward the Young River bridge crowded with spectators and vehicles. Fearing the results, there was a mad scramble as the crowd fled before the vessel struck. Bang! Down went a telephone pole, a portion of the bridge railing and timbers were splintered. The stout vessel suffered nothing but a few scratches around her stern, proving the strength of her hull.

154

Fortunately nobody was injured and the entire event just seemed to add more color to the festivities.

The superstitious declared that the misfortune was a bad omen that would launch the schooner on a jinx career, but such was not the case. Despite the decline in shipping following the war, and the competition from larger cargo steamers, the *Astoria* was still afloat in 1930, posting a worthy account of herself in the active years.

Following in the wake of the *City of Astoria*, the McEachern yard launched the schooners, *Margaret, Astri I, Madrugada, May, Pauline, Carmen,* and *Evelyn.*

When Uncle Sam declared war on Germany, one of the largest shipbuilding programs in history got underway in America. The United States Shipping Board Emergency Fleet Corporation was formed to supervise the monumental task. In addition to steel freighters, the wooden shipbuilding program was essential as well. At that time, McEachern retired from management of the shipyard and Max H. Houser replaced him. He secured, with little effort, contracts from the Emergency Fleet Corporation; unfortunately they were not for auxiliary windjammers, but for 20 wooden hulled steamers of the Hough and Ferris designs. At the termination of hostilities November 11, 1918, the curtain began dropping on the McEachern yard as well as on numerous other yards across the nation. With dwindling demand for tonnage world-wide, it appeared that the wooden shipbuilding industry was doomed, as well it was. The yard turned out four Hough steamers in 1918, and six in 1919 before contracts were cancelled. Most had brief life spans, the last of the ten launched as a barge, the final vessel produced by the McEachern yard. The wild celebration, the cheers, the fanfare of a few years earlier faded like an early morning fog under a brilliant sun.

There was a definite sadness about the oldtime sailing ship skippers who, though fully qualified, refused to go from sail into steam after the windjammers were crowded off the sealanes. There were, however, several whose pride and love of commercial sail was so deeply imbedded within that nothing except death would change their minds. Take for instance, the late Captain P.A. McDonald, who was master of some of the largest and finest of the square-riggers under the American flag. Hale and hearty into his 90's, his whole life was the ships of sail, but rather than go into steam he had to settle for many of his latter years as a watchman at a Seattle shipyard.

Granted, the romance and color of the days of commercial sail was indeed a glorious era, but time marches on, and for those who do not march with it they sometimes learn the hard way that time passes them by.

One fine, old sailing ship master was Captain James Hersey, who had a love affair with the barkentine *Conqueror*, one of the few high quality sailing vessels turned out during the World War I era. Owned by Hind, Rolph and Company, and built by the Rolph Shipbuilding Company on Humboldt Bay, the *Conqueror* was placed in service in 1918 and Captain Hersey was given command. Throughout her existence, Hersey was the only master she ever had. The two went together like salt and pepper and sometimes his wife wondered if he was married to the ship rather than to her.

The barkentine became well known in the Pacific Northwest, hauling many cargoes of lumber to South Africa and Latin America, always giving a good account of herself under sail. Unlike most of the sailing vessels built in the war period, she was a good sailer and was not accident prone. She is reported to have made an excellent passage from Victoria, B.C. to Durban, South Africa during which she averaged 231 miles a day for 20 days. She also

FOUR-MASTED SCHOONER ALICE COOKE, built by the Hall's at Port Blakely in 1891 carried a crew of 11 plus a million board feet of lumber. She rendered yoeman service throughout the Pacific, for several years in command of Captain Wm. R. Burmeister. She burned to the waterline at Prince William Sound, Alaska, November 17, 1931.

Launching the "City of Astoria" Oct 28 - 1916
McEachern - Stanaged Clarkson Ship Co.
Astoria, Oregon
Copyright 1916 by Frank Woodfield

McEACHERN SHIP COMPANY-ASTORIA, OREGON
Woodfield-Photo

Activity at the McEachern Ship Company, Astoria, Oregon, circa
1916. Upper photo, launching of the four-masted auxiliary
SCHOONER CITY OF ASTORIA, October 28, 1916, an event that
prompted an Astoria holiday and celebration. She was the initial
deepsea ship launched at the yard. Center and lower photos
show the overall view of the McEachern yard with four schooners
on the building shipways and others fitting out at dockside. Frank
Woodfield photos, courtesy Columbia River Maritime Museum.

boasted of a voyage from Puget Sound to East Africa in only 112 days. Captain Hersey was rightfully proud of the vessel, and his skills as a master mariner were readily appreciated by the vessel's owners.

Returning from a long voyage in 1928, the *Conqueror*, eking out an existence against steam competition, was laid up at Eagle Harbor on Puget Sound's Bainbridge Island. Hersey and his wife lived aboard as caretakers waiting orders to put out to sea again. With each passing month the shipmaster hoped and prayed for a call from the owners but those orders never came. Seeing the handwriting on the wall, the powers to be placed the vessel on the block in 1930. Still Hersey hung on, hoping for a miracle. He busied himself by keeping the vessel in excellent condition, painting, scraping and patching old sails. And to be sure, Mrs. Hersey kept the after cabin neat as a pin, the living quarters warm and comfortable. They even had a piano aboard.

The sheer lines of the barkentine caught the attention of many passersby, for under a coat of white she was like a greyhound at the starting post anxious to up anchor, lower her canvas and heel to the wind.

Several potential buyers surfaced, but either they lacked the money or the incentive to take the responsibility for a four-masted barkentine. In desperation, Captain Hersey, made some kind of a deal with the owners in 1931, whereby he would buy the *Conqueror*. For three more years the couple hung on awaiting a charter or even a partial cargo. But the ship was aging as

was her master and signs of deterioration appeared. An idle sailing vessel is costly to maintain and when the final curtain came down, Captain Hersey, with tears in his eyes for a vessel he'd grown to love like his own flesh and blood, had to admit that it was all over. The great depression made it obvious that a vessel like the *Conqueror* was no longer worth more than its scrap value. He reluctantly sold her to the Romano Salvage Company of Seattle, which for awhile saw some additional use for the vessel in a diving venture. When that plan fell through she was resold to the Pacific Iron and Metal Company, which stripped her to the bare bones, and towed the hull to Picnic Point, north of Edmonds. There the torch was set and the graceful windjammer went up in flames, leaping fingers of orange enveloping the masts and racing over the wooden decks.

A bit of pride was salvaged for Captain Hersey. He was given an advisory role as master of the former Arctic fur trading schooner *Nanuk* for filming purposes with Metro-Goldwyn-Mayer. It was a far cry from sailing around the Horn to South Africa but it put a little food on the table. A three-masted auxiliary schooner, the *Nanuk* was built as the *Ottilie Fjord* by Bendixsen at Fairhaven in 1892. After her trading days with Olaf Swenson were over, she was used for the filming of the documentary motion picture, *The Eskimo*. She then went Hollywood, rebuilt as the *Hispaniola* for the film *Treasure Island* and still later became the HMS *Pandora* for the initial American filming of *Mutiny on the Bounty*.

Deck scene aboard the **SCHOONER R.C. SLADE** about 1901. In the upper left is Captain Peder O. Sonerud, the vessel's master sporting a derby. Next to him is his wife Carrie and seven year old Martha Sonerud. The only other identifiable crew member is Martin Colbert, (in Apron) the ship's cook. Courtesy, Wilbur E. Hespe.

Based on research
of the late John Lyman

COMMERCIAL SAILING VESSELS OVER 100 TONS CONSTRUCTED ON THE PACIFIC COAST — 1850-1908

NAME	RIG	TONS	BUILDER	PLACE	DATE	ULTIMATE FATE
A. B. Johnson	4 m schr.	529	John Lindstrom	Aberdeen	1900	Sunk by raider Seeadler June 14, 1917 in South Pacific
A. F. Coates	4 m schr.	617	Hitchings & Joyce	Hoquiam	1901	Burned Puerto Rico July 31, 1926
A. J. West	4 m schr.	543	McWhinney & Cousins	Aberdeen	1898	Sold Greek 1920-1933, renamed
A. M. Baxter	4 m schr.	516	H. Bendixsen	Fairhaven	1898	Wrecked Suva August 8, 1918
Abbie	2 m schr.	146	H. Bendixsen	Eureka	1876	Last listed 1912
Active	2 m schr.	147	G. Buchart	Gardiner, O.	1872	Last listed 1881
Addenda	4 m bktn.	692	A. M. Simpson	North Bend	1895	Lost Palliser Bay October 14, 1904
Addie C. Hesseltine	2 m schr.	135	W. C. Wood	San Francisco	1885	Sold foreign 1888
Adelaide	2 m schr.	130	Boole & Beaton	San Francisco	1883	Last listed 1889
Admiral	4 m schr.	683	A. M. Simpson	North Bend	1899	Wrecked Columbia River Bar January 13, 1912
Advance	brig.	275	W. C. Robinson	North Bend	1862	Wrecked before 1875
Advance	3 m schr.	281	S. Danielson	Parkersburg, O.	1902	Sold Honduran 1914-1918
Advent	3 m schr.	431	A. M. Simpson	North Bend	1901	Wrecked Coos Bay Bar February 16, 1913
Aida	4 m schr.	533	Hall Bros.	Port Ludlow	1890	Vanished out of Shanghai December 1, 1896
Alaska	2 m schr.	138	Calhoun Bros.	Port Townsend	1867	Lost Bering Sea 1885
Albert	bark	682	Hall Bros.	Port Blakely	1890	Wrecked North Pt. Reyes April 2, 1919
Alberni	2 m schr,	100	————	Port Alberni, B.C.	1861	————
Albert Meyer	3 m schr.	459	H. Bendixsen	Fairhaven	1896	Wrecked Florida Keys December 31, 1927
Albion	schr.	202	J. C. Cousins	San Francisco	1861	Wrecked Mendocino Coast 1893
Alcalde	3 m schr.	321	Hall Bros.	Port Blakely	1882	Wrecked Grays Harbor February 14, 1904
Alert	4 m schr.	623	Hitchings & Joyce	Hoquiam	1902	Wrecked Niuafou, Tonga Is. June 10, 1923
Alex T. Brown	4 m schr.	788	Thomas C. Reed	Ballard	1903	Wrecked near Fremantle May 29, 1917
Alice	2 m schr.	232	C. Saunders	Beans Pt., Bainbridge Is., Wn.	1874	Abandoned San Pedro 1930
Alice	2 m schr.	146	Sebastian Ligouri	Edens Ldg., S. F. Bay	1863	Sold Mexican 1887-1910
Alice Cooke	4 m schr.	782	Hall Bros.	Port Blakely	1891	Burned Prince William Sound November 17, 1931
Alice Haake	2 m schr.	244	John C. Haake	Port Blakely	1867	Lost off Amur R., Siberia, 1875 (wreck at Sakhalin Is.)
Alice Kimball	2 m schr.	107	Thos. H. Peterson	Mendocino Coast (Little River)	1874	Wrecked Siuslaw R. bar October 12, 1904
Allen A	3 m schr.	342	H. Bendixsen	Fairhaven	1888	Abandoned 1930's Los Angeles
Aloha	4 m schr.	814	Hall Bros.	Port Blakely	1891	Foundered off Tatoosh Is. December, 1913
Alpena	4 m schr.	970	Hall Bros.	Port Blakely	1901	Hulked St. Andrews Bay, Florida, December, 1924
Alpha	3 m schr.	300	A. M. Simpson	North Bend	1903	Wrecked 9 miles north Umpqua R. February 3, 1907
Alumna	4 m schr.	696	A. M. Simpson	North Bend	1901	Abandoned 1940's Alaska
Alvena	4 m schr.	772	H. Bendixsen	Fairhaven	1901	Canadian barge 1940's
Amanda Ager	2 m schr.	110	Middlemas	San Francisco	1866	Registry dropped 1878
Amaranth	4 m bktn.	1,109	M. Turner	Benicia	1901	Wrecked Jarvis Is. August 30, 1913
Amazon	4 m bktn.	1,167	M. Turner	Benicia	1902	Burned at sea July 4, 1925
Amelia	bktn.	397	R. Murray	Marshfield	1870	Floating cannery Alaska 1920
American Boy	2 m schr.	183	H. Doncaster	Seabeck, Wn.	1882	Registry dropped 1890
American Girl	2 m schr.	225	Hall Bros.	Port Ludlow	1875	Lost W. C. Vancouver Is. November, 1899
Andy Mahony (later Mindanao)	4 m schr.	566	John Lindstrom	Aberdeen	1902	Newport Beach fish barge 1940's
Anna	2 m schr.	239	M. Turner	San Francisco	1881	Wrecked Bering Sea 1902
Annie Gee	2 m schr.	154	Hall Bros.	Port Ludlow	1874	Lost at sea 1897
Annie Larsen	3 m schr.	376	Hall Bros.	Port Blakely	1881	Wrecked Malden Is. June 9, 1918
Annie Lyle	2 m schr.	195	Hall Bros.	Port Ludlow	1875	Wrecked 1876-77
Annie Stoffin (or Stoffer)	2 m schr.	119	McDonald	Marshfield	1870	Wrecked Casper, Calif., October 11, 1879
Annie E. Smale	4 m schr.	845	————	Marshfield	1903	Stranded Point Reyes, C., July 9, 1910
Annie M. Campbell (later Antila)	4 m schr.	565	Hall Bros.	Port Blakely	1897	Sold Chile (renamed Antila); wrecked Talohae October, 1926

The fledging seaport town of Seattle where windships of old came for cargoes of coal and lumber in the early 1880,'s.
Marine Digest

Stern quarter view of the **BAR-KENTINE QUICKSTEP.** She lived up to her name on more than one occasion showing her heels to much larger square-rigged vessels. Under Captain John Johnson she was abandoned off the Oregon coast in 1904. The barkentine rig was well suited for the long runs in the trades to 'fetch'' up the Antipodes.

—*H. H. Morrison photo,*
Courtesy R. E. MacKay

NAME	RIG	TONS	BUILDER	PLACE	DATE	ULTIMATE FATE
Antelope	2 m schr.	123	M. Turner	Benicia	1887	Wrecked Nehalem, Ore. bar September 30, 1907
Arago	brig.	185	McDonald	North Bend	1859	Broken up 1905
Arago	4 m bktn.	498	A. M. Simpson	North Bend	1891	Sold Chile 1914, Peru 1937 (renamed Aurrera)
Argonaut	2 m schr.	194	White	San Francisco	1880	Registry dropped 1890
Argus	4 m schr.	566	Pacific S. B. Co.	Marshfield	1902	Burned near Destruction Is., Wn., June 13, 1906; towed in, converted to barge; lost January 8, 1916
Ariel	4 m schr.	726	M. Turner	Benicia	1900	Wrecked Inuboyesaki, Japan, 1917
Arilla	2 m schr.	107	————	Port Angeles	1899	————
Arthur I.	2 m schr.	129	M. Turner	Benicia	1889	Registry dropped 1899
Augusta	brig.	137	————	Tillamook, O.	1872	Registry dropped 1878
Aurora	2 m schr.	193	H. Bendixsen	Eureka	1873	Abandoned off C. Flattery 1886
Aurora	4 m bktn. (later schr.)	1,211	Everett S. B. Co.	Everett, W.	1901	Barge at Monterey 1940's
Azalea	3 m schr.	344	H. Bendixsen	Eureka	1890	Ended days Sausalito after 1946
B. H. Ramsdell	2 m schr.	134	J. J. Fransen	San Francisco	1866	Wrecked Kapaa, Kauai, July 10, 1879
Bainbridge	4 m schr.	566	Hall Bros.	Port Blakely	1900	Wrecked Nags Head, N. C., February 4, 1929
Balboa	4 m schr.	777	Hall Bros.	Port Blakely	1901	Wrecked Grays Harbor entrance December 1, 1913
Bangor	4 m schr.	511	Bendixsen or Peter Matthews	Eureka	1891	Beached Vallejo, C., 1928
Barbara	2 m schr.	117	T. H. Peterson	Little River C.	1877	Registry dropped 1889
Barbara Hernster	2 m schr.	148	H. Bendixsen	Fairhaven	1887	Wrecked Pt. Arena 1901, Bering Sea 1905
Bella	3 m schr.	180	————	Acme, O.	1896	Wrecked Ocean Beach, Ore., November 25, 1906
Benicia	bktn.	674	M. Turner	Benicia	1899	Wrecked Haiti October 10, 1920
Bertha Dolbeer	3 m schr.	242	H. Bendixsen	Fairhaven	1881	Burned, sank California Coast November 3, 1918 (lifeboat found N. Z)
Bertie Minor	3 m schr.	273	H. Bendixsen	Humboldt Bay	1884	Registry abandoned 1924
Berwick	2 m schr.	100	M. Turner	Benicia	1887	Wrecked Siuslaw bar, O., March 13, 1908
Beulah	3 m schr.	357	Dickie Bros.	San Francisco	1882	Laid up S. F. 1934
Big River	2 m schr.	160	Chas. Murray	Freeport (W. Seattle)	1872	Lost off Wash. Coast January, 1892 (wreckage at Grays Harbor entrance)
Blakely	bgtn.	152	(Originally tug converted to schr. 1890)	Port Blakely	1872	Wrecked Natividad Is., Mexico, December 23, 1909
Blakely	4 m schr.	751	Hall Bros.	Port Blakely	1902	Foundered Cay Verde, Cuba, September 1, 1933
Blanco	brig	284	Eldridge Simpson	North Bend	1858 or 1860	Capsized off Siletz River, O., 1864
Bobolink	2 m schr.	170	L. S. Allen	Oakland	1868	Wrecked Kent's Point, Mendocino County, March 22, 1898
Bonanza	2 m schr.	135	J. S. Nichols	San Francisco	1875	Crushed in ice Herschel Is. (King Point), Alaska, August 23, 1905
Borealis	4 m schr.	764	Bendixsen S. B. Co.	Fairhaven	1902	Wrecked in Tonga Is. February 10, 1913
Bowhead	2 m schr.	108	————	North Bend	1891	Last owned in Seattle 1900
C. A. Klose	3 m schr.	407	Hay & Wright	Alameda	1902	Capsized 124°54'W 43°52'N March 21, 1905 (drifted ashore near North Head, Wn.)
C. A. Thayer	3 m schr.	453	H. Bendixsen	Fairhaven	1895	Still afloat at S.F. Maritime Museum
C. C. Funk	bktn.	539	H. R. Reed	Marshfield	1882	Drops from registry 1899
C. S. Holmes	4 m schr.	430	Hall Bros.	Port Blakely	1893	Lost as Canadian barge off B. C. Coast 1952
C. T. Hill	2 m schr.	140	Alex Hay	San Francisco	1889	Ashore Nehalem bar July 30, 1912; salvaged registry dropped 1916
California	2 m schr.	119	Isaac Hall	San Francisco	1869	Wrecked Bowens Ldg., Calif., January 22, 1888
Camano	4 m schr.	730	Hall Bros.	Port Blakely	1902	Wrecked Arecibo, P. R., April 21, 1927
Canute	2 m schr.	118	M. Turner	San Francisco	1882	Abandoned Honolulu 1927
Caroline	4 m schr.	511	Hall Bros.	Port Blakely	1902	Beached in boneyard S. F. Bay 1925
Carrier Dove	4 m schr.	707	Hall Bros.	Port Blakely	1890	Hit reef off Molokai, sank November 2, 1921

Under the Mexican flag—**BRIG-ANTINE CONSUELO**, registered at Guaymas, is seen here off the Mexican coast about 1910. She was one of the sugar packets built by Matthew Turner at his San Francisco yard in 1880 for the sugar baron John D. Spreckels.

A total constructive loss **SCHOON-ER MARCONI** wrecked on Coos Bay bar March 23, 1909.

NAME	RIG	TONS	BUILDER	PLACE	DATE	ULTIMATE FATE
Cassandra Adams	bark	1,127	Hiram Doncaster	Seabeck	1876	Wrecked off Destruction Is. August 15, 1888
Cassie Hayward	2 m schr.	197	Hall Bros.	Port Ludlow	1875	Drops from registry 1890
Catherine Sudden	bktn.	386	Hall Bros.	Port Ludlow	1878	Wrecked Cape Nome September 8, 1900
Cecilia Sudden	4 m schr.	643	Bendixsen S. B. Co.	Fairhaven	1902	Burned off New Zealand coast September, 1920
Challenger	3 m schr.	279	Alex Cookson	Eureka	1883	Scuttled South Bend, Wn., after fire December 7, 1904
Charles E. Falk	3 m schr.	298	H. Bendixsen	Fairhaven	1889	Wrecked Copalis Beach north Grays Harbor March 31, 1909
Charles Hanson	2 m schr.	192	H. Bendixsen	Eureka	1881	Last registered Alaska 1900
Charles F. Crocker	4 m bktn.	855	C. G. White	Alameda	1890	Allowed to founder Catalina Is. 1926
Charles H. Merchant	3 m schr.	283	Hans Reed	Marshfield	1877	Wrecked Nehalem River bar August 11, 1902
Charles R. Wilson	3 m schr.	345	H. Bendixsen	Fairhaven	1891	Breakwater at Powell River, B. C., 1947
Charlotte Frances	brig.	126	J. M. Farnum	San Francisco	1863	Fate not known
Chehalis	4 m bktn.	690	T. McDonald	Hoquiam	1891	Sold to Peru 1912; still listed 1921
Chetco	2 m schr.	106	M. Turner	Benicia	1887	Burned at Summerland, Calif., February 19, 1918
Churchill	4 m schr.	655	Simpson Lbr. Co.	North Bend	1900	Wrecked French Frigate Shoal September 27, 1917
City of Papeete	bktn. (later schr.)	389	H. Bendixsen	Fairhaven	1883	Laid up San Francisco 1929
Clara Light	2 m schr.	179	————	Steilacoom, W.	1868	Lost in Arctic Ocean 1886
Claus Spreckels	2 m schr.	246	M. Turner	San Francisco	1879	Registry dropped 1887
Columbia	4 m schr.	684	G. H. Hitchings	Hoquiam	1899	Sold British 1928
Comet	3 m schr.	429	Hall Bros.	Port Blakely	1886	Wrecked San Miguel Is., C., September 2, 1911
Commerce	4 m schr.	658	Hay & Wright	Alameda	1900	Floating home Sausalito 1934
Compeer	3 m schr.	347	H. Bendixsen	Fairhaven	1877	Wrecked Bristol Bay July 17, 1912; wrecked Kvichak River August 18, 1912
Consuelo	bgtn.	293	M. Turner	San Francisco	1880	Sold Mexican 1904; still registered 1920
Coquelle	2 m schr.	103	————	Coquille River	1883	Abandoned off Calif. Coast May 21, 1923; hull drifted to Bridgeport, Calif.
Cora	2 m schr.	155	————	Port Orchard, W.	1867	Wrecked 1884
Corona	3 m schr.	394	Hall Bros.	Port Blakely	1883	Sold Peru 1909; still afloat 1920
Courser	3 m schr.	357	Hall Bros.	Port Ludlow	1876	Wrecked Shoalwater Bay 1879, salvaged; lost off Oregon Coast 1892
Courtney Ford	bgtn. (later schr.)	401	M. Turner	Benicia	1883	Wrecked Glen Is., Alaska, September 7, 1902
Crescent	5 m schr.	1,443	Bendixsen S. B. Co.	Fairhaven	1904	Abandoned on fire 1,400 miles West of S. F. June 1, 1918
Czar	2 m schr.	144	M. Turner	San Francisco	1881	Sold Mexican 1920, renamed Juan Lanzagorta
Czarina	3 m schr.	230	H. Bendixsen	Fairhaven	1891	Wrecked Nagai Is., Alaska, February 15, 1911
D. C. Haskins	2 m schr.	112	Benj. Walls	Vallejo, Cal.	1869	Registry dropped 1885
Daisy Rowe	2 m schr.	122	H. Bendixsen	Fairhaven	1879	Wrecked Pt. Bonita, Calif., November 21, 1900
Dakota	3 m schr.	335	H. R. Reed	Marshfield	1881	Registry dropped 1887
Dare	3 m schr.	259	A. M. Simpson	North Bend	1882	Wrecked Bonilla Pt., B. C., December 23, 1890
Dashing Wave	2 m schr.	148	Euphronius Cousins	Eureka	1867	Lost in Bering Sea April 16, 1891
Dauntless	4 m schr.	548	G. H. Hitchings	Hoquiam	1898	Abandoned as fish barge 1929
David Evans	4 m schr.	821	Pacific S. B. Co.	Marshfield	1901	Burned So. African Coast October, 1921
Defender	4 m schr.	446	H. Bendixsen	Fairhaven	1896	Wrecked Ongea Reef, Fiji, April 10, 1920
Defiance	4 m schr.	604	Matthews & Hitchings	Hoquiam	1897	Burned Faisai, Solomon Is., January 23, 1922
Del Norte	2 m schr.	100	M. Turner	Benicia	1887	Lost in collision off Oregon Coast, S.F. for Rogue R. 1905
Discovery	bktn.	415	Chas. Murray	Port Discovery, Wash.	1874	Vanished, Gamble for S. F., January 1896
Dora Bluhm	3 m schr.	330	Hall Bros.	Port Blakely	1883	Wrecked Santa Rosa Is., Calif., May 26, 1910
Dreadnaught	2 m schr.	183	————	Port Madison, Wash.	1866	Registry dropped 1880

SCHOONER C. S. HOLMES photographed by Pete Hurd from the Coast Guard Cutter **DUANE** in 1939. The cutter removed a sick crewman from the codfishing schooner in the North Pacific.

BARKENTINE PORTLAND off Cape Flattery. She was built way back in 1873 by John Kruse for A. M. Simpson at Marshfield, Oregon at a cost of $35,000.

NAME	RIG	TONS	BUILDER	PLACE	DATE	ULTIMATE FATE
E. B. Jackson	4 m schr.	682	J. Lindstrom	Aberdeen	1901	Wrecked Apia, Samoa, February 7, 1917
E. K. Wood	4 m schr.	520	Hall Bros.	Port Blakely	1888	Wrecked Barrier Is., B. C., November 1912
Echo	4 m schr.	707	A. M. Simpson (K. V. Kruse)	North Bend	1896	Floating home Sausalito; went to pieces 1935
Edward Parke	2 m schr.	147	Augustus Vernon	Eureka	1877	Abandoned June 6, 1899 85 miles WNW San Francisco
Edward R. West	4 m schr.	835	W. H. McWhinney	Aberdeen	1902	Wrecked Fakarava Is., Tuamotos, May 27, 1922
Eldorado	4 m schr.	881	McWhinney & Cousins	Aberdeen	1901	Abandoned June 13, 1913, 31°02'S, 121°37'W
Elida	2 m schr.	179	————	Port Madison, Wash.	1868	Abandoned off Oregon Coast December, 1874; towed in total wreck (Juan de Fuca)
Eliza Miller	2 m schr.	156	C. G. White	San Francisco	1883	Last registered 1900
Ella	bktn.	259	Wm. Bryant & C. Saunders	Freeport (W. Seattle)	1874	Out of registry 1891
Ella Johnson	2 m schr.	112	————	Port Angeles	1894	Registry dropped 1900
Ellen H. Wood	brig	——	————	Umpqua River Ore.	1850's	In Fraser gold rush 1858
Ellen Laurena	3 m schr.	223	————	Portland, Ore.	1895	Foundered December 23, 1895, off Pacific Coast
Elnorah	3 m schr.	144	James Munroe	Newport, Ore.	1871	Lost off Pacific Coast December 22, 1897
Elsie Iversen	2 m schr.	122	M. Turner	Benicia	1887	Out of registry 1888
Elvenia	2 m schr.	148	H. Bendixsen	Humboldt Bay	1872	Last listed 1900
Emma	2 m schr.	112	————	San Francisco	1854	Sold foreign 1862
Emma Augusta	bktn.	284	————	San Francisco	1867	Last registered 1890
Emma Claudina	3 m schr.	195	M. Turner	San Francisco	1882	Foundered off Grays Harbor November 14, 1906
Emma Utter	3 m schr.	279	Hall Bros.	Port Ludlow	1875	Abandoned at sea after striking Grays Harbor bar February 11, 1904
Encore	4 m schr.	651	A. M. Simpson Yard	North Bend	1897	Sunk by German raider Wolf July 19, 1917, in Pacific
Endeavor	4 m schr.	565	Hall Bros.	Port Blakely	1897	Wrecked Ongea Reef, Fiji, September 10, 1912
Ensign	4 m schr.	618	C. G. White	Everett, Wn.	1904	Wrecked near Naples, Calif., January 20, 1909
Enterprise	2 m schr.	189	James Howlett	North Bend	1863	Wrecked Crescent City Harbor September 29, 1883; raised 1884
Equator	2 m schr.	——	Wightman Bros.	Benicia	1888	Hull salvaged from Everett mudflats 1967 (historical ship)
Eric	4 m schr.	574	Hall Bros.	Port Blakely	1898	Sold British 1925
Espada	4 m schr.	777	Bendixsen S. B. Co.	Fairhaven	1902	Stranded near Levuka, Fiji, January 21, 1919
Esther Buhne	3 m schr.	287	H. Bendixsen	Fairhaven	1887	Wrecked Newport Beach February 13, 1927 (Calif.)
Ethel Zane	4 m schr.	498	Peter Matthews	Eureka	1891	Abandoned N.E. of Guam July, 1918
Eureka	bktn.	295	Charles Murray	Humboldt Bay	1868	Wrecked near Cliff House, Point Lobos, June 19, 1902
Eureka	2 m schr.	123	M. Turner	Benicia	1887	Wrecked Coquille River bar November 30, 1899
Eva	3 m schr.	277	Charles Murray	Seabeck, Wn.	1880	Wrecked Altada Bay, Mexico, April, 1910
Excelsior	3 m schr.	348	H. Bendixsen	Fairhaven	1876	Wrecked Nelson's Lagoon, Alaska, August 30, 1906
Expansion	4 m schr.	545	Hay & Wright	Alameda	1900	Wrecked near Suva, Fijis, May 20, 1918
F. M. Slade	4 m schr.	737	McWhinney & Cousins	Aberdeen	1900	Wrecked, sold Peru 1913; afloat 1920 as Helvetia
F. S. Redfield	3 m schr.	469	Hall Bros.	Port Blakely	1887	Wrecked Cape Prince of Wales August 17, 1911 (Alaska)
Falcon	3 m schr.	205	H. Bendixsen	Fairhaven	1882	Sold Chile 1901; still afloat 1924
Fannie Adele	3 m schr.	234	Dickie Bros.	San Francisco	1883	Burned at San Francisco May 23, 1904
Fanny	2 m schr.	170	Domingo Marcucci	San Francisco	1861	Sold at Hong Kong 1863
Fanny Dutard	3 m schr.	170	C. G. White	San Francisco	1882	Still afloat 1940, in Alaska as barge
Fanny Hare	2 m schr.	163	John Daly	San Francisco	1867	Sold Nicaragua 1880, Peru 1885; still afloat 1921 (Jose Pozzo)
Fanny Jane	2 m schr.	120	Jacob Sutherland	Coos Bay	1869	Registry dropped 1878
Fearless	4 m schr.	736	G. H. Hitchings	Hoquiam	1900	Wrecked Tambores, Cuba, November 25, 1927

The two-masted **SCHOONER GENERAL McPHERSON** passing the **STEAMER DISCOVERY** in Alaskan waters at the turn of the century. Launched as a steamer at San Francisco in 1867 for the Army she was converted to a schooner in 1895 and was lost in the Bering Sea September 12, 1900. Ironically, the Discovery was also lost with all hands in 1903.

Photo courtesy Bob DeArmond, Juneau, Alaska

Shorn of all but a single mast, the **SCHOONER HELENE** is seen here reduced to a barge at Seattle in 1925. Dating from 1900, the vessel a year after this photo was taken, struck a submerged object off Crescent City and was towed into San Francisco and condemned.

Stranded 14 miles north of Cape Blanco, Oregon, the **SCHOONER NOVELTY** became a total loss. She was wrecked October 23, 1907, her value listed as only $12,000. Dating from 1886, the 592 ton vessel was wrecked en route to North Bend from San Francisco. She was first of her rig on the West Coast.

NAME	RIG	TONS	BUILDER	PLACE	DATE	ULTIMATE FATE
Fidelity	3 m schr.	192	————	Eureka	1882	Capsized Humboldt bar, November 16, 1889
Forest Home	4 m schr.	763	H. E. Heuckendorff	Marshfield	1900	Sunk by German raider as Holmwood (British) in So. Pacific 1941
Forest Queen	bark	511	Hiram Doncaster	Port Ludlow	1869	Lost at sea, Tacoma for S. F., March 1898
Forester	4 m schr.	663	Hay & Wright	Alameda	1900	Beached near Antioch, Calif., 1935
Fortuna	2 m schr.	145	H. Bendixsen	Fairhaven	1886	Sold Peru 1919
Francis Alice	2 m schr.	131	W. J. Stevens	St. Helens, Ore.	1881	Wrecked India Point, Siberia, October 13, 1900 (wrecked Alaska 1905)
Fred E. Sander	3 m schr.	463	Hall Bros.	Port Blakely	1887	Sold Peru 1917; afloat as Lionelo 1930 Callao
Fred J. Wood	4 m schr.	681	G. H. Hitchings	Hoquiam	1899	Abandoned S. F. 1928
Frithiof	2 m schr.	242	Holden	Marshfield	1874	Registry dropped 1889
Fullerton	4 m bktn. (largest built till WW I)	1,554	Hay & Wright	Alameda	1902	Abandoned as fish barge at Redondo Beach, Calif., 1927
G. W. Prescott	2 m schr.	112	Thos. H. Peterson	Little River, Calif.	1874	Registry dropped 1883
G. W. Watson	3 m schr.	452	H. Bendixsen	Fairhaven	1890	Wrecked Raiatea, Society Is., April 12, 1912
Galilee	bgtn.	354	M. Turner	Benicia	1891	Club house at Sausalito in 1936
Gamble	4 m schr.	726	Hall Bros.	Port Blakely	1901	Register abandoned in Florida 1934
Garcia	2 m schr.	116	M. Turner	San Francisco	1882	Wrecked near Cape Meares, Ore., December 12, 1893
Gardiner City	4 m schr.	475	A. M. Simpson Yard	North Bend	1889	Renamed Kitsap, sunk in collision Kauai Channel, Hawaii, April 21, 1919
Gem	2 m schr.	120	————	Parkersburg, Ore.	1885	Wrecked near Double Headed Rock, Ore. February 15, 1904
General Banning	2 m schr.	177	Thos. H. Peterson	Navarro River, Calif.	1883	Sold to Mexico, afloat 1920.
General McPherson	2 m schr.	109	————	Built S.F. as Army Q. M. steamer, converted	1867 1895	Wrecked Safety Harbor, Bering Sea, September 12, 1900
General Miller	2 m schr.	108	Middlemas	San Francisco	1874	Wrecked Bering Sea 1882
Geneva	bgtn.	495	M. Turner	Benicia	1892	Burned in Gulf of Mexico June 11, 1926
George C. Perkins	bktn.	388	Hans R. Reed	Coos Bay	1880	Wrecked Topolobampo bar, Mexico, July 5, 1907
George E. Billings	5 m schr.	1,260	Hall Bros.	Port Blakely	1903	Burned for scrap San Pedro February, 1941
Geo. P. Haub	2 m schr.	122	George Buchart	San Francisco	1876	Out of registry 1878
Georgina	4 m bktn.	998	Bendixsen S. B. Co.	Fairhaven	1901	Driven ashore off So. Calif. at Redondo Beach, 1935 (fish barge)
Gleaner	bktn.	413	T. McDonald	Hoquiam	1892	Sold British at Sydney, N.S.W. 1911
Glen	2 m schr.	127	Hans R. Reed	Marshfield	1883	Wrecked Ikitak Pass, Unimak Is., 1907
Glendale	3 m schr.	296	H. Bendixsen	Fairhaven	1888	Fish barge at Point Loma 1930's
Golden Fleece	2 m schr.	127	————	Humboldt Bay	1875	Registry dropped 1895
Golden Gate	2 m schr.	——	Hans Bendixsen	Eureka	1874	Wrecked Point Arena May 18, 1889
Golden Shore	4 m schr.	699	Hall Bros.	Port Blakely	1889	Broken up at Oakland 1932
Good Templar	2 m schr.	126	Williams or Williamson	Steilacoom. W.	1866	Wrecked Manzanillo, Mexico, October 28, 1881
Gotoma	2 m schr.	198	Simpson Yard	North Bend	1872	Wrecked Willapa Harbor December 25, 1908
Grace Roberts	bktn.	268	Roberts	Port Orchard, W.	1868	Wrecked North Beach Pens. opposite Oysterville December 8, 1887
Gray Hound	2 m schr.	148	J. E. Thayer	San Francisco	1869	Registry dropped 1886
Guide	3 m schr.	144	J. H. Farnum	San Francisco	1887	Still afloat 1900
H. C. Wright	3 m schr.	290	H. Bendixsen	Fairhaven	1889	Wrecked Port Filibustero, Costa Rica, October 17, 1910
H. D. Bendixsen	4 m schr.	641	H. Bendixsen	Fairhaven	1898	Renamed Arctic, wrecked in ice Point Barrow August 10, 1924
H. K. Hall	5 m schr.	1,237	Hall Bros.	Port Blakely	1902	Sold to Peru, renamed Dante about 1924; afloat 1939

The remains of the once beautiful three-masted **SCHOONER JOHN A** at the mouth of the Nisqually River about 1950. Captain "North Pole" Hansen once described her as a wonderful little ship that maneuvered like a yacht. She was built by Peter Matthews in 1893.

The **SCHOONER RESOLUTE** reputedy aground near Dungeness, Washington. She was later refloated and ran for many years, last serving as a barge at New York in 1932. During the vessel's heyday, she once suffered a mutiny in which the master's wife sued the owner for $40,000 for her part in saving the schooner. The Resolute was built by Hitchings & Joyce at Hoquiam in 1902.

NAME	RIG	TONS	BUILDER	PLACE	DATE	ULTIMATE FATE
H. L. Tiernan	2 m schr.	153	H. L. Tiernan	San Francisco	1867	Wrecked Caspar, Calif., November, 1869, salvaged; lost Shumagin Islands 1882
Halcyon	3 m schr.	293	————	Eureka	1881	Lost near Aleutians November 27, 1918
Hannah Madison	2 m schr.	134	Thos. H. Peterson	Little River, Calif.	1876	Wrecked Navarro, Calif., November, 1885
Harriet	2 m schr.	118	————	Ballard, Wn.	1900	Lost at Nome, Alaska, September 8, 1900
Harriet Rowe	2 m schr.	114	Taylor & Rowe	San Francisco	1866	Out of registry 1877
Hayes	2 m schr.	194	John Kruse	Umpqua, Ore.	1876	Lost Navidad Bay (Jalisco), Mexico, June 2, 1895
Helen	2 m schr.	121	J. A. Hamilton	Point Arena, Calif.	1863	Wrecked Point Arena 1865
Helen N. Kimball	2 m schr.	192	Thos. H. Peterson	Cuffey's Cove Calif.	1881	Lost Fanning Is. June 27, 1901
Helene	4 m schr.	927	Hall Bros.	Port Blakely	1900	Condemned S.F. 1926 after hitting obstacle off Crescent City
Henry Wilson	4 m schr.	472	J. Lindstrom	Aberdeen	1899	Burned for scrap near Picnic Pt., Wash., March, 1937
Herman	2 m schr.	105	M. Turner	Benecia	1890	Sold to Tahiti owners, renamed Roberta; still afloat 1930
Hesper	bark	695	Hall Bros.	Port Blakely	1882	Abandoned Antofagasta 1913
Hesperian	brig	241	E. & H. Cousins	Eureka	1865	Document surrendered S. F., May, 1883
Hilo	bktn.	644	H. Bendixsen	Fairhaven	1892	Out of registry 1894
Honoipu	4 m schr.	564	Hay & Wright	Alameda	1898	Wrecked Washington Is. October 29, 1925
Howard	2 m schr.	125	Dickie Bros.	San Francisco	1881	Wrecked Navarro, Calif., December 19, 1884
Hueneme	3 m schr.	364	Hall Bros.	Port Ludlow	1877	Stranded Unimak Is. September 7, 1897 (Alaska)
Hugh Hogan	3 m schr.	392	Kruse & Banks	Marshfield	1904	Renamed Ozmo, wrecked Orford Reef, Cape Blanco, Ore., May 17, 1922
Humboldt	2 m schr.	138	H. Bendixsen	Eureka	1874	Lost Westport, Calif., September 30, 1885
Ida McKay	3 m schr.	187	H. Bendixsen	Fairhaven	1880	Wrecked at sea February 15, 1912
Ida Schnauer	2 m schr.	215	Hall Bros.	Port Ludlow	1875	Wrecked Tillamook bar June 17, 1908 (Ore.)
Inca	5 m schr.	1,014	Hall Bros.	Port Blakely	1896	Abandoned So. Pacific December, 1920; towed to Sydney and hulked
Irene	4 m schr.	772	H. Bendixsen	Fairhaven	1900	Burned purposely as "movie ship" off Long Beach, Calif., November 1, 1929
Irmgard	bktn.	670	Hall Bros.	Port Blakely	1889	Wrecked Quelelevu Reef, Fiji, June 3, 1920
Isabel	2 m schr.	184	J. H. Howlitt	North Bend	1864	Abandoned in North Pacific 1888 en route Alaska
Ivanhoe	2 m schr.	119	J. J. Walworth	Marshfield	1869	Out of registry 1893
Ivy	2 m schr.	142	Dickie Bros.	San Francisco	1882	Wrecked at Point Barrow, Alaska, September 1, 1908
J. Eppinger	2 m schr.	112	C. G. White	San Francisco	1887	Wrecked Navarro, Cal., April 14, 1887, salvaged; sunk in collision 68 miles north S. F. July 2, 1898
J. B. Ford	2 m schr.	196	————	San Francisco (brig 1877)	1860	Out of registry 1878
J. B. Leeds	2 m schr.	229	Hiram Doncaster	Umpqua, Ore.	1876	Foundered off Luzon, P. I., March 5, 1905
J. C. Ford	3 m schr.	244	M. Turner	San Francisco	1882	Wrecked and burned off Grays Harbor bar February, 1893
J. H. Lunsmann	4 m schr.	1,090	White Yard	Everett, Wn.	1902	Sunk by collision S. F. Bay July 12, 1913
J. J. Fransen	2 m schr.	120	J. J. Fransen	San Francisco	1867	Wrecked Noyo, Calif., November 18, 1869
J. M. Coleman	3 m schr.	463	Hall Bros.	Port Blakely	1888	Wrecked San Miguel Is. September 3, 1905
J. M. Griffith	bktn.	606	————	Seabeck, Wn.	1882	Sold Portuguese 1920
J. M. Weatherwax	3 m schr.	384	J. M. Weatherwax	Aberdeen, Wn.	1890	Renamed Ethel M. Sterling 1916; sold Peru 1918-1929, renamed Ballestas

Jack London went on a sealing expedition in the **SOPHIA SUTHERLAND,** seen here at berth in San Francisco. This vessel, built by A. C. McDonald at Tacoma in 1889, had the lines of a yacht and was London's inspiration for his novel, The Sea-Wolf. Purchased by Captain H. H. Bodfish for the Eskimos of Bailey Island, Alaska, she was wrecked there August 31, 1900 in a storm.
—*Courtesy San Francisco Maritime Museum*

The author took this photo in the summer of 1954 on the shores of Tillamook Bay, Oregon. It shows the remains of the **SCHOONER LILA & MATTIE** which have reposed there for more than sixty years. The vessel was badly mauled crossing Tillamook bar about 1897, run up on the beach and abandoned. She dates from 1888 when built on California's Albion River.

NAME	RIG	TONS	BUILDER	PLACE	DATE	ULTIMATE FATE
J. W. Clise	4 m schr.	845	T. C. Reed	Ballard, Wn.	1904	Abandoned 600 miles S. of New Orleans August 6, 1940
James Johnson	4 m schr.	1,149	Moran Bros.	Seattle	1901	Broken up S. F. 1924 after storm damage
James A. Garfield	3 m schr.	316	John Kruse	North Bend	1881	Sold Peru 1910, renamed G. Garibaldi; afloat till 1915
James Rolph	4 m schr.	586	H. Bendixsen	Fairhaven	1899	Wrecked Point Pedro, Calif., August 3, 1910
James Sennett	4 m schr.	766	————	Marshfield	1901	Out of registry 1904
James Townsend	schr.	168	Thos. E. Peterson	Noyo, Cal.	1867	Wrecked Point Arena 1882
James Tuft	4 m bktn.	1,274	Hall Bros.	Port Blakely	1901	Burned at Long Beach, Calif., August 22, 1935 as gambling barge named Casino
James H. Bruce	4 m schr.	533	H. Bendixsen	Fairhaven	1898	Wrecked Nicholson's Is. March 27, 1918
Jane L. Stanford	4 m bktn.	970	H. Bendixsen	Fairhaven	1892	Victim of collision August, 1929 (fish barge); remains blown up Santa Cruz Is., Calif.
Jeanette	bgtn.	298	M. Turner	Benicia	1893	Sold at Suva 1920; out of registry 1924
Jennie Stella	3 m schr.	292	H. R. Reed	Marshfield	1876	Wrecked Navidad, Mexico, December 23, 1905
Jennie Thelin	2 m schr.	145	Olaff Reed	Davenport Ldg., near Santa Cruz	1869	Out of registry San Diego 1912 wrecked Punta Maria, Baja Mexico, 1912, as Carmancita.
Jennie Walker	2 m schr.	137	Hall Bros.	Port Ludlow	1880	Hawaiian owned; fate not known
Jennie Wand	3 m schr.	171	H. R. Reed	Marshfield	1883	Wrecked La Paz, Mexico, January 2, 1906
Jessie Minor	3 m schr.	261	H. Bendixsen	Fairhaven	1883	Wrecked Nelson's Lagoon, Alaska, August 1, 1911 (longest voyage on record 58 days S. F. to Bristol Bay)
Jessie Nickerson	2 m schr.	184	Hall Bros.	Port Ludlow	1874	Wrecked Willapa bar 1880
Johanna M. Brock	2 m schr.	134	Thos. H. Peterson	Little River, Calif.	1876	Capsized Humboldt bar 1879
John A.	3 m schr.	282	Peter Matthews	Eureka	1893	Breakwater Nisqually, Wn., mudflats 1950
John Palmer	4 m bktn.	1,187	H. Bendixsen	Fairhaven	1900	Wrecked European waters October, 1920, as French schr. Yvonne
John Smith	bktn.	588	Hall Bros.	Port Blakely	1882	Sold Peru 1913; registry dropped 1922
John A. Campbell	4 m schr.	545	Hall Bros.	Port Blakely	1895	Burned at Tarawa August 1, 1922
John C. Meyer	4 m bktn.	932	Robert Banks (Hardy S. B. Co.)	Tacoma	1902	Wrecked Machias, Me., November 28, 1925
John D. Spreckels	bgtn.	266	M. Turner	San Francisco	1880	Wrecked in collision off Pt. Reyes March 29, 1913 (schr.)
John D. Tallant	4 m schr.	561	Alex Hay	Alameda	1892	Foundered at sea mid-Pacific August, 1902
John F. Miller	2 m schr.	179	L. Mortensen & B. H. Hanson	San Francisco	1882	Wrecked in Unimak Pass January 8, 1908
John G. North	3 m schr.	336	H. R. Reed	Marshfield	1881	Burned Cape San Lucas, Baja, Calif.. May 14, 1919
Joseph Perkins	bktn. or schr.	296	J. Perkins	Vallejo, Calif.	1875	Lost Waihee Reef. Maui, Hawaii, May 14, 1880
Joseph Russ	3 m schr.	247	E. Cousins	Eureka	1881	Wrecked Chirikof Is., Alaska, May 10, 1912
Jos. L. Eviston	bktn.	755	H. Heuckendorff	Marshfield	1900	Renamed Fookien, Philippine registry; dropped 1925
Juventa	2 m schr.	191	J. H. Howlett	North Bend	1865	Out of registry 1880
Kailua	4 m schr.	736	Hitchings & Joyce	Hoquiam	1901	Wrecked Kyoquot Sound, B. C., March, 1904
Katie Flickenger	bktn.	472	Bryant & Bigelow	Belltown (Seattle) Wash.	1876	Wrecked at Redondo Beach, Calif., October 20, 1905
Kauikeaouli	2 m schr.	140	Hall Bros.	Port Ludlow	1879	Hawaii owned, lost off Hawaii September 27, 1906
King Cyrus	4 m schr.	717	Hall Bros.	Port Blakely	1890	Wrecked Chehalis Point. Grays Harbor bar, July 17, 1922
Kitsap	bktn.	693	Jeniston	Port Ludlow	1881	Wrecked Palmerston Is. May 23, 1886
Kitsap	4 m schr.	791	Hall Bros.	Port Ludlow	1887	Wrecked Borodino Is. September 6, 1891
Kittie Stevens	2 m schr.	130	J. J. Fransen	San Francisco	1868	Wrecked Albion, Calif., December 10. 1883
Klikitat	bktn.	493	John Kruse	North Bend	1881	Wrecked Honlii Point, Hawaii November 11, 1912

Tugs strain in vain in 1922 to free the stranded **KING CYRUS,** at the entrance to Grays Harbor. She became a total loss. The Hall Brothers built her at Port Blakely in 1890 for the Pacific lumber trade.

At San Francisco, the little **SCHOONER ESTHER BUHNE,** built by Bendixsen at Fairhaven in 1887 operated for H. H. Buhne of Eureka. She had her sides built up to give her a greater carrying capacity.
—*Photo from Dickie Collection, courtesy San Francisco Maritime Museum*

NAME	RIG	TONS	BUILDER	PLACE	DATE	ULTIMATE FATE
Kodiak	2 m schr.	102	M. Turner	San Francisco	1881	Wrecked 1893-94 Alaska
Kodiak	2 m schr.	146	M. Turner	Benicia	1895	Last listed at S. F. 1920
Kohala	4 m bktn.	891	Bendixsen S. B. Co.	Fairhaven	1901	Fishing barge in So. Calif. 1928
Koko Head	4 m bktn.	1,084	W. A. Boole & Son	Oakland	1902	Abandoned on fire 180 miles S.W. of Java May 29, 1918
Kona	4 m schr.	679	Hay & Wright	Alameda	1901	Wrecked Kangaroo Is. February 5, 1917
LaGironde	2 m schr.	204	Hall Bros.	Port Ludlow	1875	Wrecked San Nicholas Is., Cal., October 14, 1902
Lahaina	4 m bktn.	1,067	W. A. Boole & Son	Oakland	1901	Wrecked October 5, 1933, Point Vicente, Calif.
Laura Madsen	3 m schr.	345	Holden	Gardiner, Ore.	1882	Lost October 14, 1905, at Point Barrow, Alaska
Laura May	2 m schr.	127	E. & H. Cousins	Eureka	1868	Wrecked 6 miles north Coos Bay 1874
Laura May	3 m schr.	246	H. R. Reed	Marshfield	1875	Wrecked Kvichak, Alaska, August 12, 1901
Laura Pike	2 m schr.	145	H. Bendixsen	Eureka	1875	Wrecked Humboldt bar 1878, salvaged; abandoned sinking off Cape Mendocino February 7, 1902
Legal Tender	3 m schr.	210	Meigg's Mill	Port Madison, Wash.	1863	Last registered as whaler 1886 (re-rigged as bark)
Lena Sweasey	3 m schr.	256	————	Eureka	1882	Wrecked Navidad Bay, Mexico, August 24, 1903
Lila & Mattie	2 m schr.	105	John F. Peterson	Albion River, Calif.	1888	Beached Tillamook Bay after being wrecked on bar in 1897
Lillebonne	2 m schr.	218	E. Cousins	Eureka	1883	Capsized, foundered S. F. Bay August 29, 1912
Lily	2 m schr.	142	Dickie Bros.	San Francisco	1882	Laid up Long Beach, Calif., 1935 (movie ship HMS Bounty)
Lizzie Madison	2 m schr.	131	H. Bendixsen	Humboldt Bay	1876	Out of registry 1886
Lizzie Marshall	bark	454	L. Mortensen & S. B. Peterson	Maine Prairie, Calif.	1877	Wrecked Bonilla Point, B. C., February 22, 1884
Lizzie Vance	3 m schr.	442	Hall Bros.	Port Blakely	1887	Put into Guam leaking January, 1923; sold to Japan, broken up
Lola	2 m schr.	192	————	Port Madison, Wash.	1865	Out of registry 1880
Loleta	2 m schr.	119	Hammond	Seattle	1871	Out of registry 1883
Lottie Bennett	4 m schr.	566	Hall Bros.	Port Blakely	1899	Still afloat 1940's (floating cannery) Long Beach, Calif.
Lottie Carson	3 m schr.	286	Hall Bros.	Port Blakely	1881	Laid up Newport Harbor, Calif., 1936; refitted July, 1941; appeared in three movies
Louis	5 m schr.	831	John Kruse	North Bend	1888	Wrecked South Farallon Is. June 19, 1907
Louise	3 m schr.	346	H. Bendixsen	Fairhaven	1892	Laid up Cerritos Channel, Los Angeles, 1942
Lucy	3 m schr.	309	H. Bendixsen	Fairhaven	1890	Sold Tahiti 1920; flew French flag as Raita; lost near Clooose, B. C., January 16, 1925
Ludlow	4 m schr.	762	Hall Bros.	Port Blakely	1900	Burned Gulfport, Miss., May, 1925
Lurline	bgtn.	358	M. Turner	Benicia	1887	Sunk in collision off Salina Cruz January 11, 1915
Luzon	4 m schr.	545	Hay & Wright	Alameda	1900	Sold to Chinese in 1937 under name Kaimiloa
Lyman D. Foster	4 m schr.	777	Hall Bros.	Port Blakely	1892	Abandoned off Fiji April 15, 1913; wreck towed in, sold British; refitted as barkentine in 1917
M. Turner	4 m schr.	731	M. Turner	Benicia	1902	Register abandoned in Florida 1934
Mabel Gale	4 m schr.	762	Hall Bros.	Port Blakely	1902	Register abandoned Mobile, Ala., 1933
Mable Gray	3 m schr.	205	H. Bendixsen	Fairhaven	1882	Wrecked in Redondo Beach, Calif., March 11, 1904
Maggie Johnston	2 m schr.	133	Bryant & Cummings	Navarro, Cal.	1866	Out of registry 1888
Maggie C. Russ	3 m schr.	196	Euphronius Cousins	Eureka	1881	Wrecked San Blas, Mexico, June 11, 1903
Mahukona	4 m schr.	738	Hitchings & Joyce	Hoquiam	1901	Wrecked on reef near Apia, Samoa, January 29, 1918
Maid of Orleans	2 m schr.	180	Dickie Bros.	San Francisco	1882	Last afloat as barge in Alaska 1966

Tacking against a southerly breeze **BARKENTINE NEWSBOY** is pictured around the turn of the century. She was built as a bark by the Dickie Brothers at San Francisco in 1882 and was sold to Peruvians in 1914.

The 766 ton **SCHOONER JAMES SENNETT** with all sails set off Coos Bay. She was built at Marshfield, Oregon in 1901 and was wrecked at sea a few months later.

NAME	RIG	TONS	BUILDER	PLACE	DATE	ULTIMATE FATE
Makah	bktn.	699	Hall Bros.	Port Blakely	1882	Found bottom up off Tillamook Head, Ore., October 22, 1888
Maria E. Smith	3 m schr.	365	Hall Bros.	Port Blakely	1881	Lost at sea July 12, 1904
Makaweli	4 m bktn.	899	W. A. Boole & Son	Oakland	1902	Last afloat about 1940 as fish barge Rainbow
Malolo	2 m schr.	133	Hall Bros.	Port Ludlow	1879	Hawaiian owned, fate not known
Manila	4 m schr.	731	A. M. Simpson	North Bend	1899	Sunk by raider Seeadler in South Pacific July 8, 1917
Marconi	4 m schr.	693	A. M. Simpson	North Bend	1902	Wrecked south spit Coos Bay bar March 23, 1909
Margaret Crockard	2 m schr.	169	W. H. Bryant	Port Madison	1870	Out of registry 1879
Maria G. Atkins	2 m schr.	100	J. A. Hamilton	Point Arena	1868	Last registered 1877
Marietta	2 m schr.	142	J. Foster	Port Discovery	1872	Lost on Humboldt Bar 1877
Marion	2 m schr.	235	M. Turner	San Francisco	1882	Wrecked Sanak Is., Alaska, April 11, 1906
Martha W. Tuft	2 m schr.	173	H. Bendixsen	Eureka	1876	Wrecked Katalla River, Alaska, October 11, 1907
Mary Buhne	2 m schr.	147	H. Bendixsen	Eureka	1876	Sunk collision 8 miles off Humboldt Bay December 18, 1903
Mary Dodge	3 m schr.	243	Murray	Eureka	1882	Sold Peruvian 1917
Mary Swann	2 m schr.	143	H. Bendixsen	Eureka	1875	Out of registry 1889
Mary Winkelman	bktn.	522	Hiram Doncaster	Seabeck, Wn.	1881	Lost on reef near Pago-Pago November 13, 1923
Mary D. Pomeroy	2 m schr.	114	T. H. Peterson	Little River Calif.	1879	Lost off Point Reyes January, 1880
Mary E. Foster	2 m schr.	116	Hall Bros.	Port Ludlow	1877	Sold to Hawaiian owners same year; fate not known
Mary E. Foster	4 m schr.	950	Hall Bros.	Port Blakely	1898	Beached at Waikiki after collision off Diamond Head April 26, 1923; towed in, condemned
Mary E. Russ	2 m schr.	235	E. Cousins	Eureka	1875	Wrecked Manzanillo, Mexico, April 12, 1905
Mary and Ida	2 m schr.	183	Dickie Bros.	San Francisco	1882	Wrecked February 28, 1903, Unga Is., Alaska
Maweema	3 m schr.	453	H. Bendixsen	Fairhaven	1895	Wrecked St. George Is., Alaska, August 19, 1928
Maxim	2 m schr.	117	H. Bendixsen	Humboldt Bay	1876	Lost off Calif. Coast January, 1907, S. F. for Eureka
May Queen	2 m schr.	123	Cousins	Eureka	1867	Out of registry 1880
Melancthon	bktn.	298	Murray	North Bend	1867	Hulked at Honolulu 1905
Melrose	4 m schr.	615	Hitchings & Joyce	Hoquiam	1902	Afloat in 1930's as fish barge in Calif. (afloat in 1940)
Meteor	4 m schr.	600	Hall Bros.	Port Blakely	1891	Barge in Alaska in late 1920's-1930's
Metha Nelson	3 m schr.	460	H. Bendixsen	Fairhaven	1896	Surplus end of W.W. II (Navy identification vessel)
Mildred	3 m schr.	464	H. Bendixsen	Fairhaven	1897	Wrecked south jetty Grays Harbor bar March 16, 1908
Mindoro	4 m schr.	679	Hay & Wright	Alameda	1901	Laid up S. F. September, 1921; later broken up
Mina Bell	2 m schr.	123	Bell	San Francisco	1865	Sold foreign 1875
Minnie A. Caine	4 m schr.	880	Moran Bros.	Seattle	1900	Stranded Smith Is. 1901, salvaged; blown ashore September 24, 1939, Santa Monica, Calif.; burned for metal
Modoc	bktn.	452	George Boole	Utsaladdy, Wash.	1873	Stranded February 23, 1896, Guaymas, Mexico
Monitor	bktn.	235	Domingo Marcucci	San Francisco	1862	Foundered 20 miles off Columbia River March 24, 1901
Monterey	2 m schr.	126	M. Turner	Benicia	1887	Sold to Philippine owners; last registered 1927 as Turia
Mono	2 m schr.	142	H. P. Anderson	San Francisco	1904	Fate not known
Moro	2 m schr.	111		Alameda	1894	Out of registry 1900
Muriel	4 m schr.	537	Hay & Wright	Alameda	1895	Wrecked Balboa, Calif., July, 1925 as movie ship
N. L. Drew	2 m center-board schr.	120	J. S. Nichols	San Francisco	1869	Wrecked Mendocino Coast December, 1882
Nanaimo	bark	407	Alex Allen	Nanaimo, B.C.	1882	Remained under British registry
Narwhal	bark (Steam Whaler)	523	Dickie Bros.	San Francisco	1883	Beached San Diego; burned in 1934
Nautilus	brig	173	Euphronius Cousins	Eureka	1868	Under Tahitian registry 1882
Neptune	2 m schr.	184	H. Bendixsen	Fairhaven	1882	Still afloat 1900
Newark	2 m schr.	120	M. Turner	Benicia	1887	Remains in mud San Pedro Harbor 1930's
Newsboy	bark (later bktn.)	588	Dickie Bros.	San Francisco	1882	Sold Peru 1914; registry dropped by 1920

More than one and a half million board feet of lumber was packed aboard the five-masted **INCA** when this photo was taken. Built in 1896 she was the second of her rig to be placed in service on the West Coast.

In need of a new set of canvas—**BRIGANTINE BLAKELY.** Built in 1872 as a steam tug to tow sailing vessels, she herself became a sailing vessel when rebuilt in 1890 for service as a sealer. She was lost in the guano trade off the Mexican coast in 1909.

NAME	RIG	TONS	BUILDER	PLACE	DATE	ULTIMATE FATE
Nokomis	4 m schr.	545	Hall Bros.	Port Blakely	1895	Wrecked Clipperton Is. February 28, 1914
Nomad	4 m schr.	565	Hall Bros.	Port Blakely	1897	Lost at sea December, 1897; remains drifted to Hawaii
Nome	2 m schr.	231	M. Turner	Benicia	1900	Believed lost in Alaska 1900-01
Nora Harkins	2 m schr.	209	Parker	Parkersburg, Ore.	1882	Wrecked Peterson's Point, Grays Harbor, October 16, 1894
Norma	3 m schr.	326	C. G. White	San Francisco	1883	Wrecked Ten Mile River bar, Calif., November 15, 1899
North Bend	bktn.	376	John Kruse	North Bend	1877	Last afloat as barge 1921 in B. C.
Northwest	bark	515	W. H. Bryant	Port Madison Wash.	1868	Still afloat 1907 as barge
Norway	2 m schr.	192	Jacob Bell	San Francisco	1870	Abandoned after collision off Clallam Bay, Wn., January 11, 1894; wreck drifted ashore
Novelty	4 m schr.	592	A. M. Simpson	North Bend	1886	Wrecked 14 miles north Cape Arago, Ore., October 23, 1907
Noyo	2 m schr.	195	J. C. Cousins	San Francisco	1861	Struck Coos bar, beached and burned from lime cargo 1868
O. M. Kellogg	3 m schr.	393	H. Bendixsen	Fairhaven	1892	Wrecked Mau Reef, Samoa, September, 1915
Oakland	3 m schr. (Shoal draft)	418	W. F. Stone & Son	Oakland	1902	Grounded Nehalem Beach, Ore., April, 1916, refloated 1918; renamed Mary Hanlon; foundered off Mendocino, Calif., June 24, 1924
Occident	bktn.	297	A. M. Simpson	———	1865	Wrecked Coos Bay bar May 3, 1870
Occidental	3 m schr.	209	H. Bendixsen	Fairhaven	1884	Wrecked Point Gorda February 9, 1902
Ocean Pearl	2 m schr.	195	Middlemas design	Navarro, Cal.	1868	Lost off Pacific Coast 1878
Oceania Vance	3 m schr.	445	Hall Bros.	Port Blakely	1888	Laid up as tuna transport barge 1935
Okanogan	4 m schr.	721	Hall Bros.	Port Blakely	1895	Wrecked Ahukini Point, Kauai, December 24, 1919
Olga	4 m schr.	498	H. Bendixsen	Eureka	1889	Wrecked Kahoolane, Hawaii May 25, 1906
Oliver J. Olson	4 m schr.	667	John Lindstrom	Aberdeen	1900	Wrecked Cape Falso, Mexico, October, 1911
Olympus	ship	1,110	Hiram Doncaster	Seabeck, Wn.	1880	Burned off Washington Coast September 14, 1881
Omega	bktn.	584	A. M. Simpson	North Bend	1894	Vanished at sea out of N. Z. March, 1921
Onward	3 m schr.	276	Parker	Parkersburg, Ore.	1901	Wrecked Coquille River bar February 25, 1905
Oregon	3 m schr. (Shoal draft)	343	H. Heuckendorff	Prosper, Ore.	1905	Renamed Apollo; sold Japan 1933, Apollo Maru
Oregonian	3 m schr.	247	John Kruse	North Bend	1872	Wrecked Coquille bar January 16, 1877
Orion	2 m schr.	117	Bendixsen & Peterson	Humboldt Bay	1878	Cut in half in collision off Columbia River lightship October 4, 1897
Otelia Pedersen	4 m schr.	789	C. G. White	Everett	1901	Wrecked by typhoon; wreck towed to Japan about 1902
Ottilie Fjord	3 m schr.	261	H. Bendixsen	Fairhaven	1892	Last used in movies (Mutiny on the Bounty, Treasure Island); laid up Long Beach 1942
Pacific	2 m schr.	148	John Kruse	Umpqua, Ore.	1865	Abandoned off Calif. Coast January 30, 1878
Pacific Slope	bark	824	Middlemas & Boole	San Francisco	1875	For Australian owners
Paloma	brig	223	H. Bendixsen	Humboldt Bay	1875	For Tahitian owners
Pannonia	2 m schr.	206	H. R. Reed	Marshfield	1875	Wrecked in South Seas 1891
Papeete	2 m schr.	127	M. Turner	Benicia	1891	For Tahitian owners; still afloat 1929
Parallel	2 m schr.	148	Jacobs	San Francisco	1868	Blew up under Cliff House, S. F., January 15, 1887
Parkersburg	2 m schr.	123	Parker	Parkersburg	1883	Condemned San Francisco 1905
Pathfinder	2 m schr.	105		Astoria	1891	Canadian sealer 1898
Peerless	3 m schr.	244	Peterson	Gardiner, Ore.	1878	Last registered 1925
Phil Sheridan	2 m schr.	158	T. H. Peterson	Little River, Calif.	1868	Sunk in collision 15 miles off Umpqua September 15, 1878
Philippine	4 m schr.	523	Hay & Wright	Alameda	1899	Wrecked as barge near Los Angeles about 1932 (at Brighton Beach)

The **SCHOONER EXPANSION** is reflected in a calm sea—becalmed. Built in 1900 she was lost May 20, 1918 on a reef near Suva, Fiji Islands.

The end of the four-masted **SCHOONER HENRY WILSON,** right (built in 1899 by J. Lindstrom), burned for her scrap along with the Bath-built **BARK W. B. FLINT,** left, and the wooden **STEAMER VINCENNES** at the Franzen property on Puget Sound in March 1937.   *Arvid Franzen photo*

NAME	RIG	TONS	BUILDER	PLACE	DATE	ULTIMATE FATE
Pio Benito	3 m schr.	277	Hall Bros.	Port Ludlow	1873	Wrecked in Central America August, 1875
Pioneer	3 m schr.	418	T. McDonald	Hoquiam	1886	Wrecked Nestucca Beach, Ore., December 17, 1900
Pitcairn	2 m schr. (later bgtn.)	121	M. Turner	Benicia	1890	Wrecked Mindoro, P. I., October 17, 1912
Planter	bktn.	524	Murray	Port Ludlow	1886	Abandoned in Atlantic Ocean August 15, 1921
Polaris	4 m schr.	790	————	Marshfield	1902	Wrecked on Duxbury Reef January 16, 1914
Portland	bktn.	493	John Kruse	Marshfield	1873	Burned at Tent City, Calif., for celebration 1908
Premier	3 m schr.	307	Hall Bros.	Port Ludlow	1876	Wrecked Unimak Is. May 13, 1919
Prosper	4 m schr.	605	Hall Bros.	Port Blakely	1891	Wrecked Kauai Island January, 1916
Prosper	3 m schr.	241	Pershbakers Mill	Coos Bay	1892	Burned for movie August 2, 1924, in Calif.
Puako	4 m bktn.	1,084	W. A. Boole & Son	Oakland	1902	Victoria, B. C., sawdust barge 1926; afloat 1940's as Drumwall
Puritan	4 m schr.	614	Hans Reed	Port Madison	1888	Wrecked W. C. Vancouver Is. November 12, 1896
Queen	3 m schr.	277	C. G. White	San Francisco	1882	Sold Mexican 1912; still afloat 1920
Queen of the Bay	2 m schr.	107	————	Portland, Ore.	1883	Wrecked Nehalem River entrance September 11, 1887
Quickstep	bktn.	423	Hall Bros.	Port Ludlow	1876	Foundered south of Yaquina Head November 24-25, 1904
R. C. Slade	4 m schr.	673	J. Lindstrom	Aberdeen	1900	Sunk by von Luckner's Seeadler in Pacific June 17, 1917
R. K. Ham	bktn.	569	W. H. Bryant	Port Blakely	1874	Wrecked Dungeness Spit, Wn., August, 1894
R. W. Bartlett	4 m schr.	521	H. Bendixsen	Fairhaven	1891	Sold Peru 1913; afloat as Cuatro Hermanos 1929
Rebecca	2 m schr.	161	Murray	Empire City, Ore.	1875	Registry dropped 1898
Red Rock	sloop	177	H. P. Anderson	San Francisco	1904	Fate not known
Repeat	3 m schr.	455	A. M. Simpson	North Bend	1897	Sold Tahiti 1920; last voyage 1921, battered by storm, condemned
Reporter	3 m schr.	350	Hall Bros.	Port Ludlow	1876	Wrecked March 13, 1902, near Point Lobos, Calif.
Resolute	4 m schr.	684	Hitchings & Joyce	Hoquiam	1902	Converted to barge, abandoned New York 1932
Retriever	bktn.	547	Hiram Doncaster	Seabeck, Wn.	1881	Abandoned in South Pacific March 15, 1920; wreck towed to Auckland, N. Z.
Robert Cowan	brig	220	————	Sooke, B.C.	1867	Sold Hawaiian; wrecked near Honolulu February 18, 1883 as Pomare
Robert Emmett	brig	—	H. H. Luse	Empire City, Ore.	1880	Fate not known
Robert Lewers	4 m schr.	732	Hall Bros.	Port Blakely	1889	Wrecked Pachena Point, B. C., April 11, 1923
Robert Searles	4 m schr.	608	Hall Bros.	Port Blakely	1888	Abandoned off Hawaii August 24, 1913; wreck towed to Kahului, converted to Barge 2
Robert Sudden	bktn.	616	Hall Bros.	Port Blakely	1887	Wrecked Surf, Calif., June 11, 1905
Robert R. Hind	4 m schr.	564	Hay & Wright	Alameda	1899	Broken up Sydney, N. S. W., 1924
Rosalind	3 m schr.	288	Hall Bros.	Port Blakely	1883	Wrecked 3 miles north Rogue River February 18, 1890
Rosamond	4 m schr.	1,030	M. Turner	Benicia	1900	Laid up Lake Union, Seattle, 1928
Rosario	2 m schr.	148	M. Turner	San Francisco	1878	Crushed in ice July 2, 1898, serving as whaler
Roy Somers	3 m schr.	314	H. Bendixsen	Fairhaven	1891	Last afloat 1929, French registry, at Papeete
Ruby	3 m schr. (Shoal draft)	345	J. W. Dickie & Sons	Alameda	1902	Sold Mexican 1940 (fully powered)
Ruby A. Cousins	3 m schr.	192	E. Cousins	Eureka	1882	Wrecked Eagle Harbor, Kodiak Is., Alaska, March 3, 1917 as Harold Blekum
Ruth E. Godfrey	4 m schr.	597	Hall Bros.	Port Blakely	1900	Lost in the Pacific, abandoned January 10, 1912

Under shortened sail, **BARKEN-TINE MONITOR** about 1899. She was the first of her rig built on the Pacific Coast. Domingo Marcucci turned her out for John Kentfield, San Francisco, in 1862. She foundered 20 miles off the Columbia River March 24, 1901.

Stars and stripes flying the **FOUR-MASTED SCHOONER ALERT** put out for the Antipodes with a full cargo of lumber. *Photo courtesy A. O. Anderson.*

NAME	RIG	TONS	BUILDER	PLACE	DATE	ULTIMATE FATE
S. G. Wilder	bktn.	604	Hall Bros.	Port Blakely	1889	Foundered as barge off Fenwick Is., Va., July 3, 1933
S. M. Stetson	bktn.	707	H. R. & Olaf Reed	Port Madison	1874	Wrecked off Australia coast 1880
S. N. Castle	bktn.	514	Hall Bros.	Port Blakely	1886	Burned purposely at Catalina February 17, 1926 (movie ship)
S. T. Alexander	4 m schr.	779	H. Bendixsen	Fairhaven	1899	Wrecked Toku, Tonga, September 28, 1914
Sacramento	2 m schr. (built as river barge)	130	————	San Francisco	1868	Converted to schr. 1883; wrecked Coos Bay bar October 15, 1905
Sadie	3 m schr.	310	H. Bendixsen	Fairhaven	1890	Sold Philippine 1921; afloat 1929
Sailor Boy	3 m schr.	328	Paterson	South Bend, Wash.	1883	Drops from registry Honolulu 1915
St. George	2 m schr.	100	M. Turner	San Francisco	1878	Wrecked St. Paul Harbor, Alaska, April 27, 1881
Salem	4 m schr.	767	W. F. Stone & Son	San Francisco	1902	Registry dropped Mobile 1929
Salvator	4 m schr.	467	Peter Matthews	Eureka	1890	Wrecked Seldovia Bay, Alaska, 1935
Samar	4 m schr.	710	Hay & Wright	Alameda	1901	Afloat in 1952 (machine shop); shoved aground on Mexican coast
Samson	2 m schr.	217	Alexander Hay	Alameda	1890	Wrecked Point Bonita, Calif., January 4, 1895
San Buenaventura	2 m schr.	180	H. Bendixsen	Fairhaven	1876	Wrecked near Gold Beach, Ore., January 14, 1910
Santa Paula	4 m schr.	650	Bendixsen S. B. Co.	Fairhaven	1900	Burned for scrap at Hunters Pt., Calif., July 8, 1933
Sarah	2 m schr.	142	————	Utsalady, Wash.	1861	Lost in North Pacific, codfishing, 1879
Sausalito	3 m schr. (Shoal draft)	367	W. F. Stone & Son	Oakland	1903	Wrecked Waada Is., Wash., December 27, 1915
Sehome	4 m schr.	680	C. E. Sutton	New Whatcom, Wash. (Bellingham)	1900	Abandoned as barge in Florida 1937
Selina	bgtn.	349	M. Turner	San Francisco	1883	Wrecked entering Hilo Harbor 1887
Sequoia	3 m schr.	341	H. Bendixsen	Fairhaven	1890	Sold Mexican 1933
Serena Thayer	2 m schr.	206	Clark & Webster	Port Discovery, Wash.	1872	Registry dropped 1921 in California
Seven Sisters	2 m schr.	129	M. Turner	Benicia	1888	Lost Cape Espenberg, Alaska, September 1, 1908 (one report says 8/1/05)
Siberia	brig	126	M. Turner	San Francisco	1875	Sold foreign
Skagit	bktn.	506	Hiram Doncaster	Port Ludlow	1883	Wrecked near Clo-oose, B.C., October 25, 1906
Solano	4 m schr.	728	M. Turner	Benicia	1901	Wrecked 4 miles north Ocean Park, Wn., February 15, 1907
Sophia Sutherland	3 m schr.	156	A. C. McDonald	Tacoma	1889	Stranded Bailey Is., Alaska, August 31, 1900; destroyed in storm September 26
Sophie Christenson	4 m schr.	675	Hall Bros.	Port Blakely	1901	Lost off Vancouver Is. as log barge 1950's
Soquel	4 m schr.	767	W. F. Stone & Son	San Francisco	1902	Wrecked near Pachena Bay, B.C., January 22, 1909
Sotoyome	3 m schr.	—	Andrew Peterson	Albion River, Calif.	1905	Burned off Humboldt Bay December 7, 1907
Sparrow	2 m schr.	197	L. S. Allen	Oakland	1869	Destroyed at Eureka August 9, 1904
Spokane	4 m schr.	639	Hall Bros.	Port Blakely	1890	Broken up as barge at Seattle 1941
Stag Hound	2 m schr.	136	J. H. Howlett	Marshfield	1868	Listed as casualty 1884
Staghound	2 m schr.	151	A. Hay	Alameda	1890	Sold foreign same year
Stanley	3 m schr.	355	H. Bendixsen	Fairhaven	1900	Wrecked Pauloff Harbor, Sanak Is., Alaska, March 28, 1910
State of Sonora	3 m schr.	329	————	Seabeck, Wn.	1880	Drops from registry 1885
Stimson	4 m schr.	693	T. C. Reed	Ballard, Wn.	1900	Wrecked Grand Cayman, B.W.I., September 18, 1928
Stranger	2 m schr.	124	Winslow Hall	San Francisco	1869	Drops from registry 1888
Sunshine	3 m schr.	326	Holden	Marshfield	1875	Found bottom up off Cape Disappointment November 18, 1875
Susan & Kate Deming	3 m schr.	—	John G. North	San Francisco	1854	Sold on completion to British (Australia)
Susie Merrill	3 m schr.	148	T. H. Peterson	Noyo, Cal.	1866	Lost same year Mendocino coast

180

Driven up high and dry on the beach at Miami in a hurricane in 1926 is the **SCHOONER ROSE MAHONEY.** She was later scrapped on the scene. The vessel was built at Benicia, Calif., in 1918.

Stuck on Peacock Spit January 5, 1928, **SCHOONER NORTH BEND,** Captain Theodore Hansen. *Chas. Fitzpatrick photo.*

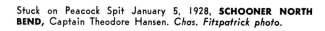

The amazing course cut by the stranded **SCHOONER NORTH BEND** is shown here in a view from Cape Disappointment looking down on Peacock Spit. The schooner made her own way across the spit to the calm waters of Baker Bay and was refloated 13 months later.
Chas. Fitzpatrick photo

NAME	RIG	TONS	BUILDER	PLACE	DATE	ULTIMATE FATE
Tahiti	bgtn.	290	M. Turner	San Francisco Bay	1881	Out of registry 1891
Tam O'Shanter	bktn.	592	A. M. Simpson	North Bend	1875	Sold Chili, renamed Antofagasta
Tamaru Tahiti	2 m schr.	145	M. Turner	Benicia	1889	For Tahitian owners
Tarawa	2 m schr.	152	Alex Hay	San Francisco	1890	Afloat Sydney, Australia, 1920
Taurus	4 m schr.	551	Pacific S. B. Co.	Marshfield	1902	Burned purposely Catalina Is. July 31, 1924 (movie ship)
Teavaroa	2 m schr.	110	M. Turner	Benicia	1892	For Tahitian owners
Thomas	brig	115	John G. North	San Francisco	1867	Out of registry 1877
Thos. P. Emigh	4 m bktn.	1,040	Tacoma S. B. Co.	Tacoma	1901	Foundered as fish barge Redondo Beach, Calif., April 20, 1932
Tidal Wave	bark	603	W. H. Bryant	Port Madison	1869	Out of registry S. F., 1909
Tolo	2 m schr.	123	Thompson	Port Ludlow	1861	Capsized off San Juan Is., Wn., February 23, 1862
Transit	4 m schr.	547	T. H. Peterson	Ballard, Wn.	1891	Wrecked in ice 5 miles S.W. of Point Barrow August 25, 1913
Tropic Bird	bktn.	347	John Kruse	North Bend	1882	Wrecked at Chamela Bay, Mexico, Jan. 10, 1907
Truckee	2 m schr.	147	Patrick Tiernan	San Francisco	1869	Out of registry 1890
Trustee	3 m schr.	280	John Kruse	North Bend	1878	Wrecked Peterson's Pt., Grays Harbor, April 24, 1886
Twilight	2 m schr.	184	Hall Bros.	Port Ludlow	1874	Still afloat 1900
Una	3 m schr.	207	Bryant	Port Blakely	1874	Last afloat 1900
Uncle John	bktn.	314	Charles Murray	Eureka	1881	Wrecked 7 miles north Carmanah Light, B. C., October 7, 1899
Uncle Sam	2 m schr.	113	T. H. Peterson	Big River, Calif.	1873	Lost Cape Foulweather, Ore., March, 1876
Undine	2 m schr. (Centerboard)	144	H. Bendixsen	Eureka	1870	Out of registry 1880
Uranus (ex SS Salinas)	3 m schr.	152	————	Built as steamer Converted to schr. 1890	1861	Laid up San Francisco 1904
Vega	3 m schr.	245	H. Bendixsen	Fairhaven	1881	Sold Peruvian 1916; afloat 1920, Callao
Venus	2 m schr.	118	Jacob Whitehouse	Point Arena	1874	Wrecked Navarro, Calif., January 25, 1881
Vesta	3 m schr.	285	M. Turner	San Francisco	1882	Wrecked near Nitinat, B. C., December 10, 1897
Viking	2 m schr.	146	H. R. Reed	Marshfield	1882	Wrecked Cape Prince of Wales, Alaska, August 7, 1904
Vine	2 m schr.	228	————	Gig Harbor, Wn.	1890	Wrecked Deering, Alaska, 1907
Virginia	4 m schr.	585	Hay & Wright	Alameda	1902	Lost off Arecibo, P. R., November 9, 1925
Volant	3 m schr.	172	H. Bendixsen	Fairhaven	1883	Wrecked Kuskokwim, Alaska, July 21, 1905
Volante	2 m schr.	125	G. L. Hobbs	North Bend	1891	Last registered 1935
Volunteer	4 m schr.	585	T. McDonald	Hoquiam	1887	Wrecked off Bodega Head, Cal., June 5, 1906
W. F. Jewett	3 m schr.	476	Middlemas & Boole	Port Ludlow	1887	Beached Magdalena Bay, Mexico, August 1928
W. H. Dimond	bktn.	390	M. Turner	San Francisco	1881	Lost Bird Is. near Unga, Alaska, February 10, 1914 (schr.)
W. H. Marston	5 m schr.	1,169	W. F. Stone & Son	San Francisco	1901	Foundered out of Mobile December 10, 1927
W. H. Meyer	2 m schr.	246	George Buchart	San Francisco	1869	Re-rigged as whaling brig; last registered 1895
W. H. Talbot	4 m schr.	816	Hall Bros.	Port Blakely	1891	Sold for breaking up in China 1925
W. J. Patterson	4 m schr.	645	J. Lindstrom	Aberdeen	1901	Broken up, Beaumont, Texas, November, 1923
W. S. Bowne	3 m schr.	421	Hall Bros.	Port Blakely	1885	Out of registry 1891
W. S. Phelps	2 m schr.	101	Olaf & H. R. Reed	Port Madison	1870	Last afloat 1900
Watson A. West	4 m schr.	818	McWhinney & Cousins	Aberdeen	1901	Wrecked San Miguel Is., Calif., February 23, 1923
Wawona	3 m schr.	468	H. Bendixsen	Fairhaven	1897	Still afloat at Seattle as museum (SOS) Inc. 1968
Web Foot	bktn.	361	A. M. Simpson	North Bend	1869	Abandoned off Tillamook Rock November 21, 1904
Wempe Bros.	4 m schr.	681	J. Lindstrom	Aberdeen	1901	Wrecked Bonilla Point, B. C., October 27, 1903
Western Belle	bktn.	275	E. & H. Cousins	Eureka	1867	Vanished on maiden voyage

Stranded amid a sea of driftwood the **SCHOONER NORTH BEND** was driven ashore on Peacock Spit at the Columbia River entrance. She stranded January 5, 1928.   *Charles Fitzpatrick photo*

Hard aground on Peacock Spit—**SCHOONER NORTH BEND** in 1928. Salvaged, she struck off Guano Rock near Coos Bay bar in September 1940 and was later allowed to drift ashore north of Cape Arago where she was eventually burned.
Chas. Fitspatrick photo

NAME	RIG	TONS	BUILDER	PLACE	DATE	ULTIMATE FATE
Western Home	2 m schr.	135	Ludwig Mortensen	Maine Prairie (Sacramento River)	1874	Wrecked north spit Coquille River November 13, 1904
Western Shore	ship (full rigged)	1,177	A. M. & R. W. Simpson, J. Kruse	North Bend	1874	Lost Duxbury Reef, Calif., July 1878
Wilbert L. Smith	4 m schr.	848	T. C. Reed	Ballard	1902	Sold French 1917; burned about 1918
Wildwood	ship (full rigged)	1,099	A. J. Westervelt	Port Madison	1871	Lost at Nushagak, Alaska, 1895
Wm. Bowden	4 m schr.	778	Hall Bros.	Port Blakely	1892	Wrecked as fish barge Redondo Beach, Calif., February 12, 1926
William Carson	4 m bktn.	890	H. Bendixsen	Fairhaven	1899	Wrecked after collision December, 1899
Wm. Nottingham	4 m schr.	1,204	T. C. Reed	Ballard	1902	Breakwater Nisqually flats, Wash., about 1946; still there 1968
William Olsen	4 m schr.	523	Hay & Wright	Alameda	1900	Wrecked Niihau Is., Hawaii, April 21, 1919
William Renton	3 m schr.	447	Hall Bros.	Port Blakely	1882	Sold Mexican about 1913
William F. Bowne	2 m schr.	136	John Kruse	Umpqua River	1864	Out of registry 1880
William F. Garms	4 m schr.	1,094	C. G. White	Everett	1901	Renamed Golden State 1913; burned in Gulf of Mexico February 17, 1922
Wm. F. Witzeman	4 m schr.	473	H. Bendixsen	Fairhaven	1887	Wrecked 4 miles north Bolinas, Calif., February 5, 1907
William G. Irwin	bgtn.	348	M. Turner	San Francisco	1881	Burned for movie Catalina May 15, 1926 (schr.)
Wm. H. Smith	4 m schr.	566	Hall Bros.	Port Blakely	1899	Laid up San Francisco 1938-1940's
Wm. H. Stevens	2 m schr.	146	James McDonald	San Francisco	1869	Out of registry 1879
William L. Beebe	3 m schr.	296	Hall Bros.	Port Ludlow	1875	Wrecked 3 miles south Cliff House, San Francisco, December 10, 1894
Willie R. Hume	4 m bktn.	665	———	North Bend	1890	Wrecked Point Santa Maria, Mexico, February, 1911
Willis A. Holden	4 m schr.	1,188	T. C. Reed	Ballard	1902	Register abandoned Florida, 1931
Winchester	2 m schr.	118	———	Prosper, Ore.	1893	Last afloat 1902
Wing & Wing	2 m schr.	141	C. G. White	San Francisco	1881	Register dropped as oil barge 1921
Winslow	4 m schr.	566	Hall Bros.	Port Blakely	1899	Sunk in Pacific by German raider Wolf June 6, 1917
Wrestler	bktn.	470	Hall Bros.	Port Ludlow	1880	Sold Nicaragua 1895; returned U. S. 1900; registry dropped 1922
York	2 m schr.	231	M. Turner	Benicia	1900	Lost same year Alaska
Z. B. Heywood	2 m schr.	107	Isaac Hall	Port Ludlow	1873	Wrecked Navarro, Calif., January, 1888
Zampa	3 m schr.	385	Hughes	Port Madison	1887	Wrecked 3 miles north Honolulu April 26, 1926

Many of the vessels in this list suffered several serious groundings from which they were salvaged—only the final fate, in most cases, is recorded. Some were fitted in latter days with auxiliary engines. The vessels built on the West Coast served as lumber carriers, sugar packets, copra carriers, general cargo vessels, lime haulers, codfishers, whalers, sealers, guano packers, and in numerous other trades, sinking even to the role of garbage barges. Most of the early windjammers that lived well into the age of steam ended their days as barges.

The **FOREST PRIDE,** right, an ex West Coast windjammer was in the unique position along with the **STEAM SCHOONER GRIFFSON** of taking part in the salvaging of the gold ship **ISLANDER.** The two vessels are seen at Green Cove, Alaska in 1934 with the **SS ISLANDER** (sunk in 1901) cradled between them after being brought up from the depths.

Ordway photo, Juneau

A disastrous fire struck the Grays Harbor Motorship Corp. shipyards May 9, 1919. Seen here at the Aberdeen yard is some of the destruction including a furiously burning hull under construction. Three other big sailing vessels building at the yard escaped damage in the $400,000 conflagration. *Jones Studio photo*

APPENDIX B

Based on the research of the late John Lyman

List of Latter Day Commercial Sailing Vessels and Auxiliary Sailing Vessels Over 100 Tons Built on the Pacific Coast — 1909-1921

(Listed by Shipyards)

WALLACE SHIPYARDS LTD., NORTH VANCOUVER, B.C.

SHIP	RIG	TONS	YEAR BUILT	FIRST FLAG	FATE
Naden	2 m schr.	100	1913	Canada	Registry dropped by 1919
Mabel Brown	5 m aux schr.	1,474	1917	Canada	Registry dropped 1925 (Norway)
Margaret Haney	5 m aux schr.	1,474	1917	Canada	Registry dropped 1921
Geraldine Wolvin	5 m aux schr.	1,472	1917	Canada	Owned in Egypt 1925
Janet Carruthers	5 m aux schr.	1,466	1917	Canada	Wrecked Jan. 22, 1919, 4 miles north Grays Harbor
Mabel Stewart	5 m aux schr.	1,472	1917	Canada	Sold Greek as Calimeris. Not afloat 1925
Marie Barnard	5 m aux schr.	1,476	1917	Canada	Cold Greek as Agapi. Afloat 1925
Jessie Norcross	5 m aux schr.	1,481	1917	Canada	Sold Alexandria, Egypt 1920's. Afloat 1925

THE WILLIAM LYALL SHIPBUILDING CO., NORTH VANCOUVER, B.C.

SHIP	RIG	TONS	YEAR BUILT	FIRST FLAG	FATE
Cap Palos	5 m aux schr.	1,468	1918	Canada	Sunk Flamborough Head, England, 1919
Cap Vincent	5 m aux schr.	1,471	1918	Canada	Registry dropped 1919
Cap Nord	5 m aux schr.	1,468	1918	Canada	Sold German 1938 (Andromeda) Schoolship
Cap Vert	5 m aux schr.	1,472	1918	Canada	Sold Italian about 1922 (renamed Isa)
Cap Horn	5 m aux schr.	1,469	1918	France	Last listed 1925. French owned
Cap Finisterre	5 m aux schr.	1,471	1918	France	Last listed 1924. French owned

CAMERON-GENOA MILLS SHIPBUILDING LTD., VICTORIA, B.C.

SHIP	RIG	TONS	YEAR BUILT	FIRST FLAG	FATE
Laurel Whalen	5 m aux schr.	1,372	1917	Canada	Registry dropped by 1925
Esquimalt	5 m aux schr.	1,373	1917	France	————————
Malahat	5 m aux schr.	1,550	1917	Canada	Afloat B.C. late 1930's
Jean Steadman	5 m aux schr.	1,577	1917	Canada	Owned in Egypt 1925
Stasia	5 m aux schr.	1,566	1917	France	Last listed 1925
Beatrice Castle	5 m aux schr.	1,566	1917	France	Last listed 1920

CHOLBERG SHIPYARD, VICTORIA, B.C.

SHIP	RIG	TONS	YEAR BUILT	FIRST FLAG	FATE
Gunn	4 m schr.	981	1919	Norway	Broken up Estonia about 1934
Vancouver (Margaret F. Sterling) (Trade Wind)	4 m schr.	988	1919	Norway U. S.	Torpedoed in Pacific 1943 as Seiki Maru (Japan)
Washington	4 m schr.	976	1919	Norway	Afloat Finland 1939, as Valborg
Sir Henry Drayton	5 m bktn.	—	1920	——	Never completed
S. F. Tolmie	5 m bktn.	1,612	1920–21	Canada	Wrecked near Victoria, B. C., 1944

THE McATEER SHIPBUILDING CO., SEATTLE, WASH.

SHIP	RIG	TONS	YEAR BUILT	FIRST FLAG	FATE
Mount Hamilton	4 m aux schr.	1,537	1918	Norway	Sold German 1924
Mount Whitney	4 m aux schr.	1,538	1919	Norway	Wrecked Carmarthen Bay 1925

NATIONAL SHIPBUILDING CO., SEATTLE, WASH.

SHIP	RIG	TONS	YEAR BUILT	FIRST FLAG	FATE
Bright	5 m schr.	2,176	1918	U. S.	Sunk in collision 1940, Chesapeake Bay
Brisk	5 m aux schr.	2,151	1918	U. S.	Burned at sea 1920

THE ELLIOTT BAY SHIPBUILDING CO., SEATTLE, WASH.

SHIP	RIG	TONS	YEAR BUILT	FIRST FLAG	FATE
Bianca	5 m schr.	2,139	1919	U. S.	Wrecked 1924 near Clallam Bay, Wn.

PUGET SOUND BRIDGE & DREDGING CO., SEATTLE, WASH.

SHIP	RIG	TONS	YEAR BUILT	FIRST FLAG	FATE
Tacoma	4 m aux schr.	1,608	1917	U. S. Norway	Foundered Tasman Sea 1922
Portland	4 m aux schr.	1,594	1917	U. S. Norway	Burned at sea 1918
Remittent	4 m aux schr.	1,616	1917	U. S. Norway	Wrecked Nicaragua 1918
Risor	4 m aux schr.	1,604	1917	U. S. Norway	Afloat Norway 1921
Barleux	4 m aux schr.	1,607	1917	France	Not afloat 1921
Douaumont	4 m aux schr.	1,608	1917	France	Not afloat 1921
Dixmude	4 m aux schr.	1,614	1917	France	Not afloat 1920
Ypres	4 m aux schr.	1,617	1918	France	Foundered near Perth Amboy, N. J., 1932
Arras	4 m aux schr.	1,617	1918	France	Afloat 1930
Peronne	4 m aux schr.	1,618	1918	France	Afloat 1930

AUXILIARY SCHOONER W. F. BURROWS about to be burned for her scrap yield at Arvid Franzen's in June 1934. She was built at the Standifer-Clarkson yard, Portland, Oregon, in 1917 for Libby, McNeill & Libby.

Ready for the torch—BARKENTINE CONQUEROR at the Arvid Franzen beach property near Picnic Point, Puget Sound, in 1947. Franzen burned scores of old wooden vessels. *Arvid Franzen photo.*

The five-masted BARKENTINE MONITOR, left, and the six-masted SCHOONER FORT LARAMIE on Puget Sound in the 1920's.

SHIP	RIG	TONS	YEAR BUILT	FIRST FLAG	FATE
THE SEABORN SHIPYARDS CO., TACOMA, WASH.					
Seaborn	5 m aux schr.	1,296	1916	U. S.	Sold German 1925 as Sierra Nevada
H. C. Hansen	5 m aux schr.	1,660	1917	Norway	————
Levi W. Ostrander	5 m schr.	1,638	1917	U. S.	Sold German 1924 as Tseng Tai
Betsy Ross	5 m schr.	1,630	1917	U. S.	Barge at Victoria, B.C., 1940's
THE BABARE MANUFACTURING CO., TACOMA, WASH.					
Else	4 m schr.	814	1916	U. S.	Registry dropped 1929
THE OLYMPIA SHIPBUILDING CO., OLYMPIA, WASH.					
Wergeland	5 m aux schr.	2,457	1917	Norway (U. S.)	Sold British, last listed 1930
General Pershing	5 m aux schr.	2,450	1918	Norway (U. S.)	Wrecked in Bahamas 1921
Korsnaes	5 m aux schr.	2,446	1918	Norway (U. S.)	Not listed 1920
MATTHEWS SHIPBUILDING CO., HOQUIAM, WASH.					
Mount Hood	4 m aux schr.	1,490	1918	Norway	Sold German 1925 as Marie Gertrude
Mount Shasta	4 m aux schr.	1,571	1918	Norway	Burned at Bremen 1935 as Comet
Vigilant (City of Alberni) (Condor)	5 m schr.	1,603	1920	U. S.	Sold Canada, then Chile; burned 1946
Undaunted	5 m schr.	2,266	1921	U. S.	Wrecked in Peru 1931
ABERDEEN SHIPBUILDING CO., ABERDEEN, WASH.					
Columbia River	5 m schr.	1,200	1916	U. S.	Wrecked Sunday Island 1921
ABERDEEN SHIPBUILDING (GRANT-SMITH-PORTER & CO.) ABERDEEN, WASH.					
Suzanne	4 m aux schr.	1,431	1918	France	Sold British 1920
Fanestrand	5 m aux schr.	2,557	1918	France	Owned Germany 1925 as Lipsia
J. H. PRICE CONSTRUCTION CO., HOUGHTON, WASH.					
Snetind	4 m aux schr.	1,501	1919	U. S.	Beached, Boston 1936
Blaatind (renamed Commodore)	4 m aux schr.	1,526	1919	U. S.	Laid up in South Africa, coal hulk 1946
MARTINOLICH YARD, DOCKTON, WASH.					
Dockton	4 m aux schr.	1,699	1918	Norway	Still afloat 1925
Ella A.	4 m schr.	1,565	1920	U. S.	Broken up Puget Sound 1930
Elinor H.	5 m schr.	1,569	1920	U. S.	Sold for scrap 1930, burned 1933
FOUNDATION CO. SHIPYARD, TACOMA, WASH.					
Gerberville	5 m aux schr.	2,032	1918	France	Laid up Brooklyn 1938
Noyon	5 m aux schr.	2,142	1918	France	————
Roye	5 m aux schr.	2,032	1918	France	————
Dannemarie	5 m aux schr.	2,022	1918	France	————
Reims	5 m aux schr.	2,142	1918	France	————
Dunkerque	5 m aux schr.	2,131	1918	France	
Thann	5 m aux schr.	2,142	1918	France	Foundered Atlantic 1926
Toul	5 m aux schr.	2,038	1918	France	
Amiens	5 m aux schr.	2,142	1918	France	————
Democratie	5 m aux schr.	2,142	1918	France	————
Vimy	5 m aux schr.	2,020	1918	France	
Fraternitie	5 m aux schr.	2,136	1918	France	Wrecked Bermuda 1919
Republique	5 m aux schr.	2,035	1918	France	
Verite	5 m aux schr.	2,142	1918	France	————
Souchez	5 m aux schr.	2,142	1918	France	————
Egalitie	5 m aux schr.	2,142	1918	France	————
Vailly (later Robin Hood)	5 m aux schr.	2,142	1918	France (U. S.)	Burned in Caribbean 1924
Justice	5 m aux schr.	2,138	1918	France	————
Givenchy	5 m aux schr.	2,031	1918	France	————
Libertie	5 m aux schr.	2,135	1918	France	————
CHILMAN SHIPYARD, HOQUIAM, WASH.					
Ady	3 m aux schr.	373	1918	Belgium	Not registered 1920
Gaby	3 m aux schr.	370	1918	Belgium	Owned Nassau 1930
GRAYS HARBOR SHIPBUILDING CO., ABERDEEN, WASH.					
Santino	5 m aux schr.	2,491	1917	U. S.	Abandoned near Nantucket 1923
Grays Harbor	5 m aux schr.	2,373	1917	U. S.	Burned in Atlantic 1918
Mount Rainier	5 m aux schr.	2,397	1917	U. S.	Burned Argentina 1921
Balestrand	5 m aux schr.	2,403	1917	U. S.	Sold Norwegian 1919
Hjeltenaes	5 m aux schr.	2,387	1917	U. S.	Sold Norwegian 1919
Marie de Ronde	5 m aux schr.	2,450	1918	U. S.	Burned off New York 1935

AUXILIARY SCHOONER GERALDINE WOLVIN silhouetted between trees as she heads to sea. She was built by the Wallace Shipyards Ltd., North Vancouver, B.C. in 1917. Her first master was Captain P. J. R. Mathieson and she was owned by the Canadian West Coast Navigation Company. She was sold to Egyptian interests at Alexandria in 1922.

Captain J. E. Shields' codfishing **SCHOONER SOPHIE CHRISTENSON** began her career as a lumber schooner in 1901.
Joe Williamson photo

SHIP	RIG	TONS	YEAR BUILT	FIRST FLAG	FATE
GRAYS HARBOR MOTORSHIP CORP., ABERDEEN, WASH.					
Forest Pride	5 m bktn.	1,600	1919	U. S.	Sold as barge 1938
Forest Dream	5 m bktn.	1,605	1919	U. S.	Burned at Stromstad 1933
Forest Friend	5 m bktn.	1,615	1919	U. S.	Hog fuel barge B. C. 1938
McEACHERN YARD, ASTORIA, OREGON					
Astoria	4 m aux schr.	1,611	1916	U. S.	Owned Canada 1932
Margaret	4 m aux schr.	1,613	1917	U. S.	Owned Germany 1930
Astri I.	4 m aux schr.	1,785	1917	Norway	Owned London 1925 as Gloria
Madrugada	4 m aux schr.	1,613	1917	Brazil-U.S.	Torpedoed 1918, Atlantic
May	4 m aux schr.	1,745	1917	U. S.	Owned Norway 1920
Pauline	4 m aux schr.	1,750	1917	Norway	Afloat 1932 in Finland as Odine
Carmen	4 m aux schr.	1,610	1917	U. S.	Owned Sweden 1920
Evelyn	4 m aux schr.	1,584	1918	U. S.	Sold Peru 1920
SOMMARSTROM BROTHERS SHIPYARD, COLUMBIA CITY, OREGON					
Kate G. Peterson	5 m bktn.	2,269	1920	U. S.	Laid up 1931, breakwater at Alameda
ST. HELENS SHIPBUILDING CO. (CHAS. R. McCORMICK), ST. HELENS, OREGON					
City of Portland	5 m aux schr.	1,791	1916	U. S.	Abandoned 1931. New York
June	3 m aux schr.	484	1916	U. S.	Registry dropped 1922
Ruby	3 m aux schr.	557	1916	U. S.	Registry dropped 1919
S. I. Allard	4 m aux schr.	1,915	1917	U. S.	Wrecked Cuba 1918
City of St. Helens	5 m aux schr.	2,135	1917	U. S.	Burned at sea 1920
Thistle	5 m schr.	1,587	1918	U. S.	Burned for scrap 1935
John W. Wells	5 m schr.	2,527	1918	U. S.	Abandoned 1931
COLUMBIA ENGINEERING WORKS, PORTLAND OREGON					
Guanacaste	4 m aux schr.	632	1917	U. S. Costa Rica	————
Tempate	4 m aux schr.	700	1917	U. S.	Wrecked Bahamas 1923
Diria	5 m schr.	1,491	1917	U. S.	Foundered off Cuba 1919
Ethel	4 m schr.	718	1917	U. S.	Foundered off Florida 1918
Chiquimula	4 m schr.	700	1917	U. S.	Broken up 1939
Elvira Stolt	4 m aux schr.	812	1918	U. S. Norway	Owned Manila 1925
Louise Bryn	4 m aux schr.	821	1918	U. S. Norway	Afloat 1921 as Pinthia
Georgette	4 m schr.	867	1918	U. S.	Dismantled Hawaii 1935
The Gardner Williams	4 m schr.	901	1918	U. S.	Owned at Mauritius 1930
Mildred	4 m aux schr.	829	1919	U. S. Norway	**Owned Buenos Aires in 1940's as Cabo Guardian**
PENINSULA SHIPBUILDING CO., PORTLAND, OREGON					
Esperanca (Alpha)	4 m aux schr.	1,601	1917	U. S. Norway	Afloat 1921, Norway
Erris (Beta)	4 m aux schr.	1,582	1917	U. S. Norway	Afloat 1921, Norway
Pechiney (Gamma)	4 m aux schr.	1,586	1917	France	Owned London 1925 as Glyndon
Adrien Bodin (L'Aiglon)	4 m aux schr.	1,622	1917	France Panama	Broken up 1933 as Monterey at Oakland
Oregon Pine (Dorothy H. Sterling later)	6 m schr.	2,526	1920	U. S.	Broken up at Adelaide 1930
Oregon Fir (Helen B. Sterling later)	6 m schr.	2,526	1920	U. S.	Broken up at Sydney, N. S. W., 1932
FOUNDATION CO. YARD, PORTLAND, OREGON					
Commandant Roisin	5 m aux schr.	2,114	1918	France	————
Capitaine Remy	5 m aux schr.	2,114	1918	France	————
Capitaine Guynemer	5 m aux schr.	2,114	1918	France	————
Lieutenant Delorme	5 m aux schr.	2,142	1918	France	————
Commandant Challes	5 m aux schr.	2,118	1918	France	————
Lieutenant Granier	5 m aux schr.	2,038	1918	France	Broken up Scotland 1924
Capitaine DeBeauchamp	5 m aux schr.	2,142	1918	France	————
Lieutenant Pegoud	5 m aux schr.	2,114	1918	France	————

Off for the codfishing grounds—the **THREE-MASTED SCHOONER JOHN A.** She is said to have been a splendid sailer and a happy ship, her life spanning six decades.

A faithful unit of the codfishing fleet, the **THREE-MASTED SCHOONER FANNY DUTARD** is seen off Kuskokwim River, Alaska, in 1920. Built as a lumber schooner at San Francisco by C. G. White in 1882 the **DUTARD** made her last commercial voyage as a codfisher in 1930, and was then converted to a barge at Seattle. *Photo courtesy W. P. McKeague.*

Full and bye—the bark **HESPER** comes home from the Antipodes.

SHIP	RIG	TONS	YEAR BUILT	FIRST FLAG	FATE
Adjutant Dorme Commandant	5 m aux schr.	2,050	1918	France	——————
DeRose	5 m aux schr.	2,142	1918	France	——————
General Baratier	5 m aux schr.	2,114	1918	France	——————
Colonel Driant	5 m aux schr.	2,117	1918	France	——————
General Serret	5 m aux schr.	2,117	1918	France	——————
Nancy	5 m schr.	2,142	1918	U. S.	Wrecked Nantasket, Mass., 1926
Aviateur DeTerlines	5 m aux schr.	2,038	1918	France	——————
Belfort	5 m aux schr.	2,142	1918	France	——————
General Galliene	5 m aux schr.	2.177	1918	France	——————
General Manoury	5 m aux schr.	2,177	1918	France	——————
Soissons	5 m aux schr.	2,117	1918	France	——————
Luneville	5 m aux schr.	2,117	1918	France	——————

THE STANDIFER-CLARKSON SHIPBUILDING CO., PORTLAND, OREGON

W. F. Burrows	4 m aux schr.	1,560	1917	U. S.	Burned, scrapped Puget Sound 1934

MONARCH SHIPBUILDING CO., PORTLAND, OREGON

Ecola	5 m schr.	2,266	1920	U. S.	Scrapped 1927, Shanghai

KRUSE & BANKS SHIPBUILDING CO., NORTH BEND, OREGON

Fort Laramie	6 m schr.	2,240	1919	U. S.	Burned for scrap Seattle 1935 (Richmond Beach)
K. V. Kruse	5 m schr.	1,728	1920	U. S.	Lost Hecate Straits 1941
North Bend	4 m schr.	981	1921	U. S.	Struck Guano Rock near Coos Bay Oct., 1940 beached, burned about 1942

ROLPH SHIPBUILDING CO., ROLPH, CALIFORNIA

Conqueror	4 m bktn.	1,395	1918	U. S.	Burned for scrap Puget Sound 1947-48
Hesperian	4 m bktn.	1,385	1918	U. S.	Broken up Antioch 1937
Annie M. Rolph	4 m bktn.	1,393	1918	U. S.	Fish barge 1944
Rolph	4 m bktn.	1,386	1919	U. S.	Broken up Antioch 1937
George U. Hind	4 m bktn.	1,389	1919	U. S.	Fish barge 1940
James Rolph III	4 m bktn.	(Not completed)	1920	U. S.	Hull broken up 1936
Thomas Rolph	4 m bktn.	(Not completed)	——	U. S.	Converted to steam schr. Viking
Phyllis Comyn (Cremona)	5 m bktn.	2,267	1920	U. S.	Broken up 1930's
Anne Comyn	5 m bktn.	2,265	1920	U. S.	Stranded; burned at Callao 1935
Russell Haviside	5 m bktn.	2,264	1920	U. S.	Scrapped 1930

HAMMOND COMPANY YARD, SAMOA, CALIFORNIA

Alicia Haviside	5 m bktn.	2,265	1919	U. S.	Scrapped 1931

BENICIA CORPORATION, BENICIA, CALIFORNIA

La Merced	4 m aux schr.	1,696	1917	U. S.	Floating cannery, hull afloat Anacortes, Wa., 1968
Oronite	4 m aux schr.	1,704	1918	U. S.	Still afloat 1935 as Aneiura
Rose Mahoney	5 m schr.	2,051	1918	U. S.	Stranded Miami 1926, scrapped
Monitor	5 m bktn.	2,247	1919	U. S.	Burned 1953, S. F. Bay

HANLON DRYDOCK & SHIPBUILDING CO., OAKLAND, CALIFORNIA

Flagstaff	5 m aux bktn.	2,101	1917	U. S.	Sold foreign 1928 (Norway)

STONE & VAN BERGEN, SAN FRANCISCO, CALIFORNIA

Neptun	2 m aux schr.	197	1909	Germany	Afloat in New Zealand as Tagua 1930's
Atlas	2 m aux schr.	209	1911	Germany	Owned in Cebu 1930's
Moana	2 m schr.	200	1912	U. S.	Owned in Tahiti 1930's

W. F. STONE YARD, OAKLAND, CALIFORNIA

Golden State	3 m schr.	353	1913	U. S.	Laid up Long Beach 1937 after movies
Hermes	2 m schr.	209	1914	Germany	Afloat as Lanikai 1940's
Mauno	2 m aux schr.	253	1917	Australia	Still afloat 1930's
Motau	2 m aux schr.	253	1917	Australia	Still afloat 1930's
Murua	2 m aux schr.	253	1917	Australia	——————
Palawan	3 m aux schr.	834	1918	U. S.	Burned off Hango 1932 (Russian flag)
Doris Crane	3 m aux schr.	351	1920	British Fanning Is.	——————

BARNES & TIBBETS, ALAMEDA, CALIFORNIA

Carolyn Frances	3 m schr.	570	1918	U. S.	Sold Russian about 1928 as Choukotka

RALPH J. CHANDLER SHIPBUILDING CO., LOS ANGELES, CALIFORNIA

Katherine Mackall (Nakoni)	5 m bktn.	2,262	1919	U. S.	Scrapped 1930, Puget Sound

192

WAWONA goes to drydock in Seattle in 1964, owned by SOS Inc.

SCHOONER WAWONA at rest at Salmon Bay in Ballard back from a Bering Sea codfishing voyage in the 1930's.

Sailing Schooner
WAWONA

Passing through the Lake Washington Ship Canal in Seattle the SCHOONER WAWONA under tow in 1964.

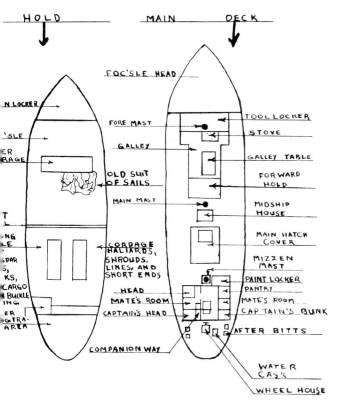

HOLD   MAIN   DECK

FOC'SLE HEAD

N LOCKER

'SLE

ER
RAGE

OLD SUIT
OF SAILS

T
L

NG
LE

SPAR
S,
KS,
CARGO
BUCKLE
ING

ER
IGERA-
AREA

FORE MAST   TOOL LOCKER
                             STOVE
GALLEY
                             GALLEY TABLE

                             FORWARD
                             HOLD
MAIN MAST
                             MIDSHIP
                             HOUSE

                             MAIN HATCH
                             COVER
CORDAGE
HALIARDS,   MIZZEN
SHROUDS,   MAST
LINES, AND
SHORT ENDS   PAINT LOCKER
                             PANTRY
HEAD
MATE'S ROOM   MATE'S ROOM
CAPTAIN'S HEAD   CAPTAIN'S BUNK

                             AFTER BITTS
COMPANION WAY

                             WATER
                             CASK

                             WHEEL HOUSE

Appendix C

WINDJAMMER VIGNETTES

The West Coast-built windjammers were all designed for specific trades. As the steam powered vessels gradually took over, many of these fine windships were forced to other trades where competition was not the pertinent factor. Perhaps more found profitable going under sail as codfishing vessels than in any other of the many trades they pursued. As has been mentioned, the potential codfishery was first recognized by Captain Matthew Turner in his brig *Timandra* as early as 1857 while he was trading in the northland as far as the Siberian coast. Actually as early as 1864, Captain Turner outfitted his command strictly for codfishing and had a successful year in the Okhotsk Sea.

It was not until several years later, however, that this business attracted the West Coast windjammers on a large scale. Some of the most colorful and interesting chapters in North Pacific maritime history revolve around these stout ships and their crews of iron men.

Among West Coast sailing vessels registering more than 100 tons, former lumber packers and sugar packets, that ultimately became codfishing vessels were the schooners *Alice, Azalea, Fortuna, General Miller, Isabel, John A., Charles R. Wilson, Maid of Orleans, Albert Meyer, John D. Spreckels, City of Papeete, S. N. Castle, Fanny Dutard, Joseph Russ, Wawona, Sophie Christenson, C. A. Thayer, Alaska, Czar, Czarina, W. H. Dimond, Glen, Ottilie Fjord, John F. Miller, Mawema, Dashing Wave, Louise, Wm. H. Smith,* the brigantine *Blakely* and others. There were also scores of West Coasters of smaller size from 45 to 90 tons engaged in the operation.

The schooner *Wawona* in 1914 came home with the largest catch of cod to that year—240,000 fish weighing 1.1 million pounds. Then, this three-masted schooner broke her own record the following year with a catch of 258,323 cod of 1,150,000 pounds. The *Wawona* under Robinson Fisheries of Anacortes went fishing every year 1914-1940, except 1921 when she was employed as a salmon packer. Her aggregate catch of 6,830,400 cod is perhaps an all-time world record.

One of the most publicized of all the events among the cod fishers involved Captain J. E. Shields and his one-man war in 1938. As master of the four-masted schooner *Sophie Christenson,* Shields became irate over foreign intervention mainly by the Japanese into the traditional Bristol Bay salmon fishing grounds. Spreading their nets across the lanes, Japanese fishermen became a threat to the huge Bristol Bay salmon packing industry and hampered the operations of the Puget Sound codfishing vessels. Gruff and direct in his approach, Shields sent a wireless message from the Bering Sea, requesting that a dozen rifles each and plenty of ammunition be sent to the schooners *Sophie Christenson* and the *Charles R. Wilson,* the latter commanded by Captain Knute Pearson.

The dispatch attracted attention all over the nation and was cabled to Japan by news agencies. A few days later another message emanated from the *Sophie Christenson.*

"Hurrah! Hurrah! All Japanese boats out of the Bering Sea. Rifles no longer needed."

The one-man war had ended, but just a couple of years later came Pearl Harbor.

One codfish shipowner who was probably in the business longer than anybody on the West Coast was Captain J. A. Matheson. He died at the age of 93 after being in the salt codfish business 76 years. He began as a hand on a North Atlantic codfishing schooner at Provincetown, Mass., at the age of 17, and four years later had his master's papers. He later acquired the fine little West Coast schooner *Fanny Dutard,* built in 1882, and operated her with great success from 1905-1930. Only when Matheson sold his charmed schooner did she go wrong. Some Ketchikan businessmen with no feeling for sailing vessels turned her into a floating brewery and the venture went "bottoms up."

During the height of her career the four-masted *Sophie Christenson* would often come to Seattle or Poulsbo, Washington, from the Bering Sea with more than 385,000 codfish salted down in her holds, a far greater load than the smaller three-masters were able to handle.

Perhaps the greatest single catches for individuals manning the dories of the codfishing vessels were set as early as 1925. In that year Danny McEachern of the schooner *Charles R. Wilson,* alone caught 20,070 fish during the

summer season. In 1933, this same rugged Newfoundlander, then second mate on the *Sophie Christenson,* took 1,051 cod in a single day, but shortly after, Ray Press set a new season's record by snagging 25,487 cod. In 1935, Billy Lund set yet another new world record with a single-day catch of 1,062 fish, according to the book Fish and Chips.

———

Some of the best known West Coast operators of windjammers in the codfishery were Pacific Marine Supply Co., San Francisco; Alaska Codfish Co., San Francisco; Union Fish Co., San Francisco; Seattle and Alaska Fish Co., Seattle; King & Winge Codfish Co., Seattle; Western Codfish Co., Seattle; Alaska Codfish Co., San Francisco; Robinson Fisheries Co., Anacortes; Blom Codfish Co., Tacoma; Northern Codfish Co., Seattle; Pacific Coast Codfish Co., Seattle and Poulsbo; Northern Fisheries Co., Anacortes; Western Canadian Fish Co., Barnet, B. C., and Canadian Fish & Cold Storage Co., Prince Rupert, B. C.

The **SCHOONER TRADE WIND** is being readied at Seattle to serve as a station ship at Kingman Atoll 1,100 miles southeast of Honolulu for Pan American Airways in the year 1937. She was formerly named **VANCOUVER** and then **MARGARET F. STERLING.** After passing to Panamanian owners she was torpedoed and sunk May 28, 1943, having passed to Japanese operation as the Seiki Maru.

Appendix D

There were so many prominent seafaring men employed as skippers of West Coast windjammers that space only permits the names of a few of the best known who were still active up to the end of the era. Capt. James Hersey, master of the barkentine *Conqueror,* who was in windjammers for fifty years; Capt. B. N. A. Krantz of the schooner *Commodore;* Capt. Charles Mellberg, of the schooner *Vigilant;* Capt. A. S. Ross of the schooner *Wilbert L. Smith;* Capt. A. J. Harris and Capt. F. D. Harris of the schooner *Lottie Bennett;* Capt. John Backland, Sr., and son Jr., of the schooner *C. S. Holmes;* Capt. J. A. Matheson, schooner *Fanny Dutard;* Capt. John Vosper, schooner *City of Alberni;* Capt. J. E. Shields and Capt. Ed Shields, schooner *Sophie Christenson* and *C. A. Thayer;* Capt. Tom Haugen, schooner *Wawona;* Capt. Louis Knaflitch, schooner *Ruby;* Capt.

Nels F. Anderson of the barkentine *Forest Pride* and *Forest Dream* etc.

* * *

Throughout the text many record passages by West Coast windjammers have been mentioned, but perhaps one of the all-time worst sailing records in the Pacific is held by the *Margaret F. Sterling,* ex *Vancouver.* In 1927 she took 49 days to sail from Cape Flattery to Honolulu. This can be compared with the all-time record passage from Honolulu to Cape Flattery by the barkentine *Thomas P. Emigh* in 1909 which was logged in 7 days, 22 hours. The average passage for sailing vessels on this route was about three weeks.

* * *

The longest passage on record from the Pacific Coast to Alaska was held by the Bendixsen-built 261 ton schooner *Jessie Minor.* She was owned by W. S. E. Jorgensen of San Francisco, and arrived at Nelson's Lagoon

Big **TUG PIONEER** tows two windjammers in from Cape Flattery to a Puget Sound lumber port. The Pioneer towed hundreds of sailing ships to and from the cape during her heyday.

June 10, 1911, after a storm-wracked, 58-day passage, during which she lost her foretopmast. Anchoring in 15 feet of water, she grounded at low tide. Her seams opened, and she became a total loss.

* * *

In November, 1917, another well known West Coast windjammer, the *Lottie Bennett,* made front page headlines when she arrived in San Francisco from Apia, after a mutiny and hand-to-hand belaying pin battle between her officers and crew.

* * *

The four-masted barkentine *Conqueror* spent almost a decade in idleness on Lake Union and at Eagle Harbor after completion of a voyage from Port Elizabeth, South Africa, January 1, 1928. Her only master was Captain James Hersey who took her over after her launching on Humboldt Bay in 1918. From Royal Roads (Victoria, B. C.) to Durban, to Callao and back to San Francisco, the *Conqueror* made the voyage in 219 days. During this passage she averaged 231 miles a day for 20 days. Mrs. Hersey traveled with her husband, and the barkentine was their home for 15 years. In 1947 the vessel was burned for her metal on upper Puget Sound.

* * *

Additional notes on Captain A. M. Simpson are supplied by Vic West of North Bend, Oregon: During the construction of the barkentine *Omega,* John Kruse, who had been in charge of Simpson's shipyard on Coos Bay for years, became ill, and died a short time later. Another man who was working at the yard completed the *Omega* for Simpson. A. M. Simpson employed Emil Heuckendorff to take charge of his yard, and he worked for Simpson till he became involved in an argument with Simpson during the construction of the schooner *Aquinaldo.* He tendered his resignation in 1899. K. V.

The **COMMODORE** departing Bellingham for Honolulu, towing out to Cape Flattery in 1931. Built for Norwegian interests as the **BLAATIND** at the J. H. Price Construction Company at Houghton on Lake Washington, the schooner had an eventful life.

Kruse was then employed to complete the schooner. Before her launching, her name was changed to *Admiral*. K. V. Kruse was with Simpson till 1901.

Simpson closed his original shipyard at his Old Town sawmill in 1902 and was able to employ Heuckendorff again to build the schooner *Alpha* at his Porter sawmill. Simpson had two sawmills on Coos Bay at that time. There had been a few small boats built at this location before the *Alpha* in 1903. That set of ways was the one that Kruse & Banks took over in 1907 when they moved from their Stove Mill yard near Marshfield, now the city of Coos Bay. Kruse & Banks was at this last location till they closed following World War II.

* * *

Some additional information on the Hall Brothers is forthcoming from Robert Fraser of Cohasset, Massachusetts.

Isaac Hall of Cohasset was born January 19, 1819, and married Catherine Hooper of Medford on January 10, 1844. They had five children. His wife died in June of 1856 at the age of 29 years and this prompted his move to California. One daughter, Catherine H. Hall, apparently went with him, for the Cohasset genealogies list her as marrying a man in California.

Richard Hall was the first of this line, landing and living at Boston. His son, James Hall, was the first in Cohasset, coming there after his marriage to a Cohasset girl in 1748. He built his house in 1750 which still stands on the east side of the Common—built of the timbers of the first Church of Cohasset (1718), removed to make way for the present First Unitarian Church built on the Common in 1747. He had a son named James Hall who was a captain-lieutenant of artillery in the Revolution and was an aide to General Washington. Most of the Halls were ship captains or shipbuilders, and sometimes both.

Isaac Hall used to work for John Bates, and commanded his fishing schooner *Frances L.*

Pleasing lines feature the fine old **BARKENTINE J. M. GRIFFITH,** circa 1882, built at Seabeck, Washington and managed by Richard Holyoke of Port Townsend. In the 1920's she was sold to Portugese interests.

This is believed to be the **SCHOONER WINSLOW.** In command of Captain Oscar Fredericks on July 28, 1907 she struck Duncan Rock near Cape Flattery, inbound from San Francisco in a storm. In a superb piece of seamanship the master kept his badly damaged vessel afloat until the tug **TACOMA** arrived the next day. Her crushed bow was repaired at Winslow.

Steele which was reputedly built at Essex. Hall sailed this schooner around Cape Horn to California, at an unrecorded date, where he lived the rest of his life. Hall built the schooners *Peerless* in 1861 and the *Morning Star* in 1866 for John Bates.

* * *

Perhaps the greatest literary hoax of all time revolved around one of the West Coast-built windjammers—the schooner *Minnie A. Caine.* It was immortalized in the best-selling book *Cradle of the Deep,* reputedly the true story of the author, Joan Lowell.

Incidently Helen Joan Wagner, Joan Lowell's real name, died in Brazil in November, 1967, but her book lives on. She was the daughter of Captain Nicholas Wagner, who was actually master of the *Minnie A. Caine.*

In the book *Cradle of the Deep,* Miss Lowell told about her rugged experiences as the only "woman-thing" aboard from the time she was 11 months old until she reached 17. It was a rip-roaring adventure tale and immediately zoomed into the best seller lists, became a Book

of the Month Club selection, and was hailed as one of the literary sensations of the day.

Part of its popularity possibly was due to the uninhibited use of salty cuss words, plus several mildly sexy passages. It was published in 1929 and in its day was considered rather controversial. The book concludes with the hair-raising account of a fire on board during which the schooner burned to the water's edge and sank. It relates how Joan, her father and the crew (who affectionately called her "skipper") managed to swim three miles through icy waters to the safety of a lightship. After that, the heart-broken captain abandoned the sea forever.

So authentically was the book written that Joan must have spent countless hours listening to her dad's experiences, and the jargon of those who sailed before the mast on his vessel.

But, as the sale of the book soared, mayhem broke loose.

Neighbors of the Wagners in San Francisco's East Bay area came out indignantly claiming that the book was so much bilge. They were backed up by records showing that Joan, who maintained her only education was received

199

from papa and the sailors on the high seas, actually had attended grammar, junior high and high school in Berkeley.

Less than a month after the book was published, a newspaperman blew the whistle on the book, when he reported the good ship *Minnie A. Caine* was moored to a dock at Oakland.

The reputed fire aboard had actually occurred in 1917, as stated in the book, but it broke out while the schooner was discharging lumber at Adelaide, Australia, and the crew had merely walked ashore via the gangplank. Moreover, the vessel had not burned to the water's edge, nor had it sunk. The *Minnie A. Caine* was repaired, and Captain Wagner, far from giving up his profession, had brought her back to San Francisco Bay.

The Book of the Month Club began advising its subscribers that they could have their money back, but the growing publicity placed the book even more in demand.

In actuality, the *Minnie A. Caine* almost ended her career before it got started. Shortly after her completion at the Moran yard in Seattle, in 1900, she ran into her first big trouble. While being towed to sea by the tug *Magic* in December, 1901, she encountered a devastating snow blizzard which slammed giant waves into the two vessels and snapped the towline. The *Caine* was swept hard aground on Smith Island, and the tug ran for Port Townsend.

At first, it was feared the schooner might be a total loss. She was hanging on a ledge within a hop, skip and jump of Smith Island Lighthouse. It took a crew of 40 men until the following May to get the schooner afloat again. Three times she was raised on temporary ways but each time storms arose to destroy the work.

Finally, in May, the tug *Tyee* was called in at flood tide and the schooner was refloated and later repaired. The novel salvage job was handled by the schooner's builder, Robert Moran, with assists from George Monk and the owner, Captain E. E. Caine.

The expose about the book inspired some hilarious spoofs of the incident but did little to dispel the original work.

Captain Wagner once was master of the San Francisco museum ship *Balclutha*. He had earned that position by going to Alaska with a salvage crew in 1905 and refloating the ship—run on a reef by another skipper the year before. The awful Alaska ship tragedy described in *Cradle of the Deep* was actually based on the loss of the bark *Star of Bengal*, wrecked on Coronation Island September 20, 1908, and Captain Wagner was master of that vessel in which 111 persons lost their lives. Captain Wagner was among the 27 survivors. Of those who died only 15 were Caucasians, the others being Oriental cannery hands. Captain Wagner actually grew very bitter over the tragedy, charging cowardice on the part of tugboat captains who, he claimed to his dying day, could have saved his vessel. Captain Wagner's license was suspended but this was later ruled unjustified in San Francisco.

The "wreck" of the *Cradle of the Deep* didn't

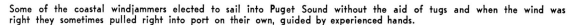
Some of the coastal windjammers elected to sail into Puget Sound without the aid of tugs and when the wind was right they sometimes pulled right into port on their own, guided by experienced hands.

shake Joan. She went on to be a newspaper reporter in Boston, write another book, marry twice and even play a small movie role with Charlie Chaplin.

* * *

One of the strangest events in West Coast windjammer annals occurred in the fall of 1916, and involved the barkentine *J. M. Griffith.*

With her arrival at San Francisco on November 27, 1916, from Sydney, Australia, with a cargo of copra, her skipper recounted a strange tale of storm and fire at sea and the unexpected salvation from destruction when two elements combated each other. Early in the voyage, the *Griffith* ran into a storm which shattered her lifeboats. Captain Griffith decided to start the donkey engine in the event it was needed for the pumps. He sent the second mate, Robert Monroe, into the donkey house on the main deck with a lighted lantern. For some unexplained reason an explosion followed. It set fire to Monroe's clothing and ultimately to the deckhouse. The crew rolled the mate on the deck and tore his blazing clothes from him. He suffered only minor burns. The vessel was afire with no means of putting it out. Then came the unexpected. A giant wave lashed by the driving

Old anchor brought to surface by Walter McCray, commercial diver, off Point Wilson, near Port Townsend, may have been off old West Coast windjammer. It was recovered in 1947.

wind, swept over the barkentine, the blazing donkey house went overboard and the fire was extinguished. *Courtesy A. O. Anderson.*

* * *

Much has been written of the famous "race" between the schooner *Commodore*, Captain B. N. A. Krantz, and the schooner *Vigilant*, Captain Charles Mellberg, in 1931, between Honolulu and Cape Flattery. The four-masted *Commodore* was owned by Lewers & Cooke of Honolulu and the five-masted *Vigilant* by the City Mill Co. of Honolulu. These two vessels were generally recognized as the last of a once great fleet of West Coast-built windjammers.

Though it was never really a race, the press played it up as such and it got the attention of the world, inasmuch as the contest marked the end of an era.

The actual story follows, as told in the words of the first mate of the schooner *Commodore.*

By JOHN WAHLBORG
(First mate, schooner *Commodore* 1931-32)

"On the trip in question (the so-called race) we came up from Honolulu to Cape Flattery on the rather long passage of 32 days. We signalled for a towboat and the tug *Goliah* of the Puget Sound Tug & Barge Company came out to pick us up. We were about 10 miles from the Cape when we took in our sails and started to take the towline aboard. In paying the towline out, the tug's mate was injured and another man took charge of the work. The towline was a heavy steel cable, but when the tug took a strain on it, it parted, due to some mishap. As it would have taken us two or three hours to haul the line in, using tackles, the master of the tug returned to port with the injured mate. At this time there was a blow coming up.

"This left us on our own, with about 1,500

One of the smaller two-masted commercial schooners built by Captain Matthew Turner at Benicia was the 66 ton **PORTIA** turned out in 1882. She is seen here a total wreck about 1899 at Stewarts Point, California.

feet of 2-inch diameter steel cable hanging straight up and down, so we set a few sails, enough to heave her to, and started to haul it in. Another towboat, the *Roosevelt,* was lying in Neah Bay, just inside Cape Flattery, so we sent a message to him, to come out to pick us up, which he did. So at ten o'clock that night we were again picked up and headed for the Cape.

"It was the 22nd of December, two days before Christmas, 1931, and everybody was happy in the anticipation of spending the holidays at home; but by now it had started to blow in earnest and by midnight it was blowing a strong gale out of the southeast and a heavy sea running, so the *Roosevelt* had all she could do to hold us against the gale. At two o'clock in the morning of the 23rd, the hawser parted. It parted in our chock this time, so at least we

didn't have to haul in another towline. The tug made a couple of heroic attempts to get connection again, but it was impossible for the two ships to get close enough together to get a line on board in that heavy sea, so she finally gave it up, and ran for safety.

"We were drifting rapidly towards Vancouver Island, and realizing that we were on our own and that if we wanted to keep from going on the rocks of that famous "Graveyard of the Pacific," we would have to do some tall sailing and act quickly. We reefed and set as many sails as she possibly could stand, and by sheer force managed to head her a little out to sea; but it was a heartbreaking as well as a backbreaking job, one sail after another would blow to pieces. Another would be gotten out of the sail locker, bent, reefed and set; and so it kept on.

One of the sleekest two-masted schooners ever seen in the Pacific Northwest was the Columbia River pilot **SCHOONER JOSEPH PULITZER.** Named for her first owner, publisher of the *New York Times,* the gaff rigged schooner yacht built at Essex, Massachusetts in 1894, was 78 feet in length with a beam of 22 feet. Later serving as a New York pilot schooner, she was reputed to be the fastest of her breed. Columbia River bar pilot, Captain Peter C. Cordiner, purchased her in 1898 for the newly formed pilots association. She arrived at Astoria in 1899 (as pictured) in command of Captain H.A. Harvey and was licensed for both Oregon and Washington pilot service. Purchased by the Port of Portland in 1909 she was fitted with an 80 horsepower gas engine for continued bar pilot service. Converted to power propulsion exclusively in 1920, she served as a mail boat on the Seward-Aleutian Island run and was wrecked at Aniakchak, Alaska, December, 18, 1920. Courtesy Columbia River Maritime Museum.

Remains of the **TWO-MASTED SCHOONER JENNIE THELIN,** built in 1869. As the **CARMANCITA** she was wrecked near Punta Maria, Baja, Mexico in 1912. Her timbers here protrude from the sands in 1982. Photo courtesy Dr. T.C. Jones, M.D. of Laguna Beach, CA.

With two million feet of lumber aboard, five-masted **SCHOONER VIGILANT** puts out for Honolulu from Puget Sound in 1930's.

"Christmas came and went, and so did New Year's, and still no letup. Once in a while it would ease up to a dead calm for an hour or so, and the ship would nearly roll over in the heavy swell. Then the gale would come down on us again as strong as ever; one thing, we had many spare sails and lots of good rope and gear and best of all, we had a crew of real old-time sailors, men, every one over fifty years of age; Oscar Swenson was 72. Just as an illustration, one night the outer jib sheet carried away, the inner jib had blown away earlier in the night and as sails had to be carried on, we had set the outer jib. When the sheet broke, everyone knew that the sail had to come down in a hurry in order to save it from slatting to pieces; no order was given, and none was necessary. The men ran for the downhaul, and I for the halyard. When the sail was hauled down, it still had to be made fast. In the clew of the sail was a chain pennant about twelve feet long and in the end of that was a hardwood block, weighing about 20 pounds; this was dancing around like a toy balloon and the ship was diving the jib-boom under in the heavy seas. I have always made it a practice not to send anybody where I wouldn't go myself, so I hesitated for a moment; but hardly was the downhaul made fast before three of these old men started out on that jib-boom,

without being told, cursing a blue streak as they went. But they got the sail fast, a new sheet was rove and the sail set again.

"What made things worse, or more interesting, if you please, another schooner, the *Vigilant,* was coming up from Honolulu at the same time, and (as we found out later), one of the Seattle newspapers made it out to be a race. Every day they had the front page all plastered up with news of the progress of the race and they had the whole country hot and bothered about it. My sister sent me a clipping which she had cut out of her little neighborhood paper back in New Jersey somewhere, telling all about it. One day the *Commodore* would be ahead, the next day the *Vigilant* and so on; they had the public seeing two ships racing neck and neck you might say, with their captains standing at the taffrails, or at the wheel as they do in the movies, shaking their fists and shouting defiance to one another. Nothing, of course, was further from the facts. The *Vigilant* left Honolulu a week after we did, and was a thousand miles behind us when we were first at the Cape; but the same gale that kept us fighting for our lives to keep off the rocks of Vancouver Island, was bringing her up from the southwest at a good clip. She arrived at the Cape, was picked up by a tug and towed into Eagle Harbor and she was declared the

Note seaman on mizzen shrouds on **BARKENTINE MARY WINKELMAN.** Hiram Doncaster built this old lumber drougher at Seabeck, Washington in 1881. She was lost near Pago Pago in 1923.

winner, while we were being driven further and further away to the northwest with all our sails in rags and everyone exhausted from loss of rest and sleep.

"Eventually the gale subsided and we managed somehow to get back to within a hundred miles of Cape Flattery where the *Goliah* again came out with a brand new hawser and picked us up, this time without mishap. They towed us into Bellingham, 46 days from Honolulu, and we had lost the race; but we were made out to be cheerful losers and were almost as popular as the winners. Then some businessman's organization in Bellingham gave a banquet and invited our captain as an honor guest, and of course he was expected to tell them all about it. But it so happened that the Seattle paper gave a blowout in Seattle on the same night, and the two captains were invited there, the winner to be presented with a gold watch, and the loser with a pair of binoculars. Our skipper went to Seattle, so when a car came down to the ship that evening in Bellingham, to take him uptown, they were told that he had gone to Seattle. They plainly showed their disappointment, and returned uptown. In about 15 minutes they came tearing back. It seemed they had gotten into a huddle somewhere and decided that a sort of a second fiddle would be better than no music at all, so I had been invited to take his place. I told them that I couldn't

possibly think of anything to say on such short notice, that I had already eaten my supper, and wanted to go to a movie; but all my protests were of no avail. I just had to come, to save the day, and so, against my better judgment, I went. When the dishes had been cleared away, the toastmaster got up to introduce the principal speaker. He spoke at length of the sporting instinct of the American people and how everybody just loved a good race and how they were to listen to a man with years of experience in sailing ships who had taken part in many ocean races and he was now to tell about this great race that had just been run. Of course the toastmaster had made up all this for introducing the captain and he was not going to let a little thing like substituting a mate for a skipper interfere with his plans. That introduction was a masterpiece. As for me, I was looking around for a trap door somewhere, through which I could nicely slide out of the picture. Disagreeable as it was out along Vancouver Island, I preferred to be there, and I was wishing I had that toastmaster along with me, just to try out his sporting instinct. When I finally got the floor, I proved to be an awful disappointment. I told them that the race was a lot of baloney gotten up by a Seattle newspaper and that the experience we had had, while it was sort of an overdose of it, it was not all together unusual in the life of a sailing ship sailor, and the evening naturally turned out to be a perfect flop."

* * *

Bald-headed schooners became very popular on the West Coast with operators who had vessels engaged in the lumber business. They were both economical and efficient to operate and in many cases proved every bit as efficient as the topsail schooners. The simplicity of handling them and their splendid performance in the hazardous coastwise trades made them the most sought after windships of their era, and most of the best known shipbuilders on the West Coast constructed them. The major builders of the bald-headed schooners included H. R. Reed, Charles Fulton, T. C. Reed, Thomas McDonald, a Mr. Hughes, Lindstrom Shipbuilding Co., and George H. Hitchings, all at Washington ports; Pacific Shipbuilding Co., John Heuckendorff and Simpson Lumber Co. at Oregon ports, and Frank Stone, Peter Matthews, H. D. Bendixsen and Bendixsen Shipbuilding Co. at California ports.

The two last survivors of the near one thousand pint-sized to large-size windjammers built on the West Coast are both bald-headed schooners—the *Wawona* and the *C. A. Thayer.* The first bald-header was the rather unorthodox five-masted schooner *Louis,* built in 1888 and commanded at one time by the well-remembered Capt. Ralph E. "Matt" Peasley of Aberdeen, whose name is kept alive by Peter B.

Kyne's Cappy Ricks novels. The last baldheader was the schooner *Oregon,* built by Heuckendorff at Prosper, Oregon, in 1905.

* * *

The vessel which served as the inspiration for the schooner *Ghost* in Jack London's immortal novel, *The Sea Wolf,* was the threemasted schooner *Sophia Sutherland* on which London was once part of the crew when the vessel was engaged as a sealing vessel, San Francisco to Alaska. Built in Tacoma in 1889 the vessel was lost at Bailey Island, Alaska in 1900. Her builder was A. C. McDonald.

* * *

The barkentines *Makaweli* and *Aurora* made historic voyages back in 1915 when they both departed Sydney, Australia, on October 8 at the same hour and reached Cape Flattery at the same time on December 14, a distance of 9,000 miles. For 21 days after leaving Sydney, the vessels were so close together that the captains would converse. Captain Nielson of the *Makaweli* and Mrs. Nielson would take dinner one day with Captain Alf Hansen of the *Aurora,* and the following day the entertainment would be reversed.

"After weeks of this, the weather became brisker and the vessels parted company. For 48 days they did not sight each other until they reached Cape Flattery. The vessels were taken in tow the same hour, and the voyage stands as a record as being undoubtedly the most even

Wooden shipbuilding and repairs were carried on at a feverish pace at the Lake Washington Shipyards, at Houghton in the early 1920's. One of the latter day windjammers in for repairs is seen at far right—the five topmast **SCHOONER BIANCA.** This vessel was lost a few months after this photo was taken while returning from Alaska with canned salmon.
Courtesy Marine Digest

race ever sailed over a course so great in length across the Pacific."

Courtesy A. O. Anderson,
Washington, D.C.

* * *

The auxiliary four-masted schooner *Mount Shasta* built by the Matthews yard at Hoquiam in 1918 had somewhat of an unusual career. After a few years under Norwegian registry she became the German flag *Comet.* In 1925 she was purchased by the famous Count Felix von Luckner and converted to a cruising yacht. Under his ownership she carried in turn the names *Seeadler, Comet, Vaterland* and *Mopelia,* mostly for the Count's famous adventure with the square-rigger (raider) *Seeadler,* during World War I. The *Mount Shasta* was destroyed by fire at Bremen in 1935.

* * *

There were many hardy characters among the windship hands, but perhaps one of the most rugged was "Contrary Gus." The schooner *John F. Miller* was engaged in a salvage operation trying to refloat the schooner *Glen* ashore in Unimak Pass, Alaska. On January 8, 1908, the *Miller,* too, was blown ashore. A rescue party sent out from Eagle Harbor found ten of the crew frozen to death, and only one man, "Contrary Gus," still alive. He was frozen to two dead men, from whom he had to be separated with axes. Gus was carefully thawed out and later went back to work on another vessel.

* * *

The first sailing vessel built on the Pacific Coast to be rigged as a three-masted schooner, was the Susan and Kate Deming, built by John G. North at San Francisco in 1854. Her builder sank all he owned in her, $28,000, and he has recorded that she was sold by her master to the British government in Australia to be used as a dispatch boat across the Tasman Sea, the skipper then skipping with the money.

Venerable trading **SCHOONER RUBY** at Seattle loaded with supplies for Alaska. The 345 ton vessel from 1914 traded to the Kuskokwim River and other northern areas of Alaska following coastwise lumber service out of Bandon. The schooner was fitted with a 140 horsepower gas engine and was used in conjunction with Alaska fisheries operations until 1936. In 1940 she was sold to Mexican interests for use as a cannery tender in Baja California under ownership of Abelardo Rodriguez and converted to a motor vessel. She was originally built in 1902.   *R. E. Mackay collection.*

Note the long bowsprit on the **SCHOONER BEULAH,** berthed at San Francisco, her homeport. She was built there in 1882 by the Dickie Brothers for Joseph Knowland. Starting out as a lumber drougher she ended her days as a codfishing vessel.
—*Courtesy San Francisco Maritime Museum*

J. H. Baxter was the first owner of the **SCHOONER ALBERT MEYER,** turned out by Hans Bendixsen in 1896. In 1912 she was under the Canadian flag but returned to U. S. registry in 1927. She was wrecked on the Florida Keys in 1927.

The rough, tough exterior of the men who sailed before the mast hardly matched the sheer beauty of a schooner becalmed on a still sea. Here is pictured the Hall Brothers' four-masted schooner **BALBOA.** She met her demise, under management of G. E. Billings, San Francisco, when she was totally wrecked at the entrance to Grays Harbor inbound from Callao, December 1, 1913.

The **SCHOONER C. A. THAYER** puts to sea on her last voyage in September 1957, under command of Capt. A. F. Raynaud, headed for San Francisco to become a museum ship. The Thayer dating from 1895 has since been completely renovated to her original splendor, and has been visited by thousands of tourists and citizens at San Francisco.

New masts stepped in 1957, the **SCHOONER C. A. THAYER** awaits a new bowsprit at the old shipyard at Winslow on Bainbridge Island, prior to her final voyage to San Francisco.

Laden down with poles at Everett, Washington—Hall Brothers' four-masted schooner **BAINBRIDGE,** foreground (note house flag), and off her starboard quarter, the Hind Rolph schooner **ROBERT R. HIND,** both preparing to sail for the fast-growing San Pedro, California. *Seeley photo*

New touch on an old stern—**C. A. THAYER** repainted at Winslow, in 1957, after purchase by the State of California for the San Francisco Maritime Museum fleet.

A rare sight—two ancient wooden-stocked anchors hang from the hawse pipes of the **BARKENTINE CONQUEROR.** The anchors outdated the **CONQUEROR** by many years having been purloined from another aging windjammer on Puget Sound or in San Francisco. *Photo courtesy Gordon Jones.*

Appendix E

Commercial sailing vessels of the Pacific Coast that were engaged in the lumber trade on the redwood coast of California often referred to as Redwood Coast schooners, or doghole schooners. The list is based on the research of Walter A. Jackson, author of the book, *The Doghole Schooners,* and the late marine historian Carl Christensen among others. Listed alphabetically, the final fate of each vessel is given when known.

A.F. Jordan, schooner, 181 tons, wrecked Cuffey's Cove, California, 1878

Abbie, schooner, 146 tons, built at Fairhaven, California, 1878

Abraham Lincoln, schooner, 66 tons, wrecked Stewarts Point, California, 1879

Acadia, schooner, wrecked Trinidad, California, March 2, 1861

Active, schooner, 185 tons, wrecked 22 miles south of Cape Mendicino, June 5, 1870

Ada May, schooner, 84 tons, wrecked Mustard Point, Sonoma County, October 27, 1880

Adelaide, schooner, 130 tons, built San Francisco 1883, wrecked New Haven, California, August 2, 1889

Agnes Nicolaisen, schooner, 68 tons, built San Francisco, 1876, wrecked Little River, California, August 23, 1886

Ajax, schooner, 74 tons, wrecked Shelter Cove, California, September 18, 1890

Albert and Edward, schooner, 96 tons, turned turtle, Humboldt Bay, August 16, 1876, with the loss of five crewmen

Albert Walker, schooner, wrecked off Point Reyes, California, December 7, 1888

Albion, schooner, 79 tons, built San Francisco, 1886

Alcyona, schooner, foundered in Noyo Harbor, California, January, 1863

Alfred, schooner, 96 tons, wrecked Mendocino, California, January 20, 1883

Alice Kimball, schooner, 107 tons, built Little River, California, 1874, wrecked Siuslaw River bar, Oregon, October 12, 1904

Amanda Agar, schooner, 110 tons, built San Francisco, 1886, wrecked Gold Bluffs, California, December 16, 1871

America, schooner, 39 tons, wrecked at Crescent City, California, June 24, 1853

American Boy, schooner 183 tons, built at Seabeck, Washington, 1882

American Girl, schooner, 225 tons, built Port Ludlow, Washington, 1875, lost off west coast Vancouver Island, November, 1899

Amethyst, schooner, 74 tons, built Benicia, California, 1883, Lost all hands (7) Coos Bay to S.F.

Anna G., schooner, 149 tons, built Port Ludlow, Washington, 1874, Salvaged after wreck at Humboldt Bay, 1875.

Annie, schooner, 38 tons, wrecked north entrance Point Arena Harbor, CA, 1874

Annie Hermine, scow schooner, 70 tons, declared wreck at Port Blakeley, Washington, 1886

Annie Stoeffer, schooner, 119 tons, built Marshfield, Oregon, 1870, wrecked Caspar, California, October 11, 1879

Annie Stoeffer, (2) scow schooner, 72 tons

Antelope, schooner 123 tons, built Benicia, California, 1887, wrecked Nehalem bar, Oregon, September 30, 1907

Aoelus, schooner, wrecked Humboldt bar, California, January 28, 1863

Arago, brig-schooner, 185 tons built North Bend, Oregon, 1859, broken up 1905

Archie and Fontie, schooner, 64 tons, built Benicia, 1890, wrecked Fort Ross, California, March 31, 1902

Argonaut, schooner, built San Francisco, 1880

Arispe, schooner, wrecked Haven's Anchorage, California, May 23, 1854

Ariziba, schooner, 69 tons, built in 1870's

Arizona, schooner, 85 tons, wrecked at Bridgeport, California, February 21, 1876, all hands (5) drowned

Artful Dodger, schooner 53 tons

Arthur I, schooner, 129 tons, built San Francisco, 1889, wrecked Iversen's Landing, California, 1898

Ashme, schooner, wrecked Gold Bluff, Klamath River, California, December 16, 1871

Aurora, schooner, 193 tons, built Eureka 1873, abandoned off Cape Flattery, 1886

B.H. Lee, schooner, 88 tons, wrecked Cuffey's Cove, California, January 6, 1878

B.H. Ramsdell, schooner, 134 tons, built San Francisco, 1866, wrecked Kapaa, Hawaii, July 10, 1879

Ballard, schooner, wrecked north Mendocino Coast, January 22, 1872

Barbara, schooner, built at Fairhaven, California, 1887

Barbara (2), schooner, 113 tons, built at Little River, California, 1887, wrecked Point Arena, California, January 24, 1901

Barbara Hernster, schooner, 148 tons, built at Eureka, 1887 (later fitted with auxiliary power; survived 4 strandings)

Barbara Johnson, schooner, built in California

Bender Bros., schooner, 84 tons, built San Francisco, 1889 (later fitted with engine; last used in Alaska as cannery)

Bertha Dolbeer, schooner, 242 tons, built Fairhaven, California, 1881, wrecked Point Gorda, California, November 3, 1918

Bertie Minor, schooner, 273 tons, built at Fairhaven, California, 1884

Berwick, schooner, 100 tons, built Benicia, 1887, wrecked Siuslaw River bar, Oregon, March 3, 1908 (fitted with engine)

Bessie Verding, schooner, 73 tons, built at San Francisco, 1876, wrecked Point Arena, September 12, 1888

Bessie K., power schooner, 98 tons, built at Alameda, California, 1893, found capsized off Cape Blanco, Oregon, February, 1907, all hands lost (7)

Bettie Danielson, scow schooner, 85 tons, wrecked Iversen's Landing, California, 1903

Big River, schooner, 160 tons, built West Seattle, 1872, wrecked Grays Harbor entrance, Washington, January, 1872

Bill the Butcher, schooner, 82 tons, built in San Francisco, 1871, wrecked Bowens Landing, California, June 15, 1893

Bobolink, schooner, 170 tons, built Oakland, California, 1868, wrecked Umpqua River bar, Oregon, 1873, salvaged, wrecked Mendocino Bay, March 22, 1898

Bonanza, schooner, 135 tons, built San Francisco, 1875, crushed in ice Hershel Island, Alaska, August 13, 1905

Brescot, schooner

Brilliant, schooner, 123 tons

C.H. Merithew, schooner, 95 tons, built Maine Prairie, California, 1875, wrecked Westport, California, June 14, 1887

C.T. Hill, schooner, 140 tons, built San Francisco, 1889, survived many strandings

Cabot, brig, wrecked Mendocino, California, November 10, 1865, all hands (6) drowned, plus 6 others on shore trying to assist

California, schooner, 98 tons, wrecked Albion, California, May 19, 1897, after having survived two other strandings in same place

California, schooner, 119 tons, built San Francisco, 1869, wrecked Bowen's Landing, January 22, 1880

California, schooner, wrecked at Pigeon Point, California, date unknown

Canute, schooner, 118 tons, built San Francisco, 1882, abandoned 1927

Caroline, schooner, 80 tons, wrecked Albion, California, California March 24, 1884

Caroline Dixon, schooner, 48 tons, built San Francisco, 1878

Caroline Medan, schooner, 73 tons, wrecked Russian Gulch, Mendocino County, California, October 24, 1887

Caroline Mills, schooner, 48 tons

Carrier Dove, schooner, 54 tons, built San Francisco, 1864

Cassie Hayward, schooner, 197 tons, built Port Blakely, Washington, 1875

Cecil, schooner, 77 tons

Centennial, schooner, wrecked Humboldt Bay bar, April 1, 1877, (2 lives lost)

Champion, schooner, 55 tons, built San Francisco, 1867, wrecked Albion, California, May 19, 1897

Charles and Edward, schooner, wrecked Point Arena, California, 1858

Charles G. Wilson, 59 tons, built San Francisco, 1875

Charles Hanson, schooner, 192 tons, built Eureka, last in Alaska, 1900

Charles T. Winslow, schooner, 55 tons, built San Francisco, 1870

Charlotte, schooner, 37 tons, built Point Arena 1861, wrecked Fish Rock, California, March 26, 1889

Chetco, schooner, 85 tons, built Benicia, 1887 (fitted with gas engine) burned Summerland, California, February 19, 1918

Christina Steffins, schooner, 70 tons, built Eureka, 1876, wrecked Timber Cove, California, April 20, 1880

City of Napa, schooner, 63 tons, wrecked Cape Blanco, Oregon, October 6, 1884

City of San Diego, schooner, 61 tons, built San Francisco, 1881

Coaster, schooner

Co-Chief, schooner, 69 tons, wrecked Fish Rock, California, 1865

Columbia, schooner, 61 tons, built San Francisco, 1865

Concordia, schooner, 110 tons, burned Humboldt Bay, April 27, 1917

Confianza, schooner, 88 tons, built Benecia, California, 1887

Constantine, schooner, wrecked Cuffey's Cove, California, November, 1862

Coquelle, schooner, 103 tons, built Coquille, Oregon (later fitted with gas engine) abandoned off California coast, May 21, 1923, drifted to Bridgeport, California

Cora, schooner, 105 tons, built Port Orchard, Washington, 1867, wrecked Caspar, California, April 12, 1884

Corinthian, power schooner, 94 tons, wrecked near Humboldt Bay, June 11, 1906 (12 crewmen drowned)

Cuffey's Cove, schooner, wrecked Cuffey's Cove, CA, 1861

D.S. Williams, schooner, 298 tons

D.W. Tietzen, schooner, 64 tons, built Eureka, 1879, wrecked Bodega Bay, CA, Nov. 20, 1900

Dashaway, schooner, wrecked off California coast, hull drifted ashore at Big Flat, Jan. 3, 1865 (14 hands perished)

Dashing Wave, schooner, 148 tons, built Eureka, 1887, crushed in Bering Sea ice, April 16, 1891

Dauntless, schooner, wrecked Klamath River bar, CA, April 20, 1894 (salvaged)

David and Edward, schooner

David and Nettie, schooner, 69 tons, built Eureka, 1876, wrecked Cuffey's Cove, CA, Dec. 22, 1880

Davisson, schooner, wrecked Iversens Landing, CA, March 31, 1903

Dawn, schooner, wrecked five miles north of Trinidad Head, CA, Aug. 15, 1903

Del Norte, schooner, 100 tons, built Benicia, 1887, wrecked in collision off Point Gorda, CA, 1905

Don Lendro, schooner, 86 tons, wrecked south side Little River harbor, CA, 1883

Donna Marie, schooner, wrecked near Cape Mendocino, CA, May 23, 1854

E. Buckley, schooner, wrecked Point Arena, CA, 1862

E. J. McKinnon, schooner, 67 tons

Edith, schooner, 96 tons, built San Francisco, 1875, wrecked near Bellingham, WA, May 1889

Eden, schooner, 43 tons, built 1860's

Edward Park, schooner, 147 tons, built Eureka, 1877, abandoned June 6, 1899, 85 miles WNW of San Francisco

Electra, schooner, 93 tons, built Little River, CA, 1875

Eliza Miller, schooner, 156 tons, last registered 1900

Ella Florence, schooner, 67 tons, wrecked Mendocino, CA, March 1872

Ellen Adelia, schooner, 53 tons, built San Francisco, 1864, foundered off Point Reyes, CA, Aug. 1884 (one drowned)

Elnorah, schooner, 144 tons, built Benton, OR, 1871, in collision off Cape Mendocino, Oct. 10, 1897, drifted ashore broke up

Elsie Iversen, schooner, 62 tons, wrecked Point Arena, CA, 1872

Elsie Iversen, schooner, 76 tons, built Whitesboro, CA, 1884, wrecked Point Arena, Dec. 7, 1886

Elsie Iversen, schooner, 122 tons, built Benicia, CA, 1887

Elvenia, schooner, 148 tons, built Fairhaven, CA, 1872, stranded Caspar, CA, April 4, 1897 (towed to S.F.)

Emily, schooner, 58 tons, wrecked south spit Coos Bay bar, OR, July 17, 1893

Emily Franssen, schooner, 69 tons, wrecked Westport, CA, Sept. 1884

Emily Schroeder, schooner, 86 tons, built San Francisco, 1869, wrecked Point Arena, 1871 (salvaged)

Emily Stevens, schooner, 98 tons, built Westport, OR, 1879, capsized off New Haven, CA, entire crew of 5 drowned; hull beached Cuffey's Cove (salvaged)

Emma, schooner, 86 tons, built San Francisco 1854 (sold foreign 1864)

Emma, schooner, 48 tons, built San Rafael, CA, 1876

Emma and Louise, schooner, 89 tons, built Little River, CA, 1873

Emma Claudine, schooner, 195 tons, built San Francisco, 1882, wrecked Grays Harbor, WA, Nov. 14, 1906

Enterprise, schooner, 189 tons, built North Bend, OR, 1863, wrecked Crescent City Harbor, CA, Sept. 29, 1883 (refloated)

Esther Cobos, schooner, 58 tons, built San Francisco, 1876

Eureka, schooner, 124 tons, built Benicia, CA, 1887

European, schooner, 30 tons, built in 1850's

Evening Star, schooner, wrecked Point Arena, CA, 1880

Ewing, schooner

Exact, schooner, (built 1830 Glastonbury, Conn.) wrecked Crescent City, CA, March 31, 1859 (carried first settlers to Seattle in 1853)

Excel, schooner, 52 tons, swamped by squall off Point Reyes, Sept. 1863, (three drowned) hull towed to San Francisco

Fairy Queen, schooner, 99 tons, built Eureka, 1869, wrecked Whitesboro, CA, Nov. 23, 1885

Falmouth, schooner, 65 tons

Fannie A. Hyde, schooner 90 tons, wrecked Point Arena, CA, Dec. 10, 1886

Fannie Gilmore, schooner, 98 tons

Fannie Hare, schooner, 163 tons, built San Francisco 1867 (sold foreign, 1880, first Nicaraguan, then Peruvian, afloat 1921 as *Jose Pozzo*)

Fannie Jane, schooner, 120 tons

Fanny Dutard, schooner, 170 tons, built San Francisco, 1882, (became codfish schr., ended days as barge 1940's)

Far West, schooner, wrecked Mendocino County coast, Jan. 15, 1863

Fayaway, schooner, operated in 1850's

Ferndale, schooner, operated in 1880's and 90's

Fidelity, schooner, 116 tons, operated in 1870's and 80's

Fidelity, schooner, 192 tons, built Eureka, 1882, wrecked Humboldt Bay bar, Nov. 6, 1889 (entire crew of 6 perished)

Five Brothers, schooner, built San Francisco, wrecked Drakes Bay, CA, Oct. 24, 1900

Fortuna, schooner, 145 tons, built Fairhaven, CA, 1886 (sold Peru 1919)

Francis Ellen, schooner, wrecked at Little River, CA, Oct. 6, 1863

Francis Ellen, schooner, operated in 1880's

Francisco, schooner, wrecked at Port Orford, OR, 1856

Free Trade, schooner, 72 tons, wrecked Noyo, CA, Feb. 2, 1881

Free Trade, schooner, 92 tons, built San Francisco, 1869

Frithee, schooner, operated in 1880's

Galatea, schooner, 98 tons, built Little River, CA, 1874, vanished at sea after departing San Francisco, July 5, 1882

Garcia, schooner, 116 tons, built San Francisco, 1882, wrecked near Cape Meares, OR, Dec. 2, 1893

Gem, schooner, 120 tons, built Parkersburg, OR, 1885, wrecked Double Headed Rock, OR, Feb. 15, 1904

General Banning, schooner, 177 tons, built Navarro River, CA, 1883 (sold Mexico 1920)

General Morgan, schooner, operated in 1850's

General Ord, schooner, 105 tons, built Port Orchard, WA, 1869, wrecked north side Point Arena Harbor, Feb. 23, 1889

George W. Prescott, schooner, 101 tons, built Little River, CA, 1874

Georgia R. Higgins, schooner, 96 tons, built Fairhaven, CA, 1875, wrecked Whitesboro, CA, Jan. 27, 1887

Glen, schooner, 127 tons, built Marshfield, OR, 1883, wrecked Ikitak, Unimak Island, Alaska, 1907

Glenarm, schooner, 82 tons, built 1870's at San Francisco

Gold Beach, schooner, wrecked Klamath River bar, CA, Feb. 5, 1856

Golden Bear, schooner

Golden Fleece, schooner, 127 tons, built Eureka 1875

Golden Gate, schooner, 98 tons, built 1874, wrecked Point Arena, CA, May 18, 1889

Golden Rule, schooner, 72 tons, built Point Arena, CA, 1860

Golden Rule, schooner, 118 tons, built 1866, wrecked Albion, CA, June 12, 1872

Golden State, schooner, sank at moorings Mendocino Bay, CA, Nov. 17, 1865

Golomi, schooner

Gotoma, schooner, 198 tons, built North Bend, OR, 1872, wrecked near Willapa Bay entrance, WA, Dec. 25, 1908

Gotoma, schooner, 189 tons, built Eureka 1875

Governor Perkins, schooner, 74 tons (formerly *Sine Johnson*)

Gracie, schooner, 105 tons

Gracie Belle Richardson, schooner, 64 tons, built Benicia, CA, 1885, wrecked Stewart's Point, CA, 1890

Gracie Belle Richardson, schooner, 68 tons, built 1889, wrecked Stewart's Point, CA, 1892

Gualala, schooner, 95 tons, built San Francisco, 1881

Glide, schooner, 144 tons, built San Francisco, 1881

Gussie Klose, schooner, 95 tons, built Fairhaven, CA, 1876, wrecked Albion, CA, March 11, 1893

H. Bendel, schooner, 74 tons, built San Francisco, 1874, wrecked Fish Rock, CA, Feb. 15, 1888

H.H. Briggs, schooner, wrecked Westport, CA, Oct. 6, 1887

H.H. Knapp, schooner, 77 tons, built San Francisco, 1878, wrecked Westport, CA, Oct. 6, 1887

H.L. Tiernan, schooner, 153 tons, built San Francisco, 1867, wrecked Caspar, CA, Nov. 18, 1869, salvaged, lost Shumagin Islands, Alaska, 1882

Hannah Madison, schooner, 134 tons, built Little River, CA, 1876, wrecked Navarro, CA, Nov. 1885

Harriet, brig, 101 tons, wrecked Mendocino, CA, Dec. 11, 1855 (3 perished)

Harriet Rowe, schooner, 110 tons

Harrison, schooner, 49 tons, operated in 1850's 60's

Helen, schooner, 65 tons, built Point Arena, CA, 1864, wrecked Point Arena, CA, 1865

Helen Blum, schooner, 66 tons, built San Francisco, 1880

Helen N. Kimball, schooner 192 tons, built Cuffey's Cove, 1881, wrecked Fanning Island, June 27, 1901

Helen Merriam, schooner, 74 tons

Hercules, schooner, 47 tons, built San Francisco, 1878

Hinda, schooner, 65 tons, built San Francisco, 1878

Home, schooner, wrecked south spit Humboldt Bay bar, Aug. 4, 1852

Hopewell, schooner, 49 tons, operated in 1850's

Howard, scow schooner, 74 tons, built San Francisco, 1869

Howard, schooner, 121 tons, built San Francisco, 1881

Humboldt, schooner, operated in the 1850's

Humboldt, schooner, wrecked at Westport, CA, Sept. 30, 1885

Humboldt, schooner, 138 tons, built Eureka, 1878, wrecked Point Gorda, CA, Sept. 1895

Hyde, schooner, 70 tons, wrecked Point Arena, CA, Dec. 1880

Ida Florence, schooner, 58 tons, built San Francisco, 1889, wrecked Rough and Ready, CA, Dec. 3, 1890

Ida May, schooner, wrecked north of San Francisco, Nov. 1880

Industry, schooner, 72 tons, wrecked Salt Point,

Industry, schooner, cont.
CA, Dec. 18, 1879

Ino, schooner, 98 tons, built Navarro River, CA, 1867 (became walrus hunter)

Iowa, schooner, wrecked Port Orford, OR, 1865

Irma, schooner, wrecked Whitesboro, CA, Dec. 27, 1887

Isabella Ebetts, schooner, operated in 1880's

Ivanhoe, schooner, 120 tons, built Coos Bay, OR, 1869, out of register, 1893

Ivy, schooner, 142 tons, built San Francisco, 1882; as Alaska trader, wrecked Point Barrow, Alaska, Sept. 1, 1908

J. B. Brown, schooner, brig, operated in 1850's

J. B. Ford, schooner, 196 tons, built San Francisco, 1860, out of register, 1878

J. B. Ford, schooner, 244 tons, built San Francisco, 1882, foundered Grays Harbor, WA, Feb. 2, 1893

J. E. Haskins, schooner, foundered off Point Reyes, CA, Sept. 4, 1874

J. E. Lunt, schooner, wrecked Navarro, CA, Oct. 13, 1878

J. Eppinger, schooner, wrecked Navarro, CA, April 14, 1887 (4 lost)

J. Eppinger, schooner, built San Francisco, 1887, sunk in collision, 68 miles north San Francisco, July 2, 1895

J. F. K. Mansfield, schooner, wrecked Point Arena, CA, Sept. 1856

J. G. Wall, schooner, 98 tons, built Eureka, 1875, sank off Crescent City, CA, Dec. 1883 (2 drowned)

J. H. Congden, schooner, 41 tons, in collision off Bodega Bay, CA; came ashore Point Reyes, March 8, 1886

J. J. Franssen, schooner, 120 tons, built San Francisco, 1867, wrecked Noyo, CA, Nov. 18, 1869 (or 1880)

J. M. Ryerson, schooner, sank Humboldt Bay bar, Dec. 14, 1858, after striking tug towing her over bar

J. P. Haven, schooner, operated in 1870's 80's

J. R. Whiting, schooner, wrecked Noyo Harbor, CA, Nov. 17, 1865, entire crew of 7 drowned

James Townsend, schooner, 168 tons, built Noyo River, 1875, wrecked Wash Rock, Point Arena, CA, 1890's

Jennie Thelin, schooner, 146 tons, built Davenport Landing, near Santa Cruz, CA, 1869, sold to Mexico 1912, wrecked Punta Maria, Baja, as *Carmancita*

Jennie Wand, schooner, 172 tons, built Marshfield, OR, 1883, wrecked LaPaz, Mexico, Jan. 2, 1906

Jessie Nickerson, schooner, 184 tons, built Port Ludlow, WA, 1874, wrecked Willapa bar, WA, 1880

Jim Butler, schooner, operated in the 1890's

Johanna, schooner, wrecked Little River, CA, Oct. 22, 1877

Johanna M. Brock, schooner, 144 tons, built Little River, CA, 1876, turned turtle off Rogue River, OR, Dec. 1878, hull drifted 15 miles south of river entrance, all seven crewmen perished

John and Samuel, schooner, 74 tons, wrecked in 1870's, Newport, CA

John Frederick, schooner, 34 tons, built San Francisco, 1860

John F. Ingalls, schooner, 95 tons, built Fairhaven, CA, 1875

John F. Miller, schooner, 176 tons, built San Francisco, 1882, wrecked near Unimak Pass, Alaska, salvaging wreck of schooner *Glen*, Jan. 1, 1908

John Hancock, schooner, capsized off Humboldt Bay, Jan. 14, 1888 (salvaged)

John Hunter, schooner, 56 tons, built Point Arena, CA, 1863

John McCulloch, schooner, 72 tons, built Fairhaven, CA, 1873, wrecked Fish Rock, March 3, 1893

John Samuel, schooner, wrecked Westport, CA, Oct. 7, 1879

John S. Kimball, schooner, 98 tons, (later fitted with naptha engine)

Joseph and Henry, schooner, 105 tons, built Benicia, CA, 1892, wrecked off Big Creek, south of Waldport, OR, Jan. 3, 1901, entire crew, 7 perished

Josephine Wilcutt, schooner, 86 tons, stranded Little River, CA, 1872 (salvaged)

Joshua Grindle, 241 tons, (built Ellsworth, Maine) abandoned off Point Sur, CA, April 1887

Kaluna, schooner, 96 tons, struck by lighning, Jan. 22, 1858 off California coast

Katie, schooner, 74 tons, built San Francisco, 1874

Kingfisher, schooner, 41 tons, built Navarro River, CA, 1880's, fitted with engine in later years (1905), abandoned 1942

Kittie Stevens, schooner, 96 tons, wrecked Albion, CA, Dec. 12, 1893

Kittie Stevens, schooner, 130 tons, built San Francisco, 1868, wrecked, 1884

Kodiak, schooner, 103 tons, built San Francisco, 1881, wrecked Alaska, 1893-94

Kodiak, schooner, 146 tons, built Benicia, CA, 1895, afloat till 1920

Laguna, schooner, 121 tons, built San Francisco, 1885, later fitted with engine, wrecked Klamath River bar, CA, July 1902

Laura Pike, schooner, 146 tons, built Fairhaven, CA, capsized on Humboldt Bay bar, 1878, her crew of seven lost; salvaged, foundered off Cape Mendocino, Feb. 7, 1902

Laura Virginia, schooner, operated in the 1850's

Lila and Mattie, schooner, 105 tons, built Albion, CA, 1888, mauled on Tillamook River bar, OR, 1897, wreck beached on bay, total loss

Lillebonne, schooner, 218 tons, built Eureka, 1883, foundered San Francisco Bay, Aug. 29, 1912

Lily, schooner, 66 tons, built San Francisco, 1887, became sealer-codfisher

Lily, schooner, 143 tons, built San Francisco, 1882, laid up Long Beach, CA, 1935 after playing HMS *Bounty* in movie

Litta, schooner, wrecked Shelter Cove, CA, 1870's

Little River, schooner, 89 tons, built Little River, CA, 1869, wrecked Whitesboro Harbor, CA, Feb. 1885, hull driven into Albion school yard

Lizzie Derby, schooner, 98 tons, built California City, 1869, stranded Fort Point, S.F. Bay, March 29, 1888, salvaged

Lizzie Madison, schooner, 131 tons, built Fairhaven, CA, 1876, wrecked Cuffey's Cove, CA, Dec. 8, 1885

Lizzie Merrill, schooner, 80 tons, wrecked Whitesboro, CA, Dec. 18, 1885

Lizzie Priem, schooner, 96 tons, built Parkersburg, OR, 1884

Lizzie Shea, schooner, wrecked Big Flat, CA, Nov. 30, 1872

Lizzie Wylde, schooner, 88 tons, built Point Arena, CA, 1863

Lizzie Wylde, schooner, 89 tons, built Point Arena 1865, vanished with all hands 1868

Lola, schooner, wrecked Trinidad Bay, CA, Jan. 17, 1876

Lottie Collins, schooner, 69 tons, built Fairhaven, CA, 1875, wrecked Salt Point, CA, Dec. 18, 1879, salvaged

Lulu, schooner, 98 tons, wrecked Westport, CA, Sept. 17, 1885

Maggie Johnson, schooner, 137 tons, built Navarro River, CA, 1866, went to South seas, out of register 1888

Maggie C. Russ, schooner, 196 tons, built Eureka, 1880-81, wrecked San Blas, Mexico, June 11, 1903

Maggie Ross, schooner, wrecked Russian Gulch, CA, (Sonoma County) Sept. 21, 1892

Maria Antonia, schooner, wrecked Albion, CA, 1850's

Maria G. Atkins, schooner, 100 tons, built Point Arena, CA, 1868, out of register 1877

Marietta, schooner, 112 tons, built Port Discovery, WA, wrecked Humboldt Bay bar, Jan. 2, 1870

Martha W.Tuft, schooner, 172 tons, built

Fairhaven, CA, 1876 wrecked Katalla River bar, Alaska, 1907 (salmon packer)

Mary Ander, schooner

Mary and Ida, schooner, 183 tons, built San Francisco, 1882, wrecked Bering Sea, Alaska, Feb. 24, 1904 (codfisher)

Mary Bidwell, schooner, 66 tons, built San Francisco, 1876

Mary Buckley, schooner, 117 tons, built Eureka, 1876

Mary Buhne, schooner, 147 tons, built Fairhaven, CA, 1876, sunk in collision eight miles west of Eureka, Dec. 18, 1903, one life lost

Mary Cleveland, schooner, 91 tons, wrecked Noyo Harbor, CA, Nov. 16, 1887

Mary Deleo, schooner, 49 tons, built San Francisco, 1868

Mary D. Pomeroy, schooner, 150 tons, built Little River, CA, 1879, flipped over Crescent City to San Francisco, Dec. 1879, all 13 aboard died, hull drifted to Point Reyes and broke up

Mary E. Anderson, schooner, 40 tons, built San Francisco, 1860

Mary Etta, schooner, 61 tons, built San Francisco, 1891, wrecked, Stewart's Point, CA, Feb. 26, 1905

Mary F. Slade, schooner, wrecked near Cape Mendocino, Sept. 6, 1869

Mary Gilbert, schooner, 88 tons, built Eureka, 1875

Mary Gilbert, schooner, built Albion River, CA, 1886, wrecked Albion, early 1890's

Mary Hart, schooner, wrecked Bowen's Landing, Sept. 30, 1877

Mary Swan, schooner, 143 tons, built Fairhaven, CA, 1875, wrecked Rosalia Bay, Mexico, Dec. 19, 1888

Mary Zephyr, schooner, 79 tons, wrecked Point Arena, CA, 1882

Maxim, schooner, 117 tons, built Fairhaven, CA, 1875, wrecked south of Eureka, (S.F. for Eureka) Jan. 1907

Mayflower, schooner, 95 tons, wrecked near Gig Harbor, WA, Nov. 17, 1897

May Queen, schooner, 84 tons, built in California, 1866

Mendocino, schooner, 93 tons, built Coos Bay, OR, 1861, wrecked Humboldt Bay bar, Jan. 2, 1888

Merrimac, schooner, operated in 1860's

Messenger, schooner, operated in 1860's

Metis, schooner, wrecked Caspar, CA, Nov. 17, 1865

Monterey, schooner, operated in 1860's

N. L. Drew, centerboard schooner, 119 tons, built San Francisco 1869, wrecked Little River, CA, Dec. 20, 1882

Napa City, schooner, 47 tons, built Little River, CA, 1872, wrecked Point Reyes, CA, 1890

Navarro, schooner, 65 tons, sold to Mexican owners

Nettie Sundborg, schooner, 67 tons, built San Francisco, 1889, wrecked near entrance Siuslaw River, OR, Dec. 28, 1902

Nevada, schooner, wrecked Cache Slough, CA, 1863

Newark, schooner, 147 tons, built 1886, wrecked Coronado Shoals, CA, March 4, 1888

Newark, schooner, 120 tons, built 1887, Benicia, CA, became sardine reduction plant 1913, remains in S.F. mudflats, visible in 1930's

Nicholas Van Bergen, schooner, 49 tons, wrecked Smith River, CA

Norma, schooner, 310 tons, wrecked Fort Bragg, CA, Nov. 18, 1898

North American, schooner, wrecked Fish Rock, CA, 1859

Northwestern, schooner, wrecked Little River, CA, Feb. 4, 1880

Norwater, schooner, operated in 1870's

Noyo, schooner, 95 tons, built Eureka, 1861, stranded Coos Bay, OR, 1868, burned to water's edge when lime cargo caught on fire

Nula, schooner

Occidental, schooner, 209 tons, built Fairhaven, CA, 1884, wrecked Big Flat, CA, Feb. 9, 1902

Ocean Bird, schooner, operated in 1880's

Ocean Pearl, schooner, 142/(195) tons, built Navarro, CA, 1868, wrecked off California coast 1878

Ocean Pearl, schooner, 189 tons, built Navarro River, CA, 1886

Ocean Spray, schooner, 79 tons, built Navarro River, CA, 1868

Olive Schultz, schooner, wrecked Ferguson's Cove, CA, March 3, 1883

Olivia, schooner, 43 tons, swamped San Francisco Bay, Dec. 6, 1857 (salvaged)

Ono, schooner, 235 tons, operated out of Navarro River, CA

Ontario, brig, operated early 1850's (purposely sunk as Mendocino breakwater)

Orion, schooner, 117 tons, built Fairhaven, CA, 1878, cut in half in collision off Columbia River, Oct. 4, 1897

Osceola, scow schooner, built in 1870's, San Francisco, wrecked Fish Rock, CA, Sept. 22, 1880

Packet, schooner

Palestine, schooner, 69 tons, operated in 1850's 60's

Paradise, schooner, built 1868

Paragon, schooner, wrecked Crescent City (Paragon Bay) CA, March 1850

Parallel, schooner, 167 tons, operated in 1860's

Parallel, schooner, 148 tons, built San Francisco,

1868, wrecked Point Lobos, near S. F.'s Cliff House, Jan. 15, 1887 (cargo exploded)

Patriot, schooner, 57 tons, operated in 1870's

Pauline Collins, schooner, 69 tons, built Fairhaven, CA, 1875

Perseverence, schooner, operated in 1880's

Pet, schooner, 47 tons, built Fisherman's Bay, CA, 1868

Petrolia, schooner, 90 tons, built Eureka, CA 1867

Phil Sheridan schooner, 146 tons, built Little River, CA, 1869, foundered off Umpqua River, OR, Sept. 15, 1887

Phoebe Fay, schooner, 49 tons, wrecked near Cape Foulweather, OR, April 16, 1883

Piedmont, schooner, wrecked Humboldt Bay bar, Feb. 1, 1855

Pomona, schooner, entered Crescent City Harbor 1852

Pontiac, schooner, operated in 1850's 60's

Portia, schooner, 66 tons, stranded Stewarts Point, CA 1899 (salvaged)

Quoddy Belle, schooner, early trader

R. B. Handy, schooner, wrecked Signal Point, CA, Dec. 18, 1883, (2 lives lost)

Rachael, schooner, 80 tons, wrecked near Point Reyes, CA, 1890's

Ralph J. Long, schooner, 89 tons, built Bandon, OR, 1886

Rattler, schooner, 93 tons, later became fishing vessel

Reliance, schooner, 65 tons, built Benicia, CA, 1880, wrecked Point Arena, Jan. 22, 1885

Reliance, power schooner, 117 tons, operated in 1890's

Restless, scow schooner, 78 tons, built San Francisco, wrecked Cuffey's Cove, CA, June 22, 1886

Rincon Point, 28 tons, wrecked near Bodega Bay, CA, 1859

Rio Rey, schooner, 80 tons, built Alameda, CA, 1880, wrecked Fish Rock, CA, 1900

Rival, schooner, 35 tons, built San Francisco, 1869, wrecked Peacock Spit, Columbia River entrance, Sept. 11, 1889 (the demise of this vessel may be confused with the bark *Rival*, of 299 tons, officially recorded as a wreck on Peacock Spit Sept. 13, 1881)

Robert and Minnie, schooner, built at Port Madison, WA, 1876

Robert E. Lee, schooner, 95 tons, wrecked Point Arena, CA, Nov. 17, 1870

Rose Sparks, schooner, 51 tons, built Whitesboro, CA 1882, vanished with all hands, Ohkotsk Sea, 1892

Rough and Ready, schooner, 76 tons, built San Francisco, 1864

Ruth, schooner, 68 tons, built Trinidad, CA, 1863, wrecked Bihlers Point, CA, Sonoma

County, May 11, 1893

S.F. Blunt, schooner, wrecked near Point Arena, CA, May 30, 1868

S.M. Coombs, schooner, built Little River, CA, 1876, wrecked near Fort Point, S.F. Bay, Oct. 30, 1881

Sacramento, schooner, 124 tons, built San Francisco, 1868 as barge, rebuilt at schooner, 1883

Sacramento, schooner, 72 tons, (believed to have been built as the *Constantine* by Russians at Fort Ross in early 1800's.

Sadie Danielson, schooner, 88 tons, built Grubes Mill, OR, 1883

Sam McKim, schooner, operated in the 1850's.

San Buenaventura, schooner, 180 tons, built Fairhaven, CA, 1876, abandoned off Rogue River, OR, January, 1910; wreck came ashore at Rogue River

San Jose, schooner, 55 tons, built Benicia, CA, 1886

San Pablo, schooner, 46 tons, operated in 1850's.

Sarah Alexander, schooner, 51 tons, built San Francisco, 1883, wrecked north side Point Arena Harbor, Oct. 28, 1889

Sea Foam, schooner, 92 tons, built Mendocino River, 1873, wrecked Westport, CA, Sept. 30, 1885

Sea Nymph, schooner, 91 tons, built Navarro River, CA

Selma, schooner, 87 tons, operated 1860's—70's

Seven Sisters, schooner, 123 tons, built Benicia, CA, 1868, crushed by ice Kotzbue, Alaska, Sept. 1906

Silas Coombs, schooner, 116 tons, built Little River, CA, 1874, wrecked south side Little River bay, July 1875

Silver Cloud, schooner, 48 tons, built San Francisco, 1870's.

Silver Springs, schooner, 66 tons

Sine Johnson, schooner, 74 tons, later renamed *Governor Perkins*

Solano, schooner, 67 tons, built Benicia, 1865

Sophie Wengar, schooner, 64 tons, wrecked Crescent City, CA, Nov. 19, 1874

Sotoyome, schooner, 270 tons, built Albion, CA, 1905, later fitted with engine, wrecked north spit Humboldt Bay, Dec. 3, 1907,

Sparkling Sea, schooner, 127 tons, wrecked Westport, CA, Oct. 7, 1882

Sparrow, schooner, 197 tons, built Oakland, CA, 1869, wrecked Umpqua River bar, OR, 3 lives lost, Dec. 1873, (salvaged)

Stimson, schooner

Stina Nicolaisen, schooner, 45 tons, flipped over after collision early 1880's, derelict drifted to Noyo, CA, sank offshore

Storm Cloud, schooner, 118 tons, wrecked Mendocino Bay, CA, Nov. 1865

Sue Merrill, schooner, 148 tons, built Russian Gulch, CA, 1866, wrecked at entrance to Noyo Harbor same year

Surprise, schooner, operated in 1870's

Susan A. Owen, schooner, 48 tons, wrecked north side Mendocino Harbor, CA, Jan. 1878

Susan A. Wardwell, schooner, wrecked Humboldt Bay bar, March, 1854

T.H. Allen, schooner, 48 tons, wrecked Humboldt Bay bar, Jan. 12, 1862

Talo, schooner, wrecked Caspar, CA, 1873

Taranto, schooner, 65 tons, wrecked Humboldt Bay bar, May 17, 1865

Therese, schooner, 74 tons, built California City, CA, 1869

Three Brothers, schooner, 37 tons, built San Francisco, 1861

Three Sisters, schooner, 62 tons, built San Francisco, wrecked Gualala, CA, Oct. 1, 1880

Truckee, schooner, 104 tons, built San Francisco, 1869, twice salvaged in major efforts at Albion, 1884, 1886, out of register 1890

Twilight, schooner, 175 tons, built Port Ludlow, WA, 1874, wrecked Whitesboro, CA, 1892, salvaged, afloat 1900

Two Brothers, schooner, 58 tons, built San Francisco, 1880's

U.S. Nelson, schooner, wrecked Mendocino, CA, June 29, 1878

Umpqua, schooner, 50 tons, operated in 1870's—80's

Una, schooner, 207 tons, built Port Blakeley, WA, 1874, last afloat 1900

Uncle Abe, schooner, 36 tons

Uncle Sam, schooner, 113 tons, built Mendocino River, CA, 1873, capsized off Cape Foulweather, OR, March 4, 1876, all hands, 6 lost

Undaunted, schooner, 65 tons, built Davenport Landing, CA, 1873

Undine, schooner, 144 tons, built Eureka, 1870, out of register 1880

Union Forever, schooner, wrecked at Trinidad, CA, Nov. 15, 1886

Urania, schooner, 80 tons

Vanderbilt, schooner, 93 tons, built San Francisco, 1867, served as lumber carrier, sealer, whaler, codfisher and South Seas trader

Vega, schooner, 245 tons, built Fairhaven, CA, 1881, became codfisher 1912, sold to Peru, 1916, afloat till 1920

Venus, schooner, 118 tons, built at Point Arena, CA, 1875, wrecked at Navarro, CA, Jan. 25, 1891, entire crew of 5 perished

Viking, schooner, 146 tons, built Marshfield, OR, 1882, wrecked Cape Prince of Wales, Alaska, Aug. 7, 1904

Volant, schooner, 172 tons, built Fairhaven, CA, 1883, capsized off San Simeon, CA, Jan. 1893, entire crew of eight lost, hull towed to S.F., rebuilt, wrecked Kuskokwim, Alaska, July 21, 1905

W. S. Phelps, schooner, 96 tons, built Port Madison, WA, 1870, wrecked near Eureka, Feb. 1899

Wanderer, schooner, operated in 1850's

Water Witch, schooner, wrecked out of Noyo, CA, March 1853

Western Home, schooner, 135 tons, built Sacramento River (Maine Prairie), 1874, wrecked Coquille River, OR, Nov. 13, 1904

Wild Pigeon, schooner, wrecked Sonoma County coast, CA, late 1880's

William Ireland, schooner

William Sparks, schooner, 56 tons, built Whitesboro, CA, 1881, wrecked New Haven, CA, Oct. 5, 1889, refloated, wrecked 3 weeks later at Russian River, CA

Wing and Wing, schooner, 141 tons, built San Francisco, 1881, last, oil barge 1921

Winslow, schooner, wrecked in 1880's

Z. B. Heywood, schooner, 107 tons, built Port Ludlow, WA, 1873, wrecked Navarro, CA, Dec. 15, 1887, hull sank being towed away

Zuella, schooner, wrecked at Point Arena, CA

FULL-RIGGED SHIP WESTERN SHORE, the only sailing ship of its type built on the Pacific Coast was Oregon's answer to the famous clipper ships of the east coast. Photo from a watercolor by W.S. Stephenson, the ship, flagship of the Simpson fleet was built at North Bend in 1874 and pictured here with most of her sails set flying the Simpson banner from the crest of the mainmast.

Appendix F

THE SEALING SCHOONERS UNDER SAIL

One of the lusty, colorful eras in the history of the Pacific Northwest centered around the pelagic sealing industry. It gained great proportions by the 1890's when every year more than 100 small schooners, propelled only by canvas, set sail from Victoria, B.C. and Puget Sound ports fanning throughout the North Pacific, in the harsh open seas of the Bering Sea, and often into Siberian and Japanese waters. The little schooners often carried large crews of hunters who were adept to the wild waters off the Aleutians, Pribilofs and Kurille islands. It was a harsh life and sometimes cruel. Several units of the fleet vanished without trace and others were swept up on hostile shores, their wooden hulls battered to match wood, the survivors forced to eke out an existence on barren, rocky terrain hoping that rescue would come.

Captain William Spring of Victoria B.C. was perhaps the pioneer of modern sealers in the 1850's. He and his associate Captain Hugh McKay utilized the little schooners *Surprise* and *Alert* to hunt seals in the Pacific rookeries, followed by Captain J.D. Warren in the *Kate*.

Anti-dating them were sealers in the early 1800's, the Russians taking skins from the Farallons to Alaska. The great slaughter didn't begin for several decades, however, when Canadian and American sealers hunted the seal to near extinction before the American and British governments enforced laws for the protection of the mammals, especially in the far north.

Victoria B.C. was for several years the head-quarters of the sealing fleet. They lined the harbor during the winter months awaiting the beginning of a new season. Four-fifths of the Northwest fleet headquartered there. By the 1890's licenses were issued and certain areas prohibited, the valued Pribilofs getting special protection. It was in 1868 that the first American flag sealer went to the Pribilofs and came back with a large cargo of skins. The following year the Americans discovered that they didn't have to sail to that lonely part of the world when the Port Townsend pilot boat, *Lottie*, went out to the Makah's seal hunting area off Cape Flattery and took 70 skins in three days.

The overhunting of the seal rookeries caused the catches to decline, despite the controls in the 1890's. The United States and Britain had tried to make restrictions and controls work which forced units of the fleet to move over to the Asiatic side, sometimes risking capture by Russian gunboats in Siberian waters. The traditional sealing fleet that had gone north from the Pacific Northwest and to some degree from San Francisco, was very much on the decline by 1898. That year the well known Canadian schooners, *Mermaid, Mary Ellen, Otto, Pathfinder, Ocean Belle, Triumph, Viva* and *Walter L. Rich* withdrew from the trade. In fact, the *Zillah May* was the only newly fitted out vessel for the sealing trade in 1898. Soon after, the vast fleet were seeking other trades, and many were on the block at cheap prices in Victoria.

An unfortunate backlash of the Russo-Japanese War was the withdrawal of the Russian patrol vessels and guards that had protected the Siberian side of the Bering Sea from seal poachers. Japanese sailing schooners took over the slaughter, unrestricted in their efforts, and devastated the Siberian rookeries for several years thereafter until restrictions were reinforced. The Japanese take was greater than the Canadian and American counterparts at the peak of their industry.

The pioneer sealers of the Pacific Northwest were the Indians that inhabited the shores of Washington, Oregon, British Columbia and Southeast Alaska. For centuries before white man ever set foot on these shores, the skilled Indians hunted both seal and whale from their dugout canoes. From one generation to another, those skills were handed down, and the white pioneers had to admit that no one was more adept at handling a canoe in all ocean conditions and at hunting whale and seals than the Indian. Though his methods were crude, they were most effective.

In July 1957, funeral services were held for Chief Maquinna Jongie Claplanhoo, 81, traditional chief of the Makah Indian tribe at Neah Bay, Washington. He was the last of the tribe's seal hunters. Born at Neah Bay, June 15, 1876, the son of Chieftan Captain John, he played a colorful role among his people. His father was one of the 41 chiefs and sub-chiefs of the Northwest Indian tribes that signed a treaty with the U.S. government, January 31, 1855. Governor Isaac I. Stevens of the territory of Washington, sailed to Neah Bay on a sloop to negotiate the treaty.

As a youth, young Claplanhoo went to sea on sealing schooners. The vessels carried a number of Indians and their canoes. When a seal herd was spotted, the Indians went after them in their canoes, armed with harpoons.

Continuing in the trade, Claplanhoo owned three schooners when the federal government outlawed that type of sealing at the turn of the century. A U.S. Naval officer who brought the news about regulations outlawing pelagic sealing promised him compensation for his schooners. For a half century he attempted to get the promised compensation, but it was never paid.

Under the terms of the treaty, the Makahs were still allowed to take seals in their "accustomed manner" in hand paddled canoes, but sailing schooners were ruled out.

Following is a list of sailing vessels engaged in the pelagic sealing industry that were built on the Pacific Coast. Based on the research of the late Captain H.J. Snow, in his book *Forbidden Seas;* by the late marine historian John Lyman; Alaska's R.N. D'Armond; Lewis & Dryden's *Marine History of the Pacific Northwest;* also the Seattle maritime trade weekly, *Marine Digest.* (Unless otherwise denoted, vessels are of American registry)

Achilles, schooner, 46 tons, built Portland, OR, 1892

Active, schooner, 77 tons, built Port Ludlow, WA, 1884

Active, schooner (Canadian), 42 tons, built Mayne Island, B.C., 1885, foundered off Cape Flattery, April 1, 1887

Adeline, schooner, 18 tons, built San Francisco, 1858

Adventure, schooner, 13 tons, built Seattle, 1886

Albert Walker, schooner, 46 tons, built San Francisco, 1888, wrecked near Kodiak, Alaska, Sept. 23, 1893

Alexander, schooner, 50 tons, built San Francisco, 1877, wrecked 1892

Alexandra, schooner, built Kodiak, Alaska, 1886

Alice, schooner, 13 tons, built Seattle, 1888

Ainoko, schooner (Canadian), 75 tons, built 1890

Allie I. Algar, schooner (American and Canadian), 79 tons, built Seattle, 1886, missing with all hands (7), Dec. 15, 1915, Honolulu for Japan

Alpha, schooner, 28 tons, built Westport, OR, 1877

Alton, schooner, 89 tons, built Marshfield, OR, 1886

Amateur, schooner, built Seattle, 1892

American, schooner, 39 tons, built San Francisco, 1852

Amethyst, schooner, 74 tons, built Benicia, CA, 1883, wrecked Barkley Sound B.C., April, 1902

Anaconda, schooner, 40 tons, built Seattle, 1891

Anastasia Cashman, schooner, 51 tons, built Coos Bay, OR, 1880, renamed *Felix,* lost with all hands, Robben Island, Alaska, Nov. 1885

Angel Dolly, schooner, 20 tons, built San Francisco, 1860

Ann Beck, schooner (Canadian), 40 tons, built San Francisco, 1865, renamed *James Swan*

Anna Mathilda, schooner, 35 tons, built San Francisco, 1862

Annie, schooner, 25 tons, lost with all hands, Alaskan waters, 1889

Beatrice, schooner (Canadian), 48 tons, built Vancouver B.C., 1891

Bering Sea, schooner, 49 tons, built Tacoma, WA, 1895

Bessie Reuter, schooner, 31 tons, built Astoria, OR, 1889, lost with all hands, Alaskan waters, 1892

Bonanza, schooner, 160 tons, built San Francisco, 1875, crushed in ice, Herschel Island, Alaska, Aug. 23, 1905

Borealis, schooner (Canadian), 37 tons, built Victoria, B.C., 1891

Bowhead, schooner, 108 tons, built Coos Bay, 1891

Buffandeau, schooner, 37 tons, built San Francisco, 1872, wrecked Yeterup Island, 1875

C.C. Perkins, schooner, 25 tons, built Seattle, 1874

C.D. Rand, schooner (Canadian), 51 tons, built Vancouver, B.C., 1891

Challenge, power schooner, 37 tons, built Seattle, 1888

Champion, schooner, 55 tons, built Port Townsend, WA, 1860's, wrecked Nitinat, B.C., 1887

C.H. White, schooner, 86 tons, built San Francisco, 1888

C.G. White, schooner, 77 tons, built San Francisco, 1887, wrecked off Kodiak Island, Alaska, 11 souls lost

C.S. White, schooner

Cape Beale, schooner (Canadian), 13 tons, built James Island, B.C., 1892

Carlotta Cox, schooner (Canadian), 76 tons, built Victoria, B.C., 1891

Carolena (Carolina), schooner, 32 tons, built on Puget Sound

Casco, schooner (Canadian), 73 tons, built Oakland, CA, 1878

Charles G. Wilson, schooner, 60 tons, built San Francisco, 1875

City of San Diego, schooner, 48 tons, built San Francisco, 1871

Columbia, schooner, 43 tons, built Seattle, 1893

Dart, schooner, 10 tons, built Lummi Island, WA, 1890, wrecked Carmanah Point, B.C., April 1895

Dashing Wave, schooner, 149 tons, built Eureka, 1867, wrecked Bering Sea, 1891

Dawn, schooner, 15 tons, built Oakland, CA,

1883

Dawn, schooner, 12 tons, built Bandon, OR, 1891

Deeahks, schooner, 43 tons, built Seattle, 1892

Diana, schooner (Canadian), 50 tons, built Victoria, B.C., 1889

Dolphin, sloop, 8 tons, built Port Townsend, WA, 1876, wrecked same year off Japan coast, all 3 crew lost

Dolphin, schooner (Canadian), 60 tons, built Victoria, B.C., 1882, later American schooner *Louis Olsen*

Eliza Edwards, power schooner (Canadian), 37 tons, built Vancouver, B.C., 1891

Ella Johnson, schooner, 112 tons, built Port Angeles, WA, 1894, registry dropped 1900

Ellen, scow schooner, 13 tons, built San Francisco, 1885

Elsie, schooner, 57 tons, built Port Townsend, WA, 1894

Emma, schooner, 22 tons, built Shokan, Alaska, 1892

Emma, schooner, 25 tons, built Benicia, CA, 1890

Emma and Louisa, schooner, 90 tons, built Little River, CA, 1874

Favourite (Favorite), schooner (Canadian), 80 tons, built Sooke, B.C., 1869, wrecked Sydney Inlet, B.C., Dec. 1919

Fawn, schooner (Canadian), 58 tons, built Chemanus, B.C., 1892, wrecked Carmanah Point, B.C., Oct. 1905

Felix, (see Anastasia Cashman)

Fisher Maid, schooner (Canadian), 21 tons, built Astoria, 1892

Flying Mist, schooner, 57 tons, built on Puget Sound 1861, lost with entire crew off the Kurilles, 1873

Garcia, schooner, 116 tons, built San Francisco, 1882, wrecked Cape Meares, OR, Dec. 12, 1893

Golden Fleece, schooner, 127 tons, built Humboldt Bay 1875, lost off Japan 1898

Grace, power schooner (Canadian), 87 tons, built Victoria, B.C., 1881, later renamed *James Hamilton Lewis*

H.C. Wahlberg, schooner, 29 tons, built Rosehill, OR, 1892

Halcyon, schooner, 64 tons, built San Francisco, 1887

Hatzic, schooner (Canadian), 72 tons, built Victoria, B.C., 1882

Helen, schooner, 30 tons, built Seattle, 1892

Helen Blum, schooner, 66 tons, built San Francisco 1886, lost with entire crew, between Chirikof and Kodiak Islands, Alaska, 1893

Henrietta, schooner, 47 tons, built Benicia, CA, 1884

Henrietta, schooner (Canadian), 30 tons, built

Lopez Island, WA, 1886

Herman, schooner, 106 tons, built Benicia, CA, 1890, sold in Tahiti, renamed *Roberta*

Hunter, schooner, 63 tons, built Benicia, CA, 1892

Ida Etta, schooner, 73 tons, built Seattle, 1894

Idler, schooner, 11 tons, built Seattle, 1892

Ivanhoe, schooner, 119 tons, built Coos Bay, OR, 1869

J. Eppinger, schooner, 113 tons, built San Francisco, 1887, sunk in collision 45 miles west Point Reyes, July 2, 1898

James Hamilton Lewis, (see *Grace*)

James Swan, (see *Ann Beck*)

Jennie, schooner, 15 tons, built San Francisco, 1875

Jessie, schooner, 38 tons, built Port Angeles, 1894, wrecked near Nome, Alaska, 1900

Juanita, schooner (Canadian), 40 tons, built Seattle, 1875, renamed *Mascotte*

Kate, schooner (Canadian), 58 tons, built San Francisco, 1863

Kate and Anna, power schooner, 31 tons, built Yaquina Bay, OR, 1879

Kodiak, schooner, 102 tons, built San Francisco, 1881, wrecked 1893-94, Alaska

Labrador, schooner (Canadian), 25 tons, built Vancouver, B.C., 1891

Laura, schooner, 20 tons, built San Francisco, 1877, wrecked Nootka Sound, B.C., Jan. 25, 1892

Letitia, schooner, 31 tons, built Sequalitche, WA, 1864

Lettie, schooner, 30 tons, built Kodiak, Alaska, 1888

Lily L., schooner, 67 tons, built San Francisco, 1887

Lookout, schooner, 19 tons, built San Francisco, 1866

Lottie, schooner, 30 tons, built Utsalady, WA, 1868, capsized off Tillamook Rock, OR, entire crew plus 28 contraband Chinese drowned; wreck towed May 1892 to Astoria

Louis Olsen, schooner (see *Dolphin*)

Lydia, schooner, 40 tons, built Benicia, CA, 1889

M.M. Morrill, schooner, 43 tons, built Seattle, 1895

Maggie C. Russ, schooner, 196 tons, built Eureka, 1881, wrecked San Blas, Mexico, 1903

Mary Brown, schooner, 45 tons, built San Francisco, 1892, wrecked Banks Island, B.C., Oct. 3, 1893, nine persons died

Mary Deleo, schooner, 49 tons, built San Francisco, 1868

Mary Ellen, schooner (Canadian), 77 tons, built San Francisco, 1863, wrecked Sand Point, Alaska, 1890

Mary Parker, schooner, 62 tons, built Utsalady, WA, 1876

Mary Taylor, schooner, American and Canadian, 43 tons, built Utsalady, WA, 1875

Mascot, schooner, 75 tons, built Pershbaker's Mill, OR, 1892, foundered off Japan coast with entire crew

Mascotte, (see *Juanita*)

Mathew Turner, schooner, 76 tons, built San Francisco, 1877, lost with entire crew off the coast of Japan, 1894

Matilda, schooner, 26 tons, built Port Angeles, WA, 1892

Matinee, schooner, 37 tons, built San Francisco, 1871, lost with entire crew in the Aleutians, 1898

May Belle, schooner (Canadian), 58 tons, lost with all hands in Asian waters, 1896

Mayflower, schooner, 90 tons, built San Francisco, 1888

Minnie, schooner (Canadian), 50 tons, built Victoria B.C., 1889

Mischief, power schooner (later Canadian), built Yaquina Bay, OR, 1886, foundered as freight boat *Alaskan*, off Pachena Point, B.C., Jan. 2, 1923, 11 drowned, no survivors

Mist, schooner, 19 tons, built Oak Point, WA, 1865

Moonlight, schooner, 71 tons, built Siuslaw River, OR, 1890

Mountain Chief, schooner (Canadian), 23 tons, built Naastic, B.C., 1881

Nor'west, schooner, 8 tons, built Kodiak, Alaska, 1884

O.S. Fowler, schooner, 33 tons, built Humboldt Bay, CA, 1874

Ocean Rover, schooner (Canadian), 55 tons, built Cordova Bay, B.C., 1896

Ocean Spray, schooner, 83 tons, built Mendocino, CA, 1865, wrecked off Siuslaw River bar, OR, Nov. 1903

Olga, schooner, 21 tons, built Kodiak, Alaska, 1883

Olga, schooner, 46 tons, built Benicia, CA, 1890

Onward, schooner (Canadian), 35 tons, built in California, 1871

Otter, schooner, 74 tons, built San Francisco, 1881, lost with all hands in North Pacific, Sept. 1888

Pachwellis, schooner (Canadian), built James Island, B.C., 1894

Pearl, schooner, 87 tons, built Benicia, CA, 1888

Penelope, schooner, 41 tons, built San Diego, as yacht, 1890

Puritan, schooner, 15 tons, built Tacoma, WA, 1892

R. Eacrett, schooner, 31 tons, built Port Angeles, WA, 1894, wrecked St. Lawrence Island, Alaska, Nov. 3, 1899, six lives lost, one survivor

Rosa Lee, schooner (Canadian), built Victoria, B.C., 1888

Rose Sparks, schooner, 44 tons, built San Francisco, 1882, lost with entire crew off Japan, 1894

Rosie Olsen, American and Canadian schooner, 39 tons, built E. Portland, OR, 1886, as power schooner, engine later removed, wrecked Hakodate, Japan, June, 1895

Rustler, schooner (Canadian), 29 tons, built East Sound, WA, 1883, wrecked near Nitinat, B.C., 1887

Sadie Turpel, schooner (Canadian), 56 tons, built Victoria, B.C., 1892

St. Lawrence, schooner, 41 tons, built Seattle, 1893

St. Paul, schooner, 49 tons, built Benicia, CA, 1890

San Jose, schooner, 55 tons, built Benicia, CA, 1886, became pilot schooner

Sarah Louise, schooner, 49 tons, built San Francisco, 1863, lost in North Pacific with all hands, 1880's

Saucy Lass, schooner, 38 tons, built Victoria, B.C., 1892

Sea Foam, schooner, 92 tons, built Mendocino, CA, 1873

Sea Gull, sloop, 16 tons, built Port Ludlow, WA, 1889, wrecked Cape St. James, B.C., May 10, 1891

Sea Gull, sloop, 12 tons, built Seattle, 1891

Sea Lion, schooner (Canadian), 51 tons, built Victoria, B.C., 1889, lost with all hands, North Pacific, 1895

Seventy Six, schooner, 38 tons, built Mayhews Landing, CA, 1876

Shelby, schooner (Canadian), 16 tons, built Victoria, B.C., 1893

Sierra, schooner, 28 tons, built Marysville, CA, 1854

Sitka, schooner, 18 tons, built Sitka, Alaska, 1889

Sophia Sutherland, schooner, 157 tons, built Tacoma, 1889, wrecked northern Alaska, Sept. 26, 1900

South Bend, schooner, 21 tons, American and Canadian, built 1881 at South Bend, WA, as steamer, converted to sail

Stella Erland, schooner, 49 tons, built Ballard, WA, 1894

Sylvia Handy, schooner, 71 tons, built San Francisco, 1886, renamed *Walter A. Earle* (Canadian flag), wrecked off Cape St. Elias, Alaska, all aboard, 32, drowned

Teazer, schooner, 33 tons, built Upper Cascades, WA, 1874

Therese, schooner, 74 tons, built California City, CA, 1869

Thistle, power schooner (Canadian), 222 tons, built Vancouver, B.C., 1890

Thornton, power schooner (Canadian), 29 tons, built Dungeness, WA, 1861, went to pieces Unalaska, after 1886

Three Sisters, schooner, 62 tons, built San Francisco, 1869

Triumph, sloop (Canadian), 15 tons, built Cowichan, B.C., 1872, wrecked 1890

Undaunted, schooner, 68 tons, built Davenport, CA, 1873

Unga, schooner, 24 tons, built San Francisco, 1876, lost North Pacific, 1894

Vancouver Belle, schooner (Canadian), 73 tons, built Vancouver, B.C., 1891

Vanderbilt, schooner, 98 tons, built San Francisco, 1867, wrecked North Pacific, Sept. 1888

Venture, schooner, 24 tons, built Ilwaco, WA, 1886

Venture, schooner (Canadian), 49 tons, built Vancouver, B.C., 1888

Victoria, schooner (Canadian), 62 tons, built Victoria, 1892

Volunteer, schooner, 13 tons, built Ballard, WA, 1892

W.P. Sayward, schooner (Canadian), 59 tons, built Victoria, B.C., 1882

Walter A. Earle, schooner, (see *Sylvia Handy*)

Wanderer, schooner, 25 tons, built San Juan Island, WA, 1872, wrecked Vancouver Island, Feb. 1896

Willard Ainsworth, schooner, 41 tons, built Seattle, 1892

Winchester, schooner, 118 tons, built Prosper, OR, 1893

Winnifred, schooner (Canadian), 13 tons, built Whatcom, WA, 1869

Worlock, power schooner (Canadian), 45 tons, built Victoria, B.C., 1893

Zillah, schooner (Canadian), 66 tons, built Ballard, WA, 1896, became halibut fishing vessel

Pacific sealing vessels that engaged in the pelagic sealing industry that were built elsewhere than on the Pacific Coast.

Abbie M. Deering, schooner (Canadian), 101 tons, built Kennebunk, ME, 1883, wrecked on reef Akutan Pass, Alaska, Sept. 4, 1903

Ada, schooner (Canadian), 97 tons, built St. John, N.B., 1880

Adele, schooner, (German), 50 tons, built Shanghai, 1877, wrecked Queen Charlotte Islands, April 8, 1891

Agnes McDonald, schooner (Canadian), 107 tons, built Shelburne, N.S., 1891, wrecked, Japan coast, 1897

Ainoko, schooner (Canadian), 75 tons (place of construction unknown)

Aldina, schooner

Alexander, steam bark, 294 tons, built New York, 1855

Alfred Adams, schooner (Canadian), 68 tons, built Essex, Mass., 1851, sank Dodge Cove, B.C., 1891

Annie C. Moore, schooner (Canadian), 113 tons, built New Foundland, 1883

Annie E. Paint, schooner (Canadian), built Port Hawkesbury, N.S., 1885

Annie F. Briggs, schooner, 94 tons, built as government vessel, 1852

Araumah (Arammah), schooner (Canadian), built Lunenburg, N.S., 1881

Arctic, schooner (British), (see *Pointer*)

Ariel, schooner (Canadian), 90 tons, built Wickham, N.B., 1880

Ariel, schooner (Canadian), 74 tons, built Bridgewater, N.S., 1884

Arietis, schooner (Canadian), 86 tons, built Lunenburg, N.S., 1887

Beatrice, schooner (Canadian), 66 tons, built Yokohoma, 1877

Brenda, schooner (Canadian), 100 tons, built Shelburne, N.S., 1888

C.H. Tupper, schooner (Canadian), 99 tons, built Shelburne, N.S., 1888

Carmolite, schooner (Canadian), 99 tons, built Liverpool, Nova Scotia, 1888

Carrie, C.W., schooner (Canadian), 92 tons, built Mahone Bay, N.S., 1888

Director, schooner (Canadian), 87 tons, built Lunenburg, N.S., 1890

Dora Steward, schooner (Canadian), 93 tons, built Lunenburg, N.S., 1891

E.B. Marvin, schooner (Canadian), (see *Mollie Adams*)

Edward E. Webster, schooner, 99 tons, built Gloucester, Mass., 1875

Henry Dennis, schooner, 96 tons, built Essex, Mass., 1883

Jane Gray, schooner, 112 tons, built Bath, Maine, 1887, foundered off Cape Flattery, May 1898, 30 drowned, 26 saved

John Hancock, schooner, 176 tons, built Boston Navy Yard, 1850, wrecked Sand Point, Alaska, April 6, 1893

Kaiso, schooner, wrecked on Yetorup Island, 1875

Khiva Elizabeth, schooner, lost in Asian waters, 1880's

La Ninfa, schooner, 126 tons, built Port Jefferson, N.Y., 1887, served as supply vessel during construction of St. George Reef Lighthouse

Maggie Mac, schooner (Canadian), 71 tons,

Maggie Mac, schooner, cont.
built Jordans River, N.S., 1886. Lost in the North Pacific Jan. 1892, all hands, 23 souls died; some wreckage came ashore at Cape Scott, Vancouver Island, B.C.

Marie, schooner (Canadian), 97 tons, built Nova Scotia, 1890

Mary H. Thomas, schooner, 98 tons, built Essex, Mass., 1885, lost with all hands in the Pacific, 1894

Mattie T. Dyer, schooner, 109 tons, built Kennebunk, Maine, 1884, lost 1895, Asian side of the Pacific

Maude S., schooner (Canadian), 97 tons, built at Shelburne, N.S., 1886, wrecked Queen Charlotte Islands, 1897

Mermaid, schooner (Canadian), built Nova Scotia, 1892

Mollie (Molly) Adams, schooner, 123 tons, built Kennebunk, Maine, 1884

Nemo, schooner, 146 tons, built Yokohama, 1882, lost on Shantraski Island, Okhotsk Sea

Ocean Belle, schooner (Canadian), 83 tons, built Lunenburg, N.S., 1883

Oscar and Hattie, American and Canadian, schooner, 86 tons, built Essex, Mass., 1884

Otto, schooner (Canadian), 85 tons, built Mahone Bay, N.S., 1889

Otome, schooner, 40 tons, built Yokohama, 1878

Ottosei, schooner, built Yokohama, 1877

Otsego, schooner, lost with all hands, N.E. end Yetorup Island, Kuriles, 1885

Pathfinder, schooner (Canadian), 70 tons, built Kingston, N.B., 1879

Penelope, schooner (Canadian), 70 tons, built Yokohama, 1882, lost in Strait of Juan de Fuca about 1898

Pointer (formerly *Arctic*) (British), built Kanagawa, Japan, 1886, wrecked Skotan Island, 1897

Rattler, schooner, 98 tons, built Essex, Mass., 1886

San Diego, schooner, 38 tons, built Sag Harbor, N.Y., 1850, lost on Asiatic side of the Pacific, 1894

Sapphire, schooner (Canadian), 124 tons, built Port Clyde, N.S., 1884, burned in North Pacific, 1897

Swallow, schooner (Japanese), 118 tons, purchased in 1873, when already old, at Nagasaki, dismantled 1874

Snowdrop, schooner, 60 tons, built Yokohama, 1874, wrecked Yetorup Island, 1874, a few months later

Snowflake, schooner, wrecked at Yezo Island, 1886

Teresa, American and Canadian, schooner 63 tons, built San Salvadore, 1883

Triumph, schooner (Canadian) 98 tons, built Shelburne, N.S., 1887

Umbrina, schooner, 98 tons, built Shelburne, N.S., 1888

Viva, schooner (Canadian), 92 tons, built Chester, N.S., 1885

Walter P. Hall, schooner (Canadian), 99 tons, built Gilberts Cove, N.S., 1886, later sold in Japan, renamed *Iolanthe*

Walter L. Rich, American and Canadian schooner, 80 tons, built Boothbay, Maine, 1877

William McGowan, schooner (Canadian), 116 tons, built Shelburne, N.S., 1892

Pacific Coast sealing vessels, without register, that may or may not have been built on the West Coast of North America.

Ainoko, Canadian schooner, 75 tons

Aldina, schooner

Alert, Canadian schooner

Arctic, schooner, capsized off Yetorup Island, April 23, 1886

Arctic, Japanese schooner, later named *Pointer*, wrecked on Shikotan Island, Alaska, date unknown

Argonaut, Canadian schooner, built in 1880's

Banner, schooner, 32 tons, wrecked Kurile Islands, 1877

Benten, schooner, lost at Paramushiro Island, Kurilles

Black Diamond, Canadian schooner, built before 1870, renamed *Katherine*

Buffandeau, schooner, 37 tons, wrecked Yetorup Island, Kuriles, about 1876

C.D. Meyers, schooner

C.S. White, schooner

Caroline I, schooner, lost with all hands in the Kuriles, 1877

Caroline II, schooner, lost with all hands north of Japan

Clara, schooner

Clyde, schooner, also listed as *Sadie Clyde*

Cygnet, schooner, 28 tons, lost with all hands, Bering Sea, 1876

Czarine, schooner

Diana, schooner, 150 tons, sunk by Russian steamer, Okhotsk Sea, 1904

Dido, schooner, wreckage found on beach, Shikotan Island, April 24, 1879

Eliza, schooner, wrecked Yetorup Island, no date given

Eliza, schooner, sunk by Russian patrol boat, no date given

Emma, schooner

Fisherman, schooner

Halcyon, schooner, 60 tons, originally Japanese as *Vera*, fitted with engine as

Halcyon, American
Helene, schooner, (German)
Josephine, schooner
Kadiak, schooner
Katherine, schooner (Canadian), 19 tons
Katherine, schooner (Canadian) see *Black Diamond*
Lama, schooner (Canadian), 19 tons
Lewis White, schooner
Louis D., or *Louisa D.*, schooner, later British flag
Mario III, schooner
Myrtle, schooner, lost in Aleutians, late 1870's

Mystery, schooner, lost in North Pacific, no date given
Newton, schooner
North Star, schooner
Retriever, schooner
Rosa Lee, schooner, (Canadian)
Sadie Clyde, schooner, (see *Clyde*)
Sanborn, schooner, lost with all hands off Cape Horn, 1875
Sea Otter, schooner
Vera, schooner, (Canadian) (see *Halcyon*)
Victor, schooner

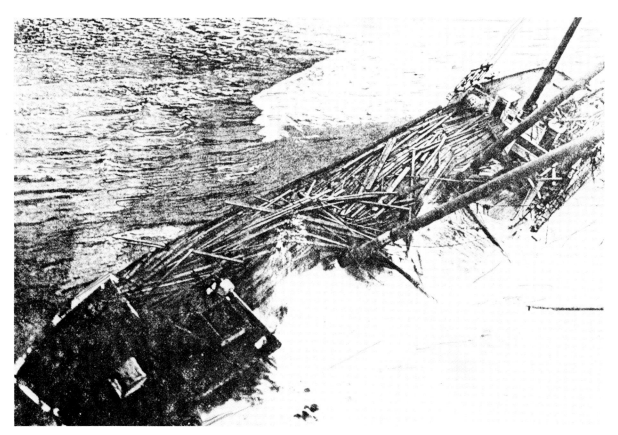

Trapped in the surf near the Coos Bay bar, the **FOUR-MASTED SCHOONER MARCONI** writhes in agony as her deckload of lumber is scattered like ten pins. Typical of the Simpson owned vessels, they were never insured. The wreck occurred March 23, 1909.

225

Appendix G

Early sailing schooners, 100 tons and under, built on the southern Oregon coast for the timber trade, based on information compiled by Victor C. West, Oregon historian.

Alaska, schooner, 48 tons, built at Port Orford, 1857

Alton, schooner, 83 tons, built at Marshfield, 1886

Anastasia Cashman, 51 tons, built at Empire City, 1880 (renamed Felix) (became sealer)

Bowhead, schooner, 90 tons, built North Bend, 1891

Coquelle, schooner, 92 tons, built Parkersburg, 1883

Cyclone, schooner, 31 tons, built Sixes River, 1891

Dawn, schooner, 41 tons, built Bandon, 1891

Enterprise, schooner, 100 tons, built North Bend, 1863

General Siglin, schooner, 80 tons, built Marshfield, 1894 (became Alaska trader)

Hannah Louise, schooner, 83 tons, built North Bend, 1863

Ivanhoe, schooner, 86 tons, built Marshfield, 1869

Kate Piper, schooner, 71 tons, built Empire City, 1868

Lizzie Priem, schooner, 94 tons, built Parkersburg, 1884

Louisa Morrison, schooner, 95 tons, built Marshfield, 1869

Mascot, schooner, 70 tons, built Prosper, 1892

Mendocino, schooner, 84 tons, built North Bend, 1861

Mizpah, schooner, 70 tons, built Prosper, 1898

Nonoha, schooner, built North Bend, 1892

Parkersburg, schooner, 100 tons, built Parkersburg, 1883

Ralph J. Long, schooner, 87 tons, built Bandon, 1888

Robert Emmett, schooner, 34 tons, built Empire City, 1880

Ruby, schooner, 41 tons, built Parkersburg, 1885

S. Danielson, schooner, 91 tons, built Parkersburg, 1883

Santa Rosa, schooner, 61 tons, built Marshfield, 1879

Silver Wave, schooner, 54 tons, built Bandon, 1889

Volante, schooner, 87 tons, built North Bend, 1891

Winchester, schooner, 98 tons, built Prosper, 1893

Zenith, schooner, 54 tons, built Bandon, 1900

Captain Peder O. Sonerud, and his wife Carrie at Berkeley, California in 1913. A seasoned commercial sailing vessel skipper, he commanded the **SCHOONER CHALLENGER** in the 1890's and the **SCHOONER R.C. SLADE** from 1900-1912 and was one of the most respected master mariners in the business. Courtesy, Wilbur E. Hespe, grandson of the late Captain Sonerud.

FOUR-MASTED SCHOONER R.C. SLADE, building at Aberdeen, Washington in 1900, was a Lindstrom product, a well constructed vessel that made many fine passages, for 12 years in command of Captain Peder O. Sonerud. Photo courtesy Wilbur E. Hespe. The **SLADE** ended her days in 1917 when sunk by the German raider, the **SEEADLER,** commanded by Count Felix van Luckner, a legendary figure in his time.

INDEX TO PHOTOS

Wash day on **SCHOONER MAHUKONA** berthed at San Pedro, Calif. Built at Hoquiam, Wash. in 1901, this handsome lumber and copra packer ended her days on a reef near Apia, Samoa, January 29, 1918 while being towed out of the port. The tow line broke and she drifted onto the reef.   *Courtesy R. E. Mackay collection*

A quartet of West Coast windjammers loads lumber on the Columbia River at the Columbia Mills, Knappton, Washington in the early years.
Courtesy Mr. and Mrs. Richard Benson

Built by J. W. Dickie & Sons, the **SCHOONER RUBY** later became a northern trader with an auxiliary engine.

On drydock at Everett—**SCHOONER SAMAR**, several decades back. The vessel was photographed by Seeley of Everett and is from the R. E. Mackay collection. The schooner built in 1901 at Alameda was shoved aground on a remote Mexican beach about 1953 after last serving as a fishing barge in Southern California.

Misty morning in Mukilteo Harbor—at anchor in background, four-masted schooner believed to be the **AURORA.**
Courtesy Pete Hurd.

All flags flying—**BARKENTINE MAKAWELI:** foremast—country of destination; mainmast—house flag; mizzenmast—name of vessel; jiggermast—nationality (USA).
Courtesy A. O. Anderson

Peaceful scene at Poulsbo, Washington in the 1940's—**SCHOONERS SOPHIE CHRISTENSON, C. A. THAYER** and **MV NORDIC MAID.** This was homeport of the Shield's codfishing fleet. *Courtesy R. E. Mackay collection.*

Photo by Lindsley

The schooner **JOHN A. CAMPBELL** ended her days carrying copra from the Gilbert Islands to San Francisco or Sydney. She caught on fire and burned at Tarawa, August 1, 1922. The Hall Brothers built her in 1895.